The Writer's FAQs

A POCKET HANDBOOK

SIXTH EDITION

New!
2016
MLA
Updates

MURIEL HARRIS
Purdue University

JENNIFER L. KUNKA
Francis Marion University

D1710515

PEARSON

Boston Columbus Indianapolis New York San Francisco
Amsterdam Cape Town Dubai London Madrid Milan Munich Paris
Montréal Toronto Delhi Mexico City São Paulo Sydney Hong Kong
Seoul Singapore Taipei Tokyo

Vice President and Editor in Chief: Joseph Opiela
Program Manager: Eric Jorgensen
Field Marketing Manager: Mark Robinson
Product Marketing Manager: Ali Arnold
Project Manager: Savoula Amanatidis
Project Coordination, Text Design, and Electronic Page Makeup: SPi Global

Program Design Lead and Cover Designer: Beth Pacquin
Cover Image: Aliaksei 7799/Getty Images
Senior Manufacturing Buyer: Roy L. Pickering, Jr.
Printer and Binder: LSC Communications–Crawfordsville
Cover Printer: Lehigh-Phoenix Color Corporation–Hagerstown

Credits and acknowledgments borrowed from other sources and reproduced, with permission, in this textbook appear on the appropriate page within text or on page 272.

PEARSON, ALWAYS LEARNING, and MyWritingLab are exclusive trademarks owned by Pearson Education, Inc. or its affiliates in the United States and/or other countries.

Unless otherwise indicated herein, any third-party trademarks that may appear in this work are the property of their respective owners and any references to third-party trademarks, logos, or other trade dress are for demonstrative or descriptive purposes only. Such references are not intended to imply any sponsorship, endorsement, authorization, or promotion of Pearson's products by the owners of such marks, or any relationship between the owner and Pearson Education, Inc., or its affiliates, authors, licensees, or distributors.

Library of Congress Cataloging-in-Publication Data
Harris, Muriel.
  The Writer's FAQs: a pocket handbook / Muriel Harris, Purdue University; Jennifer L. Kunka, Francis Marion University. — Sixth Edition.
     pages cm
  Includes index.
  ISBN 978-0-13-413305-8 (Student edition) — ISBN 0-13-413305-6 (Student editon) — ISBN 978-0-13-413973-9 (Instructor's Review Copy) — ISBN 0-13-413973-9 (Instructor's Review Copy)
  1. English language—Rhetoric—Handbooks, manuals, etc.   2. English language—Grammar—Handbooks, manuals, etc.   I. Kunka, Jennifer L. II. Title.
  PE1408.H3458 2016
  808'.042—dc23
                                                          2015035171

1   17

Student Edition
ISBN-10: 0-13-467884-2
ISBN-13: 978-0-13-467884-9

www.pearsonhighered.com

Brief Contents

How to Use This Book

- **Need to know what's in this book?** Check the Detailed Contents inside the back cover of the book. The beginning of each major section also lists what's covered there.

- **Have a question this book can answer?** On pp. vi–viii you'll find a list of questions that writers often ask and the page numbers to turn to for answers. And there are more questions to help you at the beginning of each part.

- **What can you learn in each chapter?** There are Learning Objectives listing the skills and processes covered in the pages that follow.

- **What are FAQ and Try This boxes?** Throughout the book, you'll find FAQ boxes that answer "frequently asked questions" about writing. The Try This boxes have suggestions for you to use when planning, researching, revising, and editing.

- **Do you have questions about confusing words such as *affect/effect* or *fewer/less*?** Look through the Glossary of Usage, on pp. 263–267, to see if the words you want to check are listed there.

- **Do you want to know the meaning of some grammatical term?** On pp. 267–272 are the definitions of the most commonly used grammatical terms.

- **Is there an index for looking up the information I need?** On pp. 273–278 is an alphabetical list of topics covered in this book.

- **Do you want to know what some correction symbols refer to?** On page 279 is a list of correction symbols some instructors use and the page numbers in this book to explain them.

We hope you find this book easy to use and so helpful that it becomes a writing friend to keep nearby as you write. We offer special thanks to the student writers who shared their writing in this book. We are deeply indebted to our faithful in-house support team members, Sam Harris (and family) and Andrew Kunka.

Muriel Harris
Jennifer L. Kunka

Question and Correct

Mechanics p. 97

Multilingual Speakers p. 111

Research p. 127

Documentation   p. 167

I

Composing, Conversing, Collaborating

Contents

Question and Correct

1 Writing Processes and Strategies

Your **writing process** refers to the various steps or actions you take to complete a writing project. The **global** or **higher-order concerns (HOCs)** you'll be thinking and writing about include developing and possibly revising your purpose. You'll also be considering your audience, topic, thesis, organization, and paragraphing. When you edit and proofread, you'll look closely at **local** or **later-order concerns (LOCs).** These include grammar, punctuation, spelling, and formatting. The order in which you focus on any of these concerns depends on your personal writing process.

1a Purpose

When we write, we have a **purpose** or goal in mind. Perhaps we want to share information or to persuade readers to act or believe in certain ways. Or we may want to explore what is on our minds. There are many goals for writing, so a useful way to begin is to ask ourselves questions such as these:

- What do I want my readers to know or believe?

- What do I want my readers to do after reading my paper?

FAQ

What are common purposes for writing?
- **Summarizing.** Briefly stating the main points of a work
- **Defining.** Explaining the meaning of a word or concept
- **Analyzing.** Breaking the topic into parts and examining how these parts work
- **Persuading.** Convincing readers of your point of view
- **Reporting or informing.** Examining evidence and data on a subject and presenting an objective overview
- **Evaluating.** Setting up criteria (points of evaluation) and judging the quality or importance of a subject
- **Discussing or examining.** Considering main points, implications, and relationships to other topics
- **Interpreting.** Explaining the meaning or implications of a topic

3

If we write in response to an assignment, we have another important question: "Does my purpose fit the purpose stated in the assignment?" For example, if the assignment is to review a movie, to decide whether or not it's good, writing a plot summary won't fit the assignment.

1b Audience

Is the audience you are writing to appropriate for your assignment and purpose? The information you include, your tone, and your assumptions about your readers' level of interest or knowledge of a subject will shape your writing.

TRY THIS

Defining Your Audience

Ask yourself the following questions:

- **Who is my audience?** Is it my peers? a potential boss? a general, educated audience? readers of a particular publication? people who are likely to agree or disagree?
- **What is the audience's attitude?** Are they interested? sympathetic? not likely to agree? neutral?
- **What is the audience's background?** What is their education, specialized knowledge, religion, race, cultural heritage, political views, occupation, and age?
- **What information should be included?** What do my readers already know about the subject? What will they need to know to understand my topic and point of view?

1c Topic

The topic of a piece of writing may be something the writer chooses, or it may be assigned. To choose a topic, try one or more of the strategies suggested here.

TRY THIS

Finding a Topic

- What is a problem you'd like to solve?

  _____ is a problem, and I think we should _____.

- What is something that pleases, puzzles, irritates, or bothers you?

  _____ annoys (or pleases) me because _____.

- What is something you'd like to convince others of?

  I think that _____ because _____.

- What is something that seems to contradict what you read or see around you?

  Why does _____? (or) I've noticed that _____, but _____.

- What is something you'd like to learn more about?

  I wonder how _____.

- What is something you know about that others may not know?

  I'd like to tell you about _____.

1d Thesis

A **thesis** statement is the main idea or subject of your paper. It's the promise you make to your readers: if they read the paper, this is what they'll read about. In an **informative** paper, your thesis statement summarizes your discussion about your topic. In an **argumentative** paper, your thesis communicates your primary position, solution, or interpretation to your audience. Thesis statements are often written as a single, concise sentence. For longer or more complex works, your thesis might be written in two or three sentences or even a short paragraph.

FAQ

How do I write an effective thesis statement?

There are two parts to an effective thesis statement: the **topic** and a **comment** that makes an important point about the topic.

Topic	Comment
Effective document design	helps technical writers present complex material more clearly.
Crowdfunding	has become a successful method for financing the development of innovative new products.

An effective thesis statement should have a topic that interests your readers, is as specific as possible, and is limited enough to make it manageable.

Once you have drafted a thesis statement, review and, if necessary, revise it to make sure it is focused and clearly written.

Narrow thesis statements that are too general

Thesis statements that are too general are often hard to prove within the limits of a paper.

Too General	What specific	More Specific
Climate change is a problem we should deal with.	solution would help to address the problem? What aspect of the problem will be addressed? Causes? Effects?	**Developing environmentally safe wind farms** can reduce the **effects of climate change.**

Strengthening thesis statements that are too vague

Thesis statements that are too vague can leave too much to readers' interpretation and leave room for readers to oppose your argument.

Too Vague	What does "help	More Specific
College graduates who **help the public** should receive full repayment of their federal student loans.	the public" mean? College graduates who volunteer a few hours each week? work in specific types of communities? take specific high-need jobs?	College graduates who **teach math and science in rural communities for five years** should receive full repayment of their federal student loans.

Adding qualifying words to your thesis

Sometimes using words such as *may* or *can* instead of *will* makes your thesis more provable because they are not as absolute as *will*.

Too Broad	Will this solution	Qualified
Increased drilling for natural gas in the United States **will end** America's dependence on foreign oil.	end the problem? Can you prove this? If not, more qualified words such as **can reduce** or **may lessen** would make this thesis easier to prove.	Increased drilling for natural gas in the United States **can reduce** America's dependence on foreign oil.

1e Organization

As you read over your draft, check to see if your topic sentences clearly communicate the central idea of each paragraph. Then ask yourself if each paragraph contributes to the thesis in some way and if each paragraph leads logically to the next one. With any organizational strategy, you want to avoid jumps in the development of your thesis that might confuse your reader. For suggestions on how to organize your paragraphs and whole papers, see 1f.

FAQ

What is an outline?

Outlines are plans that can be helpful before or after you draft your paper. They allow you to group related ideas together and rearrange material to create a logical structure to your work. If you find that some idea or subtopic doesn't seem to fit, it may not belong in your paper.

There are two types of outlines:

- **Informal**—Make a simple jot list using bullets or numbers. Indent minor points under major points.

- **Formal**—Use Roman numerals or decimal numbers. Pay attention to the logical relationships between major ideas, subheadings, and supporting ideas.

Roman Numerals	Decimal Numbers

I. Main idea
   A. First subheading
   B. Second subheading
     1. Supporting idea
     2. Supporting idea
II. Main idea
	1.0. Main idea
	  1.1. First subheading
	  1.2. Second subheading
	    1.2.1. Supporting idea
	    1.2.2. Supporting idea
	2.0. Main idea

1f Paragraph development

A paragraph is well developed when it has enough details, examples, specifics, supporting evidence, and information to back up your thesis. You may need to delete material that is no longer relevant or add material to strengthen your thesis and help you achieve your purpose. Try to read your paper as an uninformed reader would, and ask yourself what else you'd need to know.

Consider these strategies for organizing your ideas as you develop your paragraphs:

- **Chronological order.** Show historical development or explain a process.

- **General-to-specific order.** Provide basic information before giving specific details and examples.

- **Cause-and-effect order.** Describe how someone or something affects someone or something else.

- **Compare-and-contrast order.** Discuss similarities and differences between groups.

1g Transitions

Every paragraph should be written so that each sentence flows smoothly into the next. If your ideas, sentences, and details fit together clearly, your readers can follow along easily and not get lost. To help your readers, try repeating key terms and phrases and using synonyms, pronouns, and transitional devices between sentences and paragraphs. (See Chapter 13 for a list of transition words and phrases.) Also check for missing information that causes a break in your explanation or argument.

To create a transition between paragraphs on two different subjects, try writing a sentence that has

1. an introductory phrase or clause that refers to the topic of the previous paragraph, and

2. an independent clause that introduces the topic of the following paragraph.

See Figure 1.1 for an example.

Topic A: Paragraph on strategies corporations use to make environmentally friendly workplaces

While corporations can employ many strategies for creating environmentally friendly workplaces, homeowners also have many options for renovating their homes to conserve natural resources.

Topic B: Paragraph on ways homeowners can make their houses more environmentally friendly

▲ Figure 1.1 **Transitioning Between Paragraphs**

1h Introductions

The introduction brings readers into your world, builds interest in your subject, and announces topics. Think of an introduction as a plan or map: by the end of it, your readers should have a clear sense of what your topic is and how the paper will be organized. Try one or more of the following strategies for writing an introduction:

- Introduce a relevant quotation from a credible source.
- Cite an interesting statistic.
- Offer a concrete example.
- Provide a vivid description.
- Pose a question.
- Relate an anecdote.
- Suggest a future possibility (something that hasn't happened yet but could reasonably occur).

1i Conclusions

The conclusion signals that the paper is ending and helps put the whole paper in perspective. It is your opportunity to summarize your major points and make a memorable or persuasive final statement. Consider the following strategies as you write your conclusion.

Look back through your paper. If the paper has a complex discussion, try any of the following:

- *Summarize the main points* to remind the reader of what was discussed.
- *Emphasize points* you don't want the reader to forget.
- *Refer to something in the introduction*, thus coming full circle.

Look forward to the future implications of your topic. If the paper is short or doesn't need a summary, try the following:

- *Pose a question* for the reader to consider.
- *Offer advice.*
- *Call for action* the reader can take.
- *Consider possible outcomes and effects* of your topic.

1j　Revision

An important part of writing is **revising**, which means re-seeing how effectively the paper communicates your ideas and checking that the ideas and paragraphs are ordered appropriately. Spending time on revision can make your writing more persuasive and interesting. As you write, consider these questions to revise for global issues or higher-order concerns (HOCs):

* **Purpose.** What is the purpose of this paper? Have you achieved the purpose? If not, what's needed?
* **Audience.** Who is the audience for this paper? What assumptions have you made about your audience members? Did you tell them what they already know? Did you leave out anything your audience needs to know?
* **Topic.** Is your topic narrowed down sufficiently so you can discuss it effectively, given the expected length of your assignment?
* **Thesis.** Is the thesis clearly stated? Has it been narrowed sufficiently? Is it appropriate for the assignment? Can you summarize your thesis?
* **Organization.** What is the central idea of each paragraph? Does that idea contribute to the thesis? Do the paragraphs progress in an organized, logical way?
* **Development.** Are there paragraphs where more details, examples, or specifics would help? Are there irrelevant details that should be omitted?
* **Transitions.** Are there places where the paper doesn't flow? Are there sentence or paragraph gaps where transitions may be needed?
* **Introduction.** Does your introduction grab the reader's attention and introduce your topic? Would another introduction strategy be more effective?
* **Conclusion.** Does the conclusion bring together the ideas of the paper? Would looking ahead to the future of your topic help to wrap up your discussion?

TRY THIS

Revising Your Draft
* When you return to a paper you started earlier, read from the beginning to the section you'll be working on now. This helps you get back into the flow of thought.
* Track your changes using word-processing software.

- **Create multiple drafts.** Save each draft with a new file name and include the date in case you want to put something back in your draft.
- **Print out and read a hard copy.** This can help you get a sense of the whole paper.
- **Look at each full page on the screen.** If one paragraph looks shorter than the others, it might need more development. If a paragraph seems too long, check if it should be divided into two.
- **Meet with a writing center tutor.** Tutors can help you take your work for a "test drive" and see if it fits the assignment.

FAQ

What should I do when I meet with a writing center tutor?

- **Plan ahead.** Give yourself enough time to prepare and ask questions, as well as time after to revise your writing.
- **Bring along your assignment and any requirements.**
- **Think about the kinds of help you want—and tell your tutor.** Do you need help developing a thesis? organizing ideas? citing sources? editing for grammatical issues?
- **Read your paper aloud, or ask the tutor to read the paper aloud to you.** You'll see and hear problems that won't be as evident when you read silently.
- **Remember that tutors do not just proofread.** They want to help you learn how to revise your own work.
- **Visit tutors for help with any project—from papers to résumés.**

1k Editing and proofreading

When you edit and proofread, look closely at the details of grammar, usage, punctuation, spelling, missing words, format requirements, and other mechanics.

TRY THIS

Proofreading for Local Issues/Later-Order Concerns (LOCs)

- Edit on hard copy pages.
- Go backward through your paper, sentence by sentence. This can help you focus on grammar and spelling.

- **Slide a card down under each line as you reread.** This will help your eyes slow down.
- **Put the paper aside for a bit after you draft it.** It's easier to see problems with fresh eyes.
- **Track your changes.** Many word processors allow you to track changes between drafts.
- **Use spell checkers and grammar checkers with care.** They catch some, but not all, spelling and grammar problems and can only offer suggestions. (See 32a.)
- **Keep a list of the particular problems you tend to have when writing.** Use the Question and Correct sections in this book to find help with specific issues.

2   Arguments

Reading and writing persuasive arguments are parts of your everyday life. People actively persuade you to believe, act on, or accept their claims, just as you want others to accept or act on your claims. You can create arguments to justify your beliefs, solve problems, or evaluate products or works of art. Position papers, reviews of films and books, and literary analyses are also forms of argument.

2a   Claims and evidence

Arguments have two basic elements.

- A **claim** is the proposition or thesis to be proved.

- The **evidence** for an argument provides the reasons used to convince the audience. Such support or proof may include facts, data, examples, statistics, and the testimony of experts. Evidence may take the form of appeals.

  - *Logical appeals* are based on reason and facts.

  - *Emotional appeals* arouse the audience's emotions: sympathy, patriotism, pride, anger, and other feelings based on values, beliefs, and motives.

  - *Ethical appeals* act on the audience's impressions, opinions, and judgments about the person making the argument.

To write a convincing persuasive paper, try to find information to prove that your view should be accepted. Also, think about presenting yourself as a knowledgeable or experienced person who deserves to be listened to.

TRY THIS

Composing Persuasive Arguments

Show that your motives are reasonable and worthwhile. Give your audience reasonable assurance that you are arguing for the general good or for a claim that shares the audience's motives.

Find common ground with your audience. Rather than thinking about how you differ from your readers, consider the values, interests, motives, or goals you share with them.

Use an appropriate tone. Employing a serious tone when writing about serious issues helps your readers recognize your professionalism and trust your judgment.

Avoid vague and ambiguous terms and exaggerated claims. Words such as *everyone, no one, always, never, best,* or *worst* usually invite someone in your audience to find an exception.

Acknowledge that you have thought about opposing arguments by including them. Readers who don't agree with you want to know that you aren't ignoring their views.

Rely upon knowledgeable, credible people as sources for your evidence. Introduce your sources by indicating who they are and why they should be trusted.

Cite your source material. Citing your sources will help show your credibility. (See Chapters 45–48.)

FAQ

What are some strategies to support my thesis?

If you were writing a paper encouraging readers to avoid texting while driving, these are some ways you could support your argument:

Logical Appeals: rely on facts and data

- Offer statistics showing the number of people injured or killed in texting-related accidents.
- Include studies comparing the effects of texting while driving with the effects of drunk driving.

Emotional Appeals: influence the audience's feelings

- Include stories about adults or children injured or killed in texting-related accidents.
- Add photos of people affected by texting-related accidents.

Ethical Appeals: demonstrate your credibility

- Discuss values you share with readers, such as safety.
- Use credible sources, cited throughout the paper.
- Consider opponents' viewpoints.

2b Visual argument

Both written and visual arguments depend on connections between claims and evidence. In visual arguments, **claims** can be in the words that accompany an image, such as a caption for a photograph or a title used for a graph or chart. More often, however, claims in visual arguments are implied rather than stated openly. **Evidence** is presented through the content and position of images as well as the words accompanying the images. See Figure 2.1 for an example.

As you look at a visual argument or create one yourself, ask yourself these questions:

- **What is the purpose of the visual?** Is it to inform? to persuade? to educate? to entertain?

- **Who is the target audience for the visual argument?** If you are creating a visual argument, to whom are you directing your image?

- **What is the claim of the visual argument?** Look carefully at the wording. The claim may be implied, however, rather than stated.

- **What kinds of evidence does the visual argument offer?**

- **What kinds of appeals do the visuals make?** Are they logical, emotional, or both?

The text is strong and bold. Its placement over the driver's face emphasizes the ad's main claim.

Our eyes are drawn to the person's face at the center of this image. The fact that we can't see the driver (and he can't see us) sends a persuasive message.

The open space on the left shows where the driver's eyesight is directed. Our eyes are pushed to the left as well, away from what is typically the focal point of a person's image—the face.

▲ Figure 2.1 **Reading a Visual Argument**

3 Writing about Literature

When you write about a creative work such as a story, poem, or play, begin by reading it closely and thinking about its meaning. To analyze the piece, consider one or more of the following strategies:

- **Analyze the theme.** What are some of the conflicts? Does the writer offer a lesson to be learned or a way of looking at life or the world?

- **Analyze the plot.** How do events connect to each other? Is the author responding to an event, recalling some past moment, or foreshadowing future actions?

- **Analyze characters.** Consider characters' actions, thoughts, words, and motives. Do the characters change or stay the same?

- **Analyze the structure of the work.** Is it chronological? Does it skip around? Are you given clues by the writer as to what will happen?

- **Analyze the narrator.** Who is telling the story? Does the narrator tell the reader the characters' thoughts? What is the narrator's tone or attitude toward characters and events?

- **Look at the type or genre of the work.** Is it a tragedy, comedy, sonnet, mystery, or a work from another specific genre? How does it compare to others of its type? Does it use elements common to this type of work?

- **Analyze the historical or cultural background.** How does the work reflect values, social conflicts, or political forces of the time and place in which it is set or written?

- **Analyze the work in terms of gender, class, or race.** How does the work portray women or men? How does it reflect treatment of a particular class or group? How does it challenge traditional views of these groups?

- **Focus on the reactions of readers to the work.** Why do readers respond as they do to this work? What would influence their reactions?

- **Research the life of the author.** What about the author's life is reflected in this particular work?

- **Resist the obvious meaning of the work.** Read skeptically, look for inconsistencies, and focus on ambiguities in the work. How do you interpret the work?

TRY THIS

Avoiding Common Pitfalls in Literature Papers

- Write an interpretive analysis, not a plot summary.
- Offer a thesis that makes an interpretive claim about the work.

  Sample thesis: In E. M. Forster's *A Room with a View*, Lucy Honeychurch learns that her personal happiness not only requires her to break Edwardian society's rules but to escape them entirely.

- Include important information, such as key plot elements or details, needed to support your claims.

4 Document Design

4a Principles of document design

These principles will help you develop well-designed, readable pages.

- **Apply design elements consistently.** Use design elements, such as bullets, white space, spacing, font types, and so on, consistently throughout your document.

- **Include white space.** Well-placed white space makes your documents more readable and offers visual relief from blocks of text. White space in the margins helps frame the text and allows a reader to make notes.

- **Avoid clutter.** Remember, less is more.

- **Use contrasting design elements for emphasis.** Fonts in bold, italics, color, or varied size add emphasis by making words stand out from regular text. Indented text, graphics, and background shading highlight selected elements.

- **Insert headings and subheadings.** These help announce new topics or subsections. Make your headings and subheadings more noticeable by using a combination of bold, italics, and larger font sizes.

- **Create lists.** In research papers and professional documents, information is often presented more efficiently in lists. Use phrases or sentences containing key points and supporting details, and organize them with bullets, dashes, or numbers.

- **Use appropriate documentation style formats.** Style guides often contain specific formatting instructions for elements such as margins, titles, headers, and page numbers. For more information about formatting papers in Modern Language Association (MLA) format, see 45d; for American Psychological Association (APA) format, see 46d; for *Chicago Manual* format, see 47c; and for Council of Science Editors (CSE) format, see 48c.

4b Incorporating visuals

Visuals such as images, graphs, charts, and tables can help you communicate clearly and concisely.

- **Images.** Photographs, diagrams, maps, and illustrations add color, variety, and meaning to your documents (see Figure 4.1). They help your readers see a subject in a new perspective, follow steps in a process, or pinpoint a location. Use multiple images placed next to each other to show contrast or changes over time.

- **Graphs and charts.** Use graphs and charts to illustrate data in visual form and explain relationships between items. These can be produced in a spreadsheet program such as Microsoft Excel (see Figures 4.2–4.7, page 20).

- **Tables.** Create tables to show relationships between items. Use word-processing software to create your tables.

Drought conditions have severely depleted water supplies in California. For example, according to the United States Geological Survey (USGS), Shasta Lake's water level has declined 50% since 2011. See Fig. 1.

Fig. 1. Shasta Lake in Feb. 2014. (USGS)

Such drastic reductions in natural water resources are forcing Californians to rethink the future of public water usage.

▲ Figure 4.1 **Insertion of a Figure in an MLA-Style Paper**

TRY THIS

Adding Visuals to a Text

- **Include a title.** Graphs, charts, and images are labeled as *figures*, and tables are labeled as *tables*. Add a title to explain the content, such as "Fig. 1. Increases in Voter Registration" or "Table 5: Number of Registered Voters in Each Wisconsin County." Figures and tables each have separate numbering systems in your document.

- **Add labels.** In graphs and charts, provide a label on the x (horizontal) axis and y (vertical) axis to specify values indicated in each area of the visual. Column headings in tables also need clear labels.

- **Place visuals in their appropriate location in the text.** Check 45d for information on placement of visuals in MLA-formatted papers and 46d for APA-formatted papers.

- **Cite your sources.** See Chapters 45–48 for documentation formats.

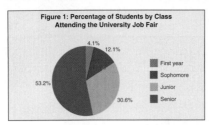

Figure 4.2 Pie Chart
Shows parts of a whole

Figure 4.3 Bar Graph ▶
Shows relationships
among items

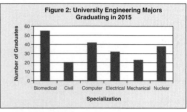

**◀ Figure 4.4 Line
Graph** Shows change
over a period of time

Figure 4.5 Map ▶
Identifies locations and
visually represents data
Source: U.S. Geological Survey

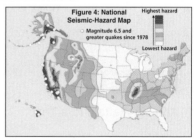

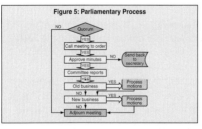

**◀ Figure 4.6 Flow-
chart** Illustrates a
process or shows
options in making
decisions

Figure 4.7 Table ▶
Summarizes large
amounts of data and
shows relationships
between items

Table 1: Available for Adoption			
Name	Breed	Age	Spayed/ Neutered
Sammy	Spaniel	8–9 years	Yes
Missy	Pomeranian	1 year	Yes
Cabot	Pointer/Beagle Mix	4–5 years	Yes
Mimi	Chihuahua	6 months	No

5 Multimedia Projects

A multimedia project combines more than one type, or mode, of communication. You can share your ideas using written text, as in a traditional academic paper, but with digital media tools, you can enhance communication with photographs, artwork, graphs, captions, video, audio, and more. Some examples include the following:

- Microsoft PowerPoint presentation
- Prezi
- Audio podcast
- Video or short film
- Website

- Blog
- Wiki
- Poster
- Advertisement
- Webzine

5a Planning

Begin planning your project by thinking about purpose, audience, and topic. Which strategies would be most likely to motivate your audience to agree with your opinions? act upon your suggestions? become interested in your topic? How can you include audio, visual, or other media to achieve your purpose?

TRY THIS

Planning Your Multimedia Project

Consider these elements as you plan your project:

- **What is your purpose?**
- **Who is your audience?**
- **What information should be included about your topic?** What do you need to say or show in order to achieve your purpose?
- **What will be the medium for your project?** Will you build a PowerPoint? Prezi? video? podcast? website? something else? What does your media format offer for sharing your views and fulfilling the purpose of your project? How will your audience view or experience your project?

5b Format

There are many options for formatting projects constructed with digital media tools. Consider these general design principles as you work:

- **Create a consistent look for all sections of your project.** Select your background colors, fonts, and animation styles and stick with them through your project. This will make your project (and you) appear organized and focused.

- **Keep paragraphs or chunks of information focused.** Long passages of text are difficult to read online. Insert a blank line between paragraphs.

- **Use easily readable fonts.** Widely available fonts such as Calibri, Cambria, Times New Roman, Arial, Georgia, Tahoma, and Verdana are good choices for digital text. Fonts that look like handwriting are difficult to read. Also, avoid using all capital letters; this is the equivalent of shouting at readers.

- **Choose contrasting background and font colors.** Use light background colors with dark font colors or vice versa. Avoid overly bright backgrounds; yellow backgrounds are particularly hard for readers to look at for long periods of time. Combinations of red on blue (and vice versa) are also difficult to read.

- **Use images that enhance your message.** Digital photographs and videos add to the impact of your project by explaining a fact or illustrating an example. Avoid clip art, which can look unprofessional.

- **Collect more than you need.** It is easier to remove images, videos, and audio clips you don't need than to go back and repeat your collection process to create new ones.

- **Back up your digital files in multiple places.**

- **Give credit to your sources.** Use the citation style requested by your instructor. In many programs, you can also insert links to the sources.

TRY THIS

Designing PowerPoint Presentations

Font Type. Use fonts that are easy to read.

Font Size. Vary your font sizes. Titles should be somewhat larger than headings, and headings should be larger than the main text. Words in fonts smaller than 20 point may be too difficult for your audience to read.

Graphics. Digital photographs that look professional serve to engage interest and reinforce your points. Cite your image sources in your presentation.

Animations. Animation can emphasize your key points and build interactions with your audience. However, too many animations can be distracting.

Layout. Balance your use of text and images to emphasize main points.

Text. Use *talking points*—words, descriptive phrases, or short sentences—on your slides rather than the full text of your speech. Set off your talking points in bullets so they are easy to read.

Organization. You have many choices for organizing your presentation. PowerPoints often contain a title slide, introductory slides that grab attention, a thesis slide that gives your main point, body slides that provide additional information and support your claims, a concluding slide that re-emphasizes your main points, and reference slides that include your list of sources.

5c Organization

Regardless of how you design your project, you'll need to think about the way you organize information. With some multimedia projects, such as podcasts and presentations, your work will have a *linear organization*, a defined beginning, middle, and end. With *hypertexts*, such as websites and wikis, audience members will choose the way they experience your project, depending on where they click. As you design your project, consider the following elements.

- **Establish an introduction, beginning, or home.** This is where your audience will begin to experience your project. Think about what readers need to understand at the beginning. Introduce your topic and purpose. If appropriate, grab your reader's attention (see 1h) to build interest in proceeding with your project.

- **Provide general and specific information.** In projects with a linear structure, give general information before specifics.

- **Create a clear navigation system.** For projects such as websites and wikis, create a menu of links to show your reader how to interact with your project and how to return to your home page.

- **Build a memorable conclusion, if you have one.** For projects with a linear organization, end on a strong note by reemphasizing your ideas or projecting the future of your topic. (See 1i.) Hypertext projects, such as websites and wikis, don't have a defined ending.

II

Sentence Choices with Style

Contents

Question and Correct

6 Clarity

6a Positive instead of negative

Use positive statements because negative statements are difficult for people to understand.

Unclear negative: Less attention is paid to commercials that lack human interest stories.

Revised: People pay more attention to commercials that tell human interest stories.

Negative statements can also make the writer seem unsure.

Evasive negative: Senator Jamison does not disagree with the governor's entire proposal.

Revised: Senator Jamison agrees with the governor's proposed education funds but would like to see more tax cuts in his budget plan.

6b Double negative

If you need a negative word, use only one in a sentence. More than one negative in a sentence is not grammatically correct and is difficult to understand.

Double negative: I **don't** think he **didn't** have money left after he paid for his dinner.

Revised: I **don't** think he had any money left after he paid for his dinner.

TRY THIS

Avoiding Double Negatives

Watch for contractions that include negatives, such as *doesn't*, *hasn't*, and *couldn't*. Also, watch for negative words such as the following:

hardly	no one	nobody	nothing	scarcely
neither	no place	none	nowhere	

Sara hardly had ~~no~~ any popcorn left.

6c Known/familiar Information to new/unfamiliar information

Begin your sentences or paragraphs with something that is generally known or familiar before you introduce new or unfamiliar material.

Familiar ⟶ Unfamiliar

Familiar to unfamiliar:

Every semester, after final exams are over, I face the problem of what to do with **lecture notes. They** might be useful someday,
(OLD) (OLD)
but **they** just keep cluttering **my computer's hard drive**. Someday,
(OLD) (NEW)
the computer will crash with all that information.
(NEW)

> *(These sentences should be clear as the discussion moves from old to new information.)*

The next example is not as clear.

Unfamiliar to familiar:

Second-rate entertainment is my description of most **movies** I've
(NEW) (OLD)
seen lately, but occasionally, some have **worthwhile themes**.
(NEW)
In the Southwest, the mysterious **disappearance** of an American
(NEW)
Indian culture is the **topic** of a recent movie I saw that I would
(OLD)
say has a **worthwhile theme**.
(OLD)

> *(These sentences are difficult to follow because the familiar information comes after the new information.)*

6d Verbs instead of nouns

Actions expressed as verbs are more easily understood and stated more briefly than actions named as nouns.

TRY THIS

Using Verbs Instead of Nouns

Try rereading your sentences to see which nouns could be changed to verbs.

Unnecessary noun form:	**The decision was** to adjourn.
Revised:	**They decided** to adjourn.

Some Noun Forms	Verbs to Use Instead
The approval of . . .	They approve . . .
The analysis of . . .	They analyze . . .
The usage of . . .	They use . . .

6e Intended subject as sentence subject

The real subject (or the doer of the action in the verb) is the grammatical subject of the sentence. Sometimes the real subject of a sentence can get buried in prepositional phrases or other less noticeable places.

Subject buried in a prepositional phrase

For music lovers, **it** is preferable to hear a live concert instead of an MP3.

> (*The grammatical subject here is* **it**, *which is not the real subject of this sentence.*)

Who prefers to hear a live concert? Music lovers, so *music lovers* is the real subject of this sentence.

Revised: **Music lovers** prefer to hear a live concert instead of an MP3.

Real subject buried in the sentence

It seems that playing games online is something **Jonas** spends too much time doing.

> (*If the real subject,* **Jonas**, *becomes the subject, the sentence becomes clearer and more concise.*)

Revised: **Jonas** seems to spend too much time playing games online.

6f Predication

A logical sentence contains a subject and a predicate (the rest of the clause) that make sense together. When the subject and the predicate are not logically connected, that is referred to as faulty predication.

Faulty predicate: The **reason** for her rapid promotion to vice president **proved** she was talented.

(*In this sentence, the subject,* **reason,** *cannot logically prove* **she was talented.**)

Revised: Her **rapid promotion** to vice-president **proved** she was talented.

Faulty predication often occurs with forms of the verb *to be* because this verb sets up an equation in which the terms on either side of the verb should be equal.

Subject	Predicate	
2 × 2	is	4
Dr. Streeter	is	our family doctor.

Faulty predication: **Success is when** you have your own swimming pool.

(*Having a pool can be one example or a result of a type of success, but it is not the equivalent of success.*)

Revised: **One sign** of financial success **is having** your own swimming pool.

6g Missing words

Words unintentionally left out of sentences can cause confusion for readers.

Words needed for parallelism

Check for prepositions (such as *in, to, for, of*) that follow verbs.

Marriages succeed when both partners have trust in and respect for each other.

(*We would have trust **in** someone, not trust **for** someone.*)

Words needed for comparisons

Check for words needed to complete a comparison. Name the two items being compared to each other.

This science class is more difficult than the one I took last semester.

(*Without **than the one I took last semester,** readers will not know what the **science class** is being compared to.*)

The job fair was in a larger room than the ~~office~~ student government had.

(*What is being compared here are the rooms. Without the missing word **office**, what is being compared are the **larger room** and the **student government**.*)

Words needed for grammatical correctness

Include words needed for correct grammatical constructions.

We have ~~celebrated~~ and will always celebrate Thanksgiving with our family.

(*The word **celebrated** is needed to complete the past tense verb.*)

7 Variety

A series of short sentences or sentences with the same subject-verb order can be monotonous to read and sound choppy. Try these strategies to add variety.

- Combine two sentences (or independent clauses) into one longer sentence by using a comma and coordinating conjunction (see 23a) or a semicolon (see 25a).

  Comedians on *Wait, Wait, Don't Tell Me* mock politicians , but the ~~. The~~ targets of the satire often miss their point.

- Combine the subjects of two independent clauses in one sentence when the verb applies to both clauses.

  Original: The **Wabash River** overflowed its banks. **Wildcat Creek** did the same.

  Revised: The **Wabash River and Wildcat Creek** overflowed their banks.

- Add a description, a definition, or other information about a noun after the noun.

  Professor Nguyen is a political science teacher , ~~. She~~ gives lectures in the community on current events.

- Turn a sentence into a *who, which,* or *what* clause.

  He was charged with breaking the city's newest law , which ~~. This law~~ states that motorcyclists must wear helmets.

- Begin with dependent clauses that start with dependent markers such as the following words:

after	because	since	when
although	if	until	while

After the trial ended, the lawyers filed an appeal.

When the stockholders met, they discussed the company's recent decline in profits.

- Add variety at the beginning of sentences by adding transitional words and phrases (see 13a).

Original: The use of social media can involve invasion of your privacy. Social media laws are being passed to prevent invasion. Such laws are not always observed.

Revised with transitions added and sentences combined: **Although** social media can involve invasion of your privacy, laws are being passed to prevent invasion. **But** such laws are not always observed.

Revised with phrases added and sentences combined: **Currently**, the use of social media can involve invasion of your privacy, though laws are being passed to prevent this. **However**, such laws are not always observed.

- Vary the sentence length so that some sentences are short and some are long.

Original: Traditionally, the game of squash has not been a popular sport in America. Recently ESPN carried some squash matches as one of their highlights. Televised squash matches are shown on terminals in Grand Central Station in New York City. This means thousands of commuters are seeing some matches. Squash is growing in popularity.

Revised: **While** the game of squash has not traditionally been a popular sport in America, ESPN recently carried some squash matches as one of their highlights. Televised squash matches **now** are shown on terminals in Grand Central Station. This means thousands of New York City commuters are seeing some matches, and **as a result**, squash is growing in popularity.

8 Conciseness

You communicate to your readers more clearly and are more likely to keep your readers' interest by cutting out extra words. This often means resisting the impulse to include everything you know or to add words that sound more formal or academic. To write concisely, omit

- what your readers do not need to know or already know
- whatever doesn't further the purpose of your paper.

How do I know if I have wordy language?

- **Check for repetition of words or phrases.** If you find you're repeating the same words in a sentence or paragraph, try eliminating some or rephrasing your sentences.

  Smart phones are helpful tools ~~. Smart phones help~~ ^{for}

  ~~with~~ tracking friends' phone numbers~~. You can also~~ ^{sending}

  ~~use smartphones to send~~ e-mail and ~~search~~ online. ^{searching}

- **Check for phrases that say the same thing twice.**

~~first~~ beginning	6 p.m. ~~in the evening~~
circular ~~in shape~~	~~true~~ facts
green ~~in color~~	each ~~and every~~
~~positive~~ benefits	the ~~end~~ result

- **Check for fillers.** Some phrases, such as the following, say little or nothing and can be omitted:

there is (or) are	I am going to discuss
in view of the fact that	I think that
what I want to say is	it is my feeling that

  He said ~~that there is~~ a storm ^{is} approaching.

  He ~~made the statement that he~~ agreed ~~with the concept~~ that inflation could be controlled.

Strategies to revise sentences and paragraphs for conciseness

- **Combine sentences.** When the same nouns or pronouns appear in two sentences, combine the two sentences into one.

  The data were entered into the reports. ~~They were also~~ ^{and} included in the graphs.

33

- **Eliminate *who*, *which*, and *that*.**

  The book ~~that is~~ lying on the piano belongs to her.

  The person ~~who is~~ responsible for this problem has not offered a solution.

  I am going to discuss artificial intelligence~~, which~~ is an exciting field of research.

  Artificial

- **Turn phrases and clauses into adjectives and adverbs.**

  all applicants who are interested → all interested applicants

  spoke in a hesitant manner → spoke hesitantly

  the piano built out of mahogany → the mahogany piano

- **Turn prepositional phrases into adjectives or possessives.**

  the entrance to the station → the station entrance

  the windows of the building → the building's windows

- **Use active rather than passive voice. (See Chapter 9.)**

  The ~~figures were~~ checked ~~by the research department~~.

  research department *the figures.*

- **Remove unnecessary words and change to verbs whenever possible.**

  The ~~function of the~~ box ~~is the storage of~~ wire connectors.

  stores

9 Active/Passive Verbs

An active verb expresses the action completed by the subject. A passive verb expresses action done to the subject. Passive voice uses forms of *to be* (*is, are, was, were*) and sometimes the word *by*.

Active: Paulo *wrote* the report.

(*The verb is* **wrote**, *and* **Paulo**, *the subject, did the writing.*)

Passive: The report *was written* by *Paulo*.

(*The verb is* **was written**, *and the* **report**, *the subject, was acted upon.*)

Using active verbs often results in clearer, more direct, and more concise sentences than those with passive verbs. Active verbs clarify who is doing the action and add a strong sense of immediacy and liveliness to your writing.

Active: After the eye of the hurricane passed, **ambulance drivers *rushed*** injured patients to the hospital. (*more immediate and direct*)

Passive: After the eye of the hurricane passed, **injured patients *were rushed*** to the hospital by **ambulance drivers**. (*wordy with weaker sense of action*)

FAQ

When is it appropriate to use passive voice?

- When the doer of the action is not important or is not known

  For the tournament game, more than five thousand **tickets were sold**.

  (*Who sold the tickets? That's not important; the number of tickets is what is being stressed here.*)

- When you want to focus on the action or the receiver of the action, not the doer

  Lara was chosen to receive the scholarship.

  (*The writer wanted to emphasize who got the scholarship, not who chose her.*)

- When you want to avoid blaming, giving credit, or taking responsibility

  It was announced that the **election was lost**.

  (*The candidate lost the election but wants to avoid stressing that.*)

- When you want a tone of objectivity, particularly in science writing

  Ten grams of sugar **were added** to the solution.

  (*The result, not who added the sugar, is important.*)

10 Voice, Formality, and Word Choice

10a Voice and formality

In writing, an appropriate voice is one that fits the level of formality in your paper and your subject.

Formal tone contains sophisticated phrasing not commonly used in conversation. Third-person pronouns *he* or *she* or *one* are often used instead of *I* or *you*. Formal tone may be expected in professional and legal documents and research writing. Jargon or language appropriate to the field and intended readers may also be used.

Formal: The tripartite narrative arc in classically constructed films requires initial exposition, rising action that delineates the central conflict, and then gradual movement toward a resolution.

Medium/semiformal tone uses standard sentence structures and vocabulary. Contractions are generally avoided. This tone is appropriate for most college writing assignments.

Medium/semiformal: The three-part narrative structure of movies follows the classical pattern of first exposing the audience to introductory information, then building action toward a conflict, and finally resolving the film's central problem.

Informal tone uses language common in daily conversation and includes slang, colloquialisms, and regionalisms. Contractions and first- and second-person pronouns such as *I* and *you* are appropriate for this tone.

Informal: Movies usually start by telling us about the people and places in the story. Then some big problem comes up, but it's worked out by the end.

Slang

Slang terms are made up (such as *salty, amped up, catfish,* and *vape*) or are given new definitions (such as *chops* for very talented or skilled). Over time, some slang may enter the general vocabulary and dictionaries of standard written English. However, slang is generally not considered appropriate for academic work. Abbreviations used on the Internet, such as LOL, IMHO, FWIW, and the shortened versions of words, such as *thanx, thru,* or *lite,* are also not appropriate for academic writing.

Jargon

Jargon is the specialized language of various trades, professions, and groups. Specialists use these terms when referring to complex concepts, objects, and techniques.

When you are writing about a specialized subject for a general audience and need to use a technical term, define the term in easily understandable language the first time you use it. You can then use the word later on and not lose the reader.

The term *jargon,* however, is also sometimes applied to *inflated expressions,* which sound pompous, and *euphemisms,* which are terms used to disguise unpleasant realities.

Specialized language: subcutaneous hemorrhage, metabolic disorders, exhaust manifold, beta decay, data integrity, cloture

Inflated expressions: learning facilitator (teacher), monetary remuneration (pay)

Euphemisms: revenue enhancement (taxes), pre-owned (used), nonmilitary collateral damage (dead civilians)

Unnecessary jargon reflects the writer's inability to write clearly. Note the wordiness and pompous tone of this example:

Original: Utilize this receptacle, which functions as a repository for matter to be removed.

Revised: Deposit litter here.

10b Tone shifts

Once you choose a formal or informal tone for a paper, keep that tone consistent in your word choices. Shifting from formal to informal or informal to formal can disrupt the tone of your writing.

Unnecessary shift: The welfare worker's responsibility is to assist in a family's struggle to obtain food and clothing children ~~stuff~~ for the ~~kids~~.

(*The use of the informal words* **stuff** *and* **kids** *illustrates a shift in tone in this formal sentence.*)

10c Emphasis

When you want to stress a point or want your readers to realize the importance of what you're writing about, you can add emphasis to your writing in several ways:

- **Use parallelism.** When you have two or more items in a group or when you want to join two ideas, write them in parallel form (see 21a):

  "**Ask not what** your country can do for you; **ask what** you can do for your country." (President John F. Kennedy)

  "Too many people spend money they haven't earned, **to buy** things they don't want, **to impress** people they don't like." (Will Rogers)

- **Use strong adjectives and adverbs.** Words that modify nouns and verbs can help you make your writing more vivid and memorable.

  Not vivid: The brightly colored sunset on the cliffs was pretty.

  Vivid: The flaming golden rays of the sunset glowed on the cliffs.

- **Use striking language.** You can use an interesting metaphor, concrete details, or an unusual way of stating something to add emphasis to your writing.

  Laughter illuminates faces and lights up our minds.

  Web browsers are portals because they open doors to the world.

- **Use visual design.** See Chapter 4 for ways to add visual impact and emphasis as you design your documents.

10d Denotation and connotation

The *denotation* of a word is the definition found in dictionaries. The *connotations* of a word are the associations, attitudes, and emotional overtones that some words have. While readers don't all share the same connotations, some connotations are widely known. Consider the word *snake:*

Denotation of the word *snake:* any of the many varieties of legless reptiles

Connotation of the word *snake:* something or someone who's evil, dangerous, treacherous

Weighing the denotative and connotative meanings of words can help you say what you really mean.

My boss is **firm** about the policy.

> (**Firm** *means strong and unwavering. It has a positive connotation.*)

My boss is **obstinate** about the policy.

> (**Obstinate** *means unwavering, but it also means stubborn and unwilling to consider other options. It has a negative connotation.*)

11 General and Specific Language

When we use general language, we are thinking of a large category or class of items, such as "dangerous driving habits." But that applies to many different types of such habits and can be too vague or large a category when specifics are needed. To be more specific, we name an instance or example in the category we want to focus on, such as the danger of talking on a cell phone while driving, which identifies a more specific item or category within the general one. General statements can be made more specific, and general words can be made more specific.

General words	Specific	More specific
animal	dog	cocker spaniel
clothing	pants	jeans

General statement: The number of problems in the service industry is growing.

More specific: Lack of adequate training among flight attendants has resulted in a rapidly increasing number of complaints by passengers.

Sometimes general terms are sufficient, depending on your purpose, but specific terms are often more precise and vivid, allowing readers to become more aware of your topic and its importance.

General term: unsafe food

More specific term: alfalfa sprouts contaminated with salmonella bacteria

12 Inclusive Language

12a Gender-inclusive language

Gender bias in English occurs when we use male pronouns and *man* as universals to indicate members of both sexes. To avoid offending readers by using language that seems to favor one sex over the other, use more inclusive terms and strategies such as the following.

- **Use alternatives to *man* or *men*.**

Instead of:	*Use:*
man	person, individual
stewardess	flight attendant
housewife	spouse
policeman	police officer
congressman	congressional representative, member of Congress
businessman	business professional
saleswoman or salesman	salesperson, salesclerk, sales specialist

- **Use the plural.**

  Not inclusive: **A nurse** is trained to understand **her** patients' emotions and physical symptoms.

  Inclusive: **Nurses** are trained to understand **their** patients' emotions and physical symptoms.

- **Eliminate the pronoun or reword to avoid it.**

  Not inclusive: If a taxpayer has questions about the form, **he** can call a government representative.

  Inclusive: A taxpayer who has questions about the form can call a government representative.

- **Replace the pronoun with *one, he or she*, or an article (*a, an, the*).**

  Not inclusive: The parent who reads to **her** infant helps increase the infant's sound discrimination.

  Revised: The parent who reads to **an** infant helps increase the infant's sound discrimination.

- **Address the reader directly in the second person.**

  Not inclusive: Each applicant must mail **his** form by Thursday.

  Revised: Mail **your** form by Thursday.

- **Address the person by his or her title when you don't know the gender.**

  Not inclusive: Dear **Sir**,

  Revised: Dear **Customer Services Representative**,

FAQ

When referring to *everyone*, do I use *he or she* or *they?*

There are different views as to when to use the indefinite pronouns *everybody, anybody, everyone,* and *anyone.* Some people use the singular pronoun (*everyone . . . he* or *she/his* or *her*) and consider the plural *they* to be wrong.

Formal: When **everyone** has completed **his or her** test, **he or she** may leave class.

However, the use of the plural pronoun (*everyone . . . they/ their*) has become acceptable in many informal contexts.

Informal: When **everyone** has completed **their** test**s, they** may leave class.

In formal writing, it is still advisable to avoid using either gender-specific or plural pronouns with these words.

12b Respectful language

Writing inclusively also means avoiding assumptions about our audience. When we write for a general educated audience, we can't assume everyone will be of the same race, religion, age, ethnicity, gender, or sexual orientation as ourselves. To be inclusive, we can acknowledge diversity by not assuming our readers share our characteristics and beliefs.

Using inclusive language

Inclusive language also does not exclude or stereotype groups. It is disrespectful to make broad generalizations—even if they are seemingly positive—about an entire group of people. Here are some examples of assumptions to avoid:

My friend is gay, so he'll be the most fashionable one at the party.

(assumes all gay men are fashionable)

Parents use their Biblical education to raise their children.

(assumes all parents are Christian)

Senior citizens will require extra help using this computer program.

(assumes all senior citizens do not know how to use computers)

Liu is Asian American, so she'll be able to help you with your math homework.

(assumes all Asian Americans are good at math)

Choosing terms for ethnic or racial groups

For ethnic or racial groups, there are preferred choices and some terms to avoid.

- Use *Native American* or *American Indian* instead of *Indian*
- Use *African American*, *Black*, or *black*
- Use *Hispanic* or *Latino* (or *Latina*, the feminine form)
- Use *Asian* instead of *Oriental*

When it's appropriate, use more specific terms, such as the name of a specific country or region of origin, as in *Cuban American*, *Chinese American*, and *Mexican American*. Current source materials, such as news or journal articles, are useful guides to the appropriate terms for groups you refer to in your writing. But it's important to remember that some people have strong preferences for one term or another.

13 Transitions

13a Transitional words and phrases

Transitions are words and phrases that build bridges between sentences, parts of sentences, and paragraphs. They help connect them and show relationships.

Using transitions between words and sentences

The state government is determined not to raise property taxes this year. **Therefore**, some legislators were in favor of an increase in the cigarette tax, **but** the majority voted for a reduction in funding for educational programs. **As a result**, teachers, parents, and students protested in the state capitol yesterday.

Using transitions between paragraphs

To find causes for the high number of car crashes by teenage drivers, the researchers gathered various types of **data** on teens with licenses, expecting to find a **connection** to risky behaviors among the various **data** that were collected.

    However, among all the behaviors studied, the only **correlation** that stood out in the **data** was that teens who sleep later have fewer accidents. . . .

Types of transitions used between paragraphs

    Data: repetition of a word

    Connection (*and*) **correlation:** synonyms

    However: transitional word

FAQ

Which transitional word(s) should I use in my sentence?

Are you doing this?	Then use one of these words:
Adding:	*and, besides, in addition, also, too, moreover, furthermore, next, first, second, third, likewise*
Comparing:	*similarly, likewise, in like manner, at the same time, in the same way*
Contrasting:	*but, yet, however, still, nevertheless, on the other hand, on the contrary, instead, rather, though, whereas, although*
Emphasizing:	*indeed, in fact, above all, and also, even more, in any event, in other words, that is, obviously*
Ending:	*after all, finally, in sum, for these reasons*
Giving examples:	*for example, for instance, to illustrate, that is, namely, specifically*
Pointing to cause and effect, proof, or conclusions:	*thus, therefore, consequently, because of this, hence, as a result, then, so, accordingly*

Are you doing this?	Then use one of these words:
Showing place or direction:	*over, above, inside, next to, underneath, to the left, just behind, beyond, in the distance*
Showing time:	*meanwhile, soon, later, now, in the past, then, next, before, during, while, at last, since then, presently, at the same time*
Summarizing:	*to sum up, in conclusion, finally, in general, to conclude, in other words*

13b Repetition of a key term or phrase

Repeating a word or phrase helps you draw connections between sentences and emphasize your main idea.

Among the recent food fads sweeping America and Europe is the interest in **molecular gastronomy**, which involves exploring the chemical composition of foods and the cooking process to create new and exciting dishes. While not all chefs agree that **molecular gastronomy** is the wave of the future, they cannot deny that it has had a significant impact on the culinary world.

13c Synonyms

Synonyms are words with similar meanings. Using synonyms helps you build connections between sentences without repeating the same word too many times.

By experimenting with the physical and chemical composition of **food**, chefs concoct **edible delights** shaped as creams, gels, spheres, and foams. Applied properly, chemicals such as calcium chloride and liquid nitrogen transform standard **fare** into **delectable cuisine** in unexpected shapes and consistencies.

13d Pronouns

Pronouns (such as *he, she, it, they*) can help you refer to people, places, and things discussed in your writing. With pronouns, you can build the flow of your writing without overusing the same words.

For one meal at Maze in London, I had a **bacon, lettuce, and tomato sandwich**, but **it** was a multilayered gel and mousse combination served in a martini glass. **It** was uniquely delicious.

Sentence Grammar

Contents

Question and Correct

14 Fragments

A sentence fragment is an incomplete sentence

To recognize a fragment, check for the basic requirements of a sentence:

- A sentence is a group of words with at least one independent clause.

- An independent clause has at least one subject and a complete verb, plus an object or complement if needed. An independent clause can stand alone as a thought, even though other sentences may be needed to clarify the thought or idea.

  Independent clause: She saw a concert last night.

  (*We don't know who* **she** *is, but a pronoun can be a subject. And we don't know what concert* **she** *saw, but this type of additional information can appear in accompanying sentences.*)

  Not an independent clause: When it rains.

  (*Say that group of words out loud, and you will hear that it's not a complete sentence because we don't know what happens as a result of the* **when** *clause.*)

14a Unintentional fragments

1. A fragment can result when a subject or verb is missing from the sentence.

   Fragment: The week I spent on the beach just relaxing with a good book and soaking up the bright sun every day we were there.

   (**Week** *is probably the intended subject here, but it has no verb.*)

2. A fragment can be caused by misplaced periods. This happens when a dependent phrase or dependent clause gets detached from the sentence to which it belongs. Some writers do this when they worry about the sentence being too long. Such fragments can be corrected by removing the period between the independent clause and the fragment.

Fragment. She decided to write her paper about the abuse of prescription drugs. **Then wondered if her choice was wise.** *(fragment)*

(The highlighted word group is a fragment with no subject for the verb **wondered.** *This phrase got disconnected from the independent clause that came before it and needs to be reattached.)*

Revision: She decided to write her paper about the abuse of prescription drugs, then wondered if her choice was wise.

Fragment: **Because he scored several three-point baskets** *(fragment)* **during the game.** Everyone applauded when he sat down on the bench.

(The highlighted word group is a dependent clause that was detached from the independent clause following it.)

Revision: Because he scored several three-point baskets during the game, everyone applauded when he sat down on the bench.

FAQ

How can I find fragments in my writing?

1. When you read your paper backward, from the last sentence to the first, you'll be able to notice a fragment more easily when you hear it without the sentence to which it belongs.

2. To find dependent clauses separated from the main clause, look at the marker word, such as *after, although, because, before, during, if, since, unless, when,* or *while.* If the clause is standing alone, attach it to the independent clause that completes the meaning.

   If this happens ──────▶? (*Then what? By itself, this is incomplete.*)

14b Intentional fragments

Writers occasionally write an intentional fragment for its effect on the reader. However, intentional fragments should be used only when the writer could have written a whole sentence but preferred a fragment.

Fragment: Dilek walked quietly into the room, unnoticed by the rest of the group. **Not that she wanted it that way.** She simply didn't know how to make an effective entrance.

15 Comma Splices and Fused Sentences

A comma splice and a fused sentence (also called a run-on sentence) are punctuation problems in compound sentences. A compound sentence is one that contains two or more independent clauses.

TRY THIS

Using Commas and Semicolons in Compound Sentences

There are three patterns for commas and semicolons in compound sentences:

1. *Comma and conjunction:*

   Independent clause, and independent clause.

   but
   nor
   so
   for
   or
   yet

   Kuljit found some sources for his research paper, **but** he still needs more information.

2. *Semicolon:* Independent clause; independent clause.

   Tiara majored in professional writing; she is now a technical writer for a biomedical firm.

3. *Semicolon and comma:*

   Independent clause; however, independent clause.
   therefore,
   moreover,
   consequently,
   (etc.)

   Dina planned to give her presentation on Tuesday; **however,** her professor asked her to speak on Thursday instead.

15a Comma splices

The comma splice is a punctuation error that occurs in one of two ways:

- When independent clauses are joined only by a comma and no coordinating conjunction.

  Comma splice: In Econ 150, students meet in small groups for
                    and
                    an extra hour each week, this helps them learn
                    from each other.

- When a comma is used instead of a semicolon between two independent clauses.

  Comma splice: The doctor prescribed a different medication,
                    ;
                    however, it's not helping.

15b Fused or run-on sentences

The fused or run-on sentence occurs when there is no punctuation between independent clauses. This causes the two clauses to be "fused" or "run on" into each other.

, and (or ;)
Fused sentence: I didn't know which job I wanted I couldn't decide.

FAQ

How can I fix comma splices, fused sentences, and run-ons?

- Between the two independent clauses, add a comma and then one of the seven joining words (*for, and, nor, but, or, yet, so*).
- Separate the independent clauses into two sentences.
- Change the comma to a semicolon.
- Make one clause dependent on the other clause.

---

16 Subjects and Verbs

16a Subject-verb agreement

Subject-verb agreement occurs when the subject and verb (or helping verb) endings agree in number and person. The subject of every sentence is either singular or plural (agreeing in number) and is in first (*I* or *we*), second (*you*), or third person (*he, she, it, they*). These determine the verb (or helping verb) ending. Verbs with singular subjects take singular endings, and verbs with plural subjects have plural endings.

Lavon   **takes**   lots of pictures with his phone.
(singular subject) *(singular verb)*

Singular nouns, pronouns, and nouns that cannot be counted, such as *news, time*, and *happiness* (see 35b), take verbs with singular endings.

I chew.   Water drips.   Time flies.   You laugh.

Plural

Plural nouns and pronouns take verbs with plural endings.

Numbers show.   The shoes are blue.   They stretch.

FAQ

How can I find the subject and verb in a sentence?

1. It's easier to find the verb first because the verb is the word or words that change when you change the time of the sentence from present to past or past to present.

Nikki **bikes** to work.   Yesterday, Nikki **biked** to work.
(verb is in present tense)   *(verb is in past tense)*

Tomorrow, Nikki **will bike** to work.
(verb is in future tense)

2. Eliminate phrases starting with the following words because they are normally not part of the subject:

including   along with   together with
accompanied by   in addition to   as well as

Everyone, including my sister, **is** here.
(subject)   *(verb)*

Buried subjects

It is sometimes difficult to find the subject word when it is buried among many other words. In such cases, disregard prepositional phrases; modifiers; *who, which*, and *that* clauses; and other surrounding words.

Almost **all** of my friends who live in Atlanta **are attending** the party.
(subject)   *(verb)*

(*In this sentence, **Almost** is a modifier of the subject **all**; of my friends is a prepositional phrase; and*

who live in Atlanta *is a who clause that describes* **friends**.)

Compound subjects

Subjects joined by *and* take a plural verb (X *and* Y = more than one, plural).

The **dog** and the **squirrel are** running around the tree.

But sometimes the words joined by *and* act together as a unit and are thought of as one thing. If so, use a singular verb.

Peanut butter and jelly is a popular filling for sandwiches.

Or and *either/or* in subjects

When the subject words are joined by *or*, *either . . . or*, *neither . . . nor*, or *not only . . . but also*, the verb agrees with the subject word closer to it.

Either **Aleeza** or her **children are** going to bed early.

Not only the **clouds** but also the **snow was** gray that day.

Clauses and phrases as subjects

When a whole clause or phrase is the subject, use a singular verb.

What I want to know is why I can't retake the test.

Saving money is difficult to do.

However, if the verb is a form of *be* and the noun after it (the complement) is plural, the verb has to be plural.

What we saw were pictures of the experiment. (*What we saw* = *pictures*).

Indefinites as subjects

Indefinite words with singular meanings, such as *each, every*, and *any*, take a singular verb when they are the subject or precede the subject word.

Each has her own preference.

Each book is checked in by the librarian.

However, when indefinite words such as *none, some, most,* or *all* are the subject, the number of the verb depends on the meaning of the subject.

Some of the book **is** difficult to follow.

(*The subject is a single portion of the book and needs a singular verb.*)

Some of us **are leaving** now.

(*The subject is several people, so it's plural and needs a plural verb.*)

Collective nouns and amounts as subjects

Collective nouns refer to a group or a collection (such as *team, family, committee,* and *group*). When a collective noun is the subject and refers to the group acting as a whole or as a single unit, the verb is singular:

Our **family has** a new car.

In most cases, a collective noun refers to the group acting together as a unit, but occasionally the collective noun refers to members acting individually. In that case, the verb is plural.

The **committee are** unhappy with each other's decisions.

When the subject names an amount, the verb is singular.

More than 125 **miles is** too far.   Six **dollars is** the price.

Plural words as subjects

Some words with an -*s* ending, such as *civics, mathematics, measles,* and *news,* are thought of as a single unit and take a singular verb.

Physics is fascinating.   Modern **economics shows** contradictions.

Some words, such as those in the following list, take a plural verb, even though they refer to one thing. (In many cases, there are two parts to these things.)

jeans are . . .   sunglasses cost . . .   thanks were . . .
riches are . . .   pants fit . . .   scissors cut . . .

Titles, company names, words, and quotations as subjects

For titles of written works, names of companies, words used as terms, and quotations, use singular verbs.

The Help **is** a good movie.

Thanks is not in his vocabulary.

Amazon is hiring.

"Cookies for sale!" she **said**.

Linking verbs

Linking verbs agree with the subject rather than the word that follows (the complement).

Her **problem is** frequent injuries.

Short **stories are** my favorite reading matter.

There is/are, here is/are, and *it*

When a sentence begins with *there* or *here*, the verb depends on the complement that follows the verb.

There is an excellent old **movie** on TV tonight.

Here are my **friends**.

However, *it* as the subject always takes the singular verb, regardless of what follows.

It was bears in the park that knocked over the garbage cans.

Who, which, that, and *one of* as subjects

When *who, which,* and *that* are used as subjects, the verb agrees with the previous word it refers to (the antecedent).

They are the **students who study** hard. He is the **student who studies** the hardest.

In the phrase *one of those who* (or *which* or *that*), it is necessary to decide whether the *who, which,* or *that* refers only to the one or to the whole group. Only then can you decide whether the verb is singular or plural.

Chang is **one of those shoppers who buy** most things online.

> (*In this case, Chang is part of a large group,* **shoppers** *who buy most things online, and acts like others in that group. Therefore,* **who** *takes a plural verb because it refers to* **shoppers**.)

The American Dictionary is **one of the dictionaries** on that shelf **that includes** Latin words.

> (*In this case,* **The American Dictionary**, *while part of a group of dictionaries, is specifically one that includes Latin words. The other dictionaries may or may not. Therefore,* **that** *refers to one dictionary and takes a singular verb.*)

16b   Verbs

Verbs that add *-ed* for the past tense and the past participle are regular verbs. The past participle is the form that has a helping verb such as "has" or "had." For a guide to using verb tenses, see 34a.

Regular Verb Forms			
	Present	**Past**	**Future**
Simple	I walk.	I walked.	I will walk.
Progressive	I am walking.	I was walking.	I will be walking.
Perfect	I have walked.	I had walked.	I will have walked.
Perfect progressive	I have been walking.	I had been walking.	I will have been walking.

Some brief samples of irregular verb forms are shown in the following tables. Consult a dictionary for more verbs.

Irregular Verb Forms				
	Present		**Past**	
Verb	Singular	Plural	Singular	Plural
be	I am	we are	I was	we were
	you are	you are	you were	you were
	he, she, it is	they are	he, she, it was	they were
have	I have	we have	I had	we had
	you have	you have	you had	you had
	he, she, it has	they have	he, she, it had	they had
do	I do	we do	I did	we did
	you do	you do	you did	you did
	he, she, it does	they do	he, she, it did	they did

Some Irregular Verbs		
Base (Present)	**Past**	**Past Participle**
be (am, is, are)	was, were	been
become	became	become
begin	began	begun
bring	brought	brought
come	came	come
do	did	done
eat	ate	eaten
find	found	found
forget	forgot	forgotten
get	got	gotten
give	gave	given
go	went	gone
grow	grew	grown
have	had	had
know	knew	known
lay	laid	laid
lie	lay	lain
make	made	made
read	read	read
say	said	said
see	saw	seen
sit	sat	sat
speak	spoke	spoken
take	took	taken
teach	taught	taught
think	thought	thought
write	wrote	written

16c Lie/lay and sit/set

Two sets of verbs, *lie/lay* and *sit/set*, can cause problems. Because they are related in meaning and sound, they are often confused with each other, but each one of each set has a different meaning.

Lie (recline)	She **lies** in bed all day. *(present)*
	She **lay** in bed all last week. *(past)*
Lay (put)	He **lays** his keys on the table. *(present)*
	He **laid** his keys on the table. *(past)*
Sit (be seated)	Please **sit** here by the window. *(present)*
	She **sat** by the window in class. *(past)*
Set (put)	Please **set** the flowers on the table. *(present)*
	He **set** the flowers on the desk before he left. *(past)*

16d Verb voice

Verb voice tells whether the verb is in the active or passive voice. In the active voice, the subject performs the action on the verb. In the passive voice, the subject receives the action. The doer of the action in the passive voice may be omitted or may appear in a "by the" phrase.

Active: The **child** **sang** the song.

Passive: The **song** **was sung** by the **child**.

16e Verb mood

The mood of a verb tells the following:

- It expresses a fact, opinion, or question (**indicative mood**).

- It expresses a command, request, or advice (**imperative mood**).

- It expresses a doubt, a wish, a recommendation, or something contrary to fact (**subjunctive mood**). In the subjunctive mood, present tense verbs stay in the simple base form and do not indicate the number and person of the subject. However, for the verb *be*, ***were*** is used for all persons and numbers.

Indicative: The new app **runs** well on this tablet computer.

Imperative: **Watch** the news to find out more about this issue.

Subjunctive: The doctor recommends that Amit **stop** smoking.
I wish I **were** rich.

17 Pronouns

17a Pronoun case

A pronoun is a word that substitutes for a noun. Pronouns change case according to their use in a sentence.

Subject case: **She** told a story.

Object case: Rosario told **them** a story.

Possessive case: The children liked **her** story.

Pronoun Cases

	Subject		Object		Possessive	
	Singular	Plural	Singular	Plural	Singular	Plural
First person	I	we	me	us	my, mine	our, ours
Second person	you	you	you	you	your, yours	your, yours
Third person	he	they	him	them	his	their, theirs
	she	they	her	them	her, hers	their, theirs
	it	they	it	them	it, its	their, theirs

TRY THIS

Correcting Common Problems with Pronouns

- Remember that *between, except,* and *with* are prepositions and take the object case.

  between you and ~~I~~ me   except Alexi and ~~she~~ her

  with ~~he~~ him and ~~I~~ me

- Don't use *them* as a pointing pronoun in place of *these* or *those.* Use *them* only as the object by itself.

  He liked ~~them~~ those socks. He liked them.

- Possessive case pronouns never take apostrophes.

  The insect spread ~~it's~~ its wings.

- Use possessive case before *-ing* verb forms.

  The crowd cheered ~~him~~ his making a three-point basket.

- Use reflexive pronouns (those ending in *-self* or *-selves*) to strengthen nouns they refer back to.

  Sarah puts too much suntan oil on herself.

- Don't use reflexive pronouns in other cases because you think they sound more correct. They aren't.

  They included ~~myself~~ me in the group.

Pronouns in compound constructions

To find the right case when your sentence has a noun and
a pronoun, temporarily eliminate the noun as you read the
sentence to yourself. You'll hear the case that is needed.

Jon and ~~him~~ went to the store.
> he

(*If* **Jon** *is eliminated, the sentence would be "***him*** *went
to the store." It's easier to notice the wrong pronoun case
this way.*)

Mrs. Weg gave the tickets to **Lutecia** and ~~I~~.
> me

(*Try dropping the noun,* **Lutecia**. *You'll be able to hear
that the sentence sounds wrong: "Mrs. Weg gave the
tickets to* **I**.*" Because* **to** *is a preposition, the noun or
pronoun that follows is the object of the preposition
and should be in the object case.*)

Who/whom

In informal speech, some people may not distinguish between
who and *whom*. But for formal writing, the cases are as
follows:

Subject	Object	Possessive
who	whom	whose
whoever	whomever	

Subject:	**Who** is going to the concert tonight? (**Who** is the subject of the sentence.)
	Give this to **whoever** wants it. (**Whoever** is the subject of **wants**.)
Object:	To **whom** should I give this ticket? (**Whom** is the object of the preposition **to**.)
Possessive:	No one was sure **whose** voice that was. (**Whose** is the possessive marker for **voice**.)

FAQ

When do I use *who* and when do I use *whom*?

If you aren't sure whether to use *who* or *whom*, turn a question
into a statement or rearrange the order of the phrase:

Question:	(Who, whom) are you looking for?
Rearranged order:	You are looking for **whom**.
	(*object of the preposition*)

Sentence:	She is someone (**who, whom**) I know well.
Rearranged order:	I know **whom** well.
	(direct object)

Pronoun case after *than* or *as*

In comparisons using ***than*** and ***as***, choose the correct pronoun case by filling in the words that are omitted.

He is taller than (**I, me**). (The omitted words here are ***am tall***.)

He is taller than **I** (am tall).

Our cat likes my sister more than (**I, me**). (The omitted words here are ***he likes***.)

Our cat likes my sister more than (he likes) **me**.

Pronoun case *we* or *us* before nouns

When ***we*** or ***us*** is used before a noun, such as "we players" or "us friends," use the case appropriate for the noun. You can hear which to use by omitting the noun.

(*We, Us*) players paid for our own equipment.

> **Test:** *Would you say "**Us** paid for the equipment" or "**We** paid for the equipment"? (**We** is the correct pronoun here.)*

The barista gave (*we, us*) customers our coffee.

> **Test:** *Would you say "The barista gave **we** our coffee" or "The barista gave **us** our coffee?" (**Us** is the correct pronoun here.)*

Pronoun case with *to* + verb (infinitive)

When you use a pronoun after an infinitive (*to* + verb), use the object case.

Mira offered to drive Orin and (*I, me*) to the meeting.

> (*Would you say "Mira offered to drive **I** to the meeting"? The correct pronoun is **me**.*)

Pronoun antecedents

Because pronouns substitute for nouns, they should agree with the nouns they refer to in number and gender.

Singular: The ***student*** turned in *her* lab report.

Plural: The ***students*** turned in *their* lab reports.

17b Pronoun reference

To avoid confusing your readers, be sure your pronouns agree with the words they refer to (their antecedents).

Unclear reference: Gina told Michelle that **she** took **her** car to the library.

(Did Gina take Michelle's car or her own car to the library?)

Revised: When Gina took **Michelle's** car to the library, she told Michelle she was borrowing it.

TRY THIS

Avoiding Vague Pronouns

Watch out for the vague uses of *they, this, it,* or *which* that don't refer to any specific group, word, or phrase (antecedent).

the screenwriters and producers
In Hollywood, ~~they~~ don't know what the American public really wants in movies.

> (Who *are the* **they** *referred to here?*)

serving as a forest ranger
Martina worked in a national forest last summer, and ~~this~~ may be her career choice.

> *(What does* **this** *refer to? Because no word or phrase in the first part of the sentence refers to the pronoun, the revised version has one of several possible answers.)*

Many people who have cell phones let their ringtones go off
and the loud ringing
loudly when sitting in movies or lectures, ~~which~~ bothers me.

> *(What does* **which** *refer to here? The fact that many people have cell phones, that they let their phones go off in movies or lectures, or maybe that the ringtones are so loud? The revised version has one of several possible answers.)*

Pronoun number

- ***Pronouns for collective nouns:*** For collective nouns, such as *group, committee,* and *family,* use either a singular or plural pronoun, depending on whether the group acts as a unit or acts separately as many individuals within the unit.

  The **committee** reached **its** decision before the end of the meeting.

  (Here the committee acted as a unit.)

The **committee** relied on **their** own consciences to reach a decision.

(*Here each member of the committee relied separately on his or her own conscience.*)

- ***Consistent pronoun use:*** Don't let your writing shift from singular to plural or plural to singular unless it's necessary.

  The **company** made a profit last year, but ~~they~~ *it* lost money when ~~their~~ *its* sales declined this year.

Pronouns with compound subjects

Compound subjects with *and* take the plural pronoun.

The **table and chair** were delivered promptly, but **they** were not the style I had ordered.

For compound subjects with *or* or **nor**, the pronoun agrees with the subject word closer to it.

The restaurant offered either regular **patrons** or each new **customer** a free cup of coffee with **his or her** dinner.

Pronouns with *who/which/that*

When ***who, which***, or ***that*** begins a dependent clause, use the word as follows:

- ***Who*** is used for people (and sometimes animals).

  He is a person **who** can help you.

- ***Which*** is used most often for nonessential clauses.

  The catalog, **which** I sent for last month, had some unusual merchandise.

  (*The **which** clause here is nonessential because the time when the catalog was ordered is not necessary to the meaning of the main clause.*)

- ***That*** is used most often for essential clauses.

  When I finished the book **that** she lent me, I was able to write my paper.

  (*The **that** clause here is essential because the reader needs to know which book helped the writer compose his paper.*)

Indefinite words

Indefinite words such as *any* and *each* usually take the singular pronoun.

Each of the boys handed in **his** uniform.

Indefinite pronouns

Indefinite pronouns are pronouns that don't refer to any specific person or thing, such as *anyone*, *no one*, *somebody*, or *each*. Some of them may seem to have a plural meaning, but in formal writing, treat them as singular. When another pronoun refers to one of these words, you can use *his or her*, switch to plural, use *they*, or use *a*, *an*, or *the*. (See 12a on inclusive language.)

Everyone brought **his or her** coat. (or)

All the people brought **their** coats. (or)

Everyone brought **their** coats.

> (*Some people view this example as incorrect. Others, such as the National Council of Teachers of English, accept this as a way to keep the language inclusive. See 12a.*)

(or) **Everyone** brought **a** coat.

18 Adjectives and Adverbs

18a Adjectives

Adjectives describe or add information about nouns and pronouns:

red	house		They	were **loud.**
(*adjective*)	(*noun*)		(pronoun)	(*adjective*)

Order of Adjectives

		Physical Description							
Determiner	Evaluation or Opinion	Size	Shape	Age	Color	Nationality	Religion	Material	Noun
a one her	lovely	big	round	old	green	English	Catholic	silk	purse

- the quiet Japanese rock garden
- a square blue cotton handkerchief
- my lazy old Siamese cat
- six excellent new movies
- many difficult physics problems
- every big green plant

To use adjectives and adverbs correctly:

- Use **-ed** adjectives (the **-ed** form of verbs, past participles) to describe nouns. Be sure to include the **-ed** ending.

  used clothing   **iced** tea   **experienced** driver

- Use adjectives following linking verbs such as **appear**, **seem**, **taste**, **feel**, and **look**.

  The sofa seemed **comfortable**. (sofa = comfortable)
  The water tastes **salty**. (water = salty)

18b Adverbs

Adverbs modify verbs, verb forms, adjectives, and other adverbs:

danced	**gracefully**		**very**	tall
(*verb*)	(*adverb*)		(*adverb*)	(*adjective*)

ran	**very**	quickly
(*verb*)	(*adverb*)	(*adverb*)

Many adverbs end in **-ly.**

Adjective	Adverb
rapid	rapidly
nice	nicely
happy	happily

However, the **-ly** ending isn't a sure test for adverbs because some adjectives have an **-ly** ending (*early, ghostly*), and some adverbs do not end in **-ly** (*very, fast, far*). To be sure, check your dictionary to see whether the word is listed as an adjective or adverb.

Use adverbs to modify verbs.

He ran ~~quick.~~ quickly.   The glass broke ~~sudden.~~ suddenly.   She sang ~~sweet.~~ sweetly.

When you use adverbs such as *so, such,* and *too,* be sure to complete the phrase or clause.

Hailey was **so** tired. that she left the office early.

Malley's is **such** a popular restaurant. that reservations are recommended.

TRY THIS

Understanding Commonly Used Adjectives and Adverbs

Be sure to use the following adjectives and adverbs correctly:

Adjective	Adverb
sure	surely
real	really
good	well
bad	badly

She ~~sure~~ ^{surely} likes to dance.   The car runs ~~bad.~~ ^{badly.}   He sings ~~good~~ ^{well} .

FAQ

What is the difference between *good* and *well*?

Good is used as an adjective to modify a noun.

This is a **good** peach.
(adjective)

Well is most often used as an adverb.

Shake **well** before using.
(adverb)

Well is used an adjective when it refers to good health.

Despite her surgery, she looks **well**.
(adjective)

18c   Comparisons

Adverbs and adjectives are often used to show comparison, and their forms indicate the degree of comparison. In comparisons, most adjectives and adverbs add *-er* and *-est* as endings or combine with the words **more** and **most** or **less** and **least**.

- **Positive form** is used when no comparison is made.

  a **large** box   an **acceptable** offer

- **Comparative form** is used when two things are being compared (with *-er, more,* or *less*).

  the **larger** of the two boxes   the **less acceptable** of the two

- **Superlative form** is used when three or more things are being compared (with *-est, most,* or *least*).

  the **largest** of the six boxes
  the **least acceptable** of all the offers

Adjectives and Adverbs in Comparison		
Positive	**Comparative**	**Superlative**
(for one: uses the base form)	*(for two: uses* **-er**, **more**, *or* **less***)*	*(for three or more: uses* **-est**, **most**, *or* **least***)*
tall	taller	tallest
pretty	prettier	prettiest
cheerful	more cheerful	most cheerful
selfish	less selfish	least selfish
Curtis is **tall**.	Curtis is **taller** than Rachel.	Curtis is the **tallest** player on the team.

Irregular Forms of Comparison		
Positive	**Comparative**	**Superlative**
(for one)	*(for two)*	*(for three or more)*
good	better	best
well	better	best
little	less	least
some	more	most
much	more	most
many	more	most
bad, badly	worse	worst

TRY THIS

Making Comparisons Correctly

Avoid double comparisons in which both the *-er* and *more* (or *-est* and *most*) are used.

the ~~most~~ farthest   ~~more~~ quicker

19 Modifiers

19a Dangling modifiers

A dangling modifier is a word or word group that refers to (or modifies) a word or phrase that has not been clearly stated in the sentence. When an introductory phrase does not name the doer of the action, the phrase then refers to (or modifies) the subject of the independent clause that follows.

Having finished the assignment, **Jillian** turned on the TV.

> (**Jillian**, *the subject of the independent clause, is the doer of the action in the introductory phrase. She finished the assignment.*)

However, when the intended subject (or doer of the action) of the introductory phrase is not stated as the subject of the independent clause, the result is a dangling modifier.

Having finished the assignment, the **TV** was turned on.

> (*This sentence says that* **the TV** *finished the homework. Because it is unlikely that TV sets can complete assignments, the introductory phrase has no logical word to refer to. Sentences with dangling modifiers say one thing while the writer means another.*)

Characteristics of dangling modifiers

- They most frequently occur at the beginning of sentences but can also appear at the end.
- They often have an *-ing* verb or a *to* + **verb** phrase near the start of the whole phrase.

TRY THIS

Revising Dangling Modifiers

1. Name the appropriate or logical doer of the action as the subject of the independent clause.

    Dangling Modifier: **Having arrived** late for practice, a **written excuse** was needed.

    Revised: **Having arrived** late for practice, the **team member** needed a written excuse.

Dangling Modifier:	After **getting** a degree in education, more **experience** in the classroom is needed to be a good teacher.
Revised:	After **getting** a degree in education, **Lu** needed more classroom experience to become a good teacher.

2. Name the doer of the action in the dangling phrase.

Dangling modifier:	Without **knowing** the guest's name, **it** was difficult for Marina to introduce him to her husband.
Revised:	Because **Marina did** not **know** the guest's name, it was difficult to introduce him to her husband.

19b Misplaced modifiers

A misplaced modifier is a word or word group placed so far away from what it refers to (or modifies) that readers may be confused. Modifiers should be placed close to the words they modify in order to keep the meaning clear.

Misplaced modifiers: The assembly line workers were told that they had been fired **by the personnel director.**

(*Were the workers told by the personnel director that they had been fired, or were they told by someone else that the personnel director had fired them?*)

Revised: The assembly line workers were told **by the personnel director** that they had been fired.

Single-word modifiers should be placed immediately before the words they modify. Note the difference in meaning in these two sentences:

I earned **nearly** $30.

(*The amount was almost $30 but not quite.*)

I **nearly** earned $30.

(*I almost had the opportunity to earn $30, but it didn't work out.*)

FAQ

What should I look for to avoid misplaced modifiers?

When you proofread, check these words to be sure they are as close as possible to the words they refer to.

almost	hardly	merely	only
even	just	nearly	simply

19c Split infinitives

Split infinitives occur when modifiers are inserted between *to* and the **verb**. Some people object to split infinitives, but others consider them grammatically correct. In some cases, inserting a modifier between *to* and the **verb** is the more natural phrasing.

To *quickly* go

> (*Some people accept this, and others prefer to revise to* ***to go quickly***.)

To *easily* reach

> (*Most writers prefer this as more natural than "He wanted* **easily** *to reach the top shelf."*)

20 Shifts

Consistency in writing involves using the same (1) pronoun person and number, (2) verb tense, and (3) tone (see 10b).

20a Shifts in person or number

Avoid shifts between first, second, and third person pronouns and between singular and plural. The following table shows the three persons in English pronouns:

Pronoun Person	Singular	Plural
First person (the person or persons speaking)	I, me	we, us
Second person (the person or persons spoken to)	you	you
Third person (the person or persons spoken about)	he, she, it, him, her, it	they, them

Unnecessary shift in person

Once you have chosen to use first, second, or third person, shift only with a good reason.

In **a person's** life, the most important thing ~~you do~~ *he or she does* is to decide
    (third)   *(second)*
on a type of job.

> (*This is an unnecessary shift from third to second person.*)

Unnecessary shift in number

To avoid pronoun inconsistency, don't shift unnecessarily in number from singular to plural (or from plural to singular).

Women face
~~A woman faces~~ challenges to career advancement. When **they**
(singular)   *(plural)*
take maternity leave, **they** should be sure that opportunities for
            (plural)
promotion are still available when they return to work.

> (*The writer uses the singular noun* **woman** *in the first sentence but then shifts to the plural pronoun* **they** *in the second sentence.*)

20b Shifts in verb tense

Because verb tenses indicate time, keep writing in the same time (past, present, or future) unless the logic of what you are writing about requires a switch.

Necessary shift: Many people today **remember** very little about the first Gulf War except the filmed scenes of fighting they **watched** on television news at the time.

> (*The verb* **remember** *reports a general truth in the present, and the verb* **watched** *reports past events.*)

Unnecessary shift: While we **were watching** the last game of the World Series, the TV picture suddenly **breaks up.**

*(The verb phrase **were watching** reports a past event, and there is no reason to shift to the present tense verb **breaks up**.)*

Revised: While we **were watching** the last game of the World Series, the TV picture suddenly **broke up**.

21 Parallelism

21a Parallel structure

Parallel structure involves using the same grammatical form for equal ideas in a list or comparison. The balance of equal elements in a sentence helps your reader see the relationship between ideas and adds emphasis. Often, the equal elements repeat words or sounds.

Parallel: The instructor explained **how to start the engine**
(1)
and **how to shift gears**.
(2)

(Phrases 1 and 2 are parallel in that both start with **how to**.*)*

Parallel: **Getting the model airplane off the ground** was even
(1)
harder than **building it from a kit**.
(2)

(Phrases 1 and 2 are parallel phrases that begin with **-ing** *verb forms.)*

Parallelism is needed in the following constructions:

- **Items in a series or list**

Parallel: Our ideal job candidate will know how to

- **manage** team projects
- **troubleshoot** computer problems
- **communicate** effectively with clients.

(parallelism with verbs)

- ***Both . . . and, either . . . or, whether . . . or, neither . . . nor, not . . . but, not only . . . but also*** (correlative conjunctions)

Parallel: Both his professional appearance and his knowledge of the company suggested he wanted to make a good impression during his job interview.

(parallelism with noun phrases)

- *And, but, or, nor, yet, for, so* (coordinating conjunctions)

Parallel: Job opportunities are **increasing** in the health fields **but decreasing** in many areas of engineering.

(parallelism using -ing verbs)

- **Comparisons using *than* or *as***

Parallel: The mayor noted that it was easier **to agree** to the new budget **than to veto** it.

(parallelism in a comparison with to + verb)

21b Faulty parallelism

Nonparallelism (or **faulty parallelism**) is grammatically incorrect and can also lead to a lack of clarity.

When the investigator took over, he started his inquiry by **calling** the
                                                                    requesting   (1)
witnesses back and ~~requested~~ that they repeat their stories.
                  ^   (2)

The article looked at **future uses of computers** and ~~what~~ **their role**
                                                      (1)   (2)
~~will be~~ in the next decade.

TRY THIS

Proofreading for Parallel Structure

As you proofread, **listen** to the sounds when you are linking or comparing similar elements. Do they provide balance by sounding alike? Parallelism often adds emphasis by the repetition of similar sounds.

Not parallel: Braden wondered **whether to search** for a full-time job or **if he should apply** to graduate school.

Parallel: Braden wondered whether **to search** for a full-time job or **to apply** to graduate school.

Parallel: Braden wondered **if he should** search for a full-time job or **if he should apply** to graduate school.

IV

Punctuation

Contents

Question and Correct

22 Sentence Punctuation Patterns (for Commas and Semicolons)

Commas and semicolons in sentences

- For simple sentences, use pattern 1.
- For compound sentences, use patterns 2, 3, and 4.
- For complex sentences, use patterns 5, 6, 7, and 8.

1. **Independent clause .**

   This novel has a memorable conclusion.

2. | **Independent clause ,** | **coordinating conjunction** | **independent clause .** |
   |---|---|---|
   | | and   or | |
   | | but   so | |
   | | for   yet | |
   | | nor | |

   Claire wanted a snack **,** **so** she ordered a pizza.

3. **Independent clause ; independent clause .**

   Jin is looking for a summer job **;** he wants to work in a hospital or a medical clinic.

4. | **Independent clause ;** | **independent clause marker ,** | **independent clause .** |
   |---|---|---|
   | | however, | |
   | | nevertheless, | |
   | | therefore, | |
   | | consequently, | |
   | | (etc.) | |

   Fewer people are buying newspapers **;** **however** **,** more people are reading news online.

5. | **Dependent clause marker** | **dependent clause ,** | **independent clause .** |
   |---|---|---|
   | Because   While | | |
   | Since   After | | |
   | If   (etc.) | | |
   | When | | |

When Oliver graduated from college **,** he started a new job as a reporter.

6. | **Independent clause** | **dependent clause marker** *because* *since* *if* *when* *while* *after* (etc.) | **dependent clause** **.** |

Emergency vehicles arrived quickly **after** the police officer called for help.

7. | **Subject ,** | **nonessential ,** **dependent clause** | **verb/predicate .** |

(Use commas before and after the dependent clause if it is nonessential.)

Sayid **,** **who is a talented mechanic** **,** repaired the helicopter.

8. | **Subject** | **essential** **dependent clause** | **verb/predicate .** |

(Do not use commas before and after essential clauses.)

The fossils **that the scientist discovered last month** have been donated to a museum.

23 Commas

23a Commas between independent clauses

Use commas when you join independent clauses.

Independent clause: a clause that can stand alone as a sentence

Compound sentence: a sentence with two or more independent clauses

Use the comma with one of the seven joining (coordinating) conjunctions. Some writers remember this list as "**FAN BOYS**," spelled out with the first letter of each word.

For   And   Nor   But   Or   Yet   So

(*Clause*)**, and** (*clause*).

The political debate covered many issues**, but** the candidates did not impress me.

Alternative: If one of the independent clauses has a comma, use a semicolon with the joining word instead.

Alesha**,** not Mateya**,** is the team captain**; but** Mateya assists the coach during practice.

Exception: A comma may be omitted if the two independent clauses are short and there is no danger of misreading.

We were tired **so** we stopped the game.

23b Commas after introductory elements

Use a comma after introductory words, phrases, and clauses that come before the main clause in your sentence.

Introductory words

Well,   In fact,   First,

Well, perhaps he meant no harm. **In fact,** he wanted to help.

Introductory phrases and clauses

Long phrases (usually four words or more) and clauses:

Without his new smartphone, Rashaad could not remember his friends' phone numbers.

23c Commas with essential and nonessential elements

When you include words, phrases, or clauses not essential to the meaning of the sentence and that could be included in another sentence, place commas before and after the nonessential element. If the word, phrase, or clause is essential to the meaning of the sentence, don't use commas.

Identifying Essential and Nonessential Words and Clauses

You can decide if an element is essential by reading the sentence without it. If the meaning changes, that element is essential.

Essential: Apples **that are green** are usually very tart.

If you remove the clause *that are green*, the statement changes to indicate that all apples are usually very tart.

Nonessential: Madison, **who is my cousin**, will move to Denver when she graduates college.

Whether or not Madison is my cousin, she will still move to Denver. *Who is my cousin* is not essential.

23d Commas in series and lists

Use commas when three or more items are listed in a series. The items can be words, phrases, or clauses. In a list of three items, some writers prefer to omit the comma before the "and."

He first spoke to Julio, then called his roommate, and finally phoned me.

My favorite sports are football, baseball, and basketball.

(The comma after baseball *is optional.)*

Do I need a comma between a list of two items or phrases?

You need at least three items or phrases in a list in order to use commas. Some writers mistakenly put a comma between two items (often verbs) in a sentence.

Misused comma: No one has ever been able to locate the source of the river, and follow it to its starting place.

| **Revised:** | No one has ever been able to locate the source of the river and follow it to its starting place. |

23e Commas with adjectives

Use commas to separate two or more adjectives that describe the same noun equally.

cold, dark water   happy, healthy baby

But when adjectives are not equal, do not use commas to separate them.

six big dogs   bright green sweater

23f Commas with dates, addresses, geographical names, and numbers

- **With dates listing month and day before the year**

  In a heading or list: May 27, 2013 (*or*) 27 May 2013

  In a sentence: The order was shipped on March 18, 2012, but not received until April 14, 2012.

- **With addresses**

  In a letter heading or on an envelope:

  Jim Johnson, Jr.
  216 Oakwood Drive
  Mineola, NM 43723-1342

  In a sentence:

  You can write to Senator Michael Jameson, Jr., 1436 West-wood Drive, Birlingham, ID 83900, for more information.

- **With geographical names**

  Put a comma after each element in a place name.

  The convention next year will be in Chicago, Illinois, and in Washington, D.C., the year after that.

- **With numbers**

  4,300,150   27,000   4,401 (*or*) 4401

23g Commas with interrupting words or phrases

Use commas to set off words and phrases that interrupt the sentence.

> The committee was, however, unable to agree.

> The weather prediction, much to our surprise, was accurate.

23h Commas with quotations

Use a comma before quotations that begin or end with words such as *he said*.

> Everyone was relieved when the chairperson said, "I will table this motion until the next meeting."

> "I forgot," Serkan explained, "to complete the materials section of my lab report."

23i Unnecessary commas

- Don't separate a subject from its verb.

  Unnecessary comma: An eighteen-year-old in most states, is now considered an adult.

- Don't put a comma between two verbs that share the same subject.

  Unnecessary comma: We turned off our phones, and began to study.

- Don't put a comma in front of every *and* or *but*.

  Unnecessary comma: We decided that we should not lend her the money, and that we should explain our decision.

  (The **and** *in this sentence joins two* **that** *clauses.)*

- Don't put a comma in front of a direct object. Remember that clauses beginning with *that* can be direct objects.

  Unnecessary comma: He explained to me, that he is afraid to fly because of terrorists.

- Don't put commas before a dependent clause when it comes after the main clause except for strong contrast.

  Unnecessary comma: She texted me, because she was going to miss class.

| **Strong contrast:** | The movie actor was still quite upset, although he did win an Academy Award. |

- Don't put a comma after *such as* or *especially*.

| **Unnecessary comma:** | There are several kinds of dark bread from which to choose, such as**,** whole wheat, rye, pumpernickel, and bran. |

24 Apostrophes

24a Apostrophes with possessives

The apostrophe shows ownership, but this is not always obvious.

TRY THIS

Testing Words for Possession

Turn the surrounding words into an **of the** phrase.

day's pay   Mike's shoes

the pay of the day   the shoes of Mike

- For singular nouns, use '*s*.

    the book**'s** author   a flower**'s** smell

- For a singular noun ending in -*s*, the *s* after the apostrophe is optional, especially if it would make pronunciation difficult.

    James**'s** car   (*or*)   James**'** car

    Euripides**'** story

    (*Saying* Euripides's story *is difficult.*)

- For plural nouns ending in -*s*, add only an apostrophe.

    both teams**'** colors   six days**'** vacation

- For plural nouns not ending in -*s* (such as *children* or *mice*), use *'s*.

  the children**'s** game   six men**'s** coats

- For indefinite pronouns (pronouns ending in -*body* and -*one*, such as *no one* and *everybody*), use *'s*.

  no one**'s** fault   someone**'s** hat

- For compound words, add *'s* to the last word.

  brother-in-law**'s** job   everyone else**'s** preference

- For joint ownership by two or more nouns, add *'s* after the last noun in the group. When individually owned, add *'s* after each noun.

  Lisa and Vinay**'s** house   (*Lisa and Vinay own the house jointly.*)

  Lisa**'s** and Vinay**'s** houses   (*Lisa and Vinay each own different houses.*)

FAQ

Where does the apostrophe go to show possession?

For singular nouns that don't end in **'s:**

Word	Possessive Marker	Result
cup	**'s**	cup**'s** handle

When you aren't sure whether the word is plural or not, remember this sequence:

- Write the word.
- Then write the plural, if needed.
- Then add the possessive apostrophe.

Thus, everything to the left of the apostrophe is the word its plural, if needed.

Word	Plural Marker	Possessive Marker	Result
cup	**s**	**'**	cup**s'** handles

24b Apostrophes with contractions

Use the apostrophe to mark the omitted letter or letters in contractions.

> it's = it is   don't = do not   that's = that is   '79 = 1979
> he's going = he is going

24c Apostrophes with plurals

Use apostrophes to form plurals of letters, abbreviations with periods, numbers, and words used to refer to the word itself, not the thing or meaning it represents. The apostrophe is optional if the plural is clear.

Plural of a word used as the word itself:

Madison uses too many *wow*'s in her e-mails.

Necessary apostrophes:

a's   B.A.'s   *A*'s

Optional apostrophes:

9s (*or*) 9's   UFOs (*or*) UFO's   ands (*or*) and's

&s (*or*) &'s   Ph.D.'s (*or*) Ph.D.s

24d Unnecessary apostrophes

Don't use the apostrophe with possessive pronouns (such as *hers* and *its*) or with the regular plural forms of nouns.

| **Not correct:** | it's sound | yours' | I bought five apples'. |
| **Correct:** | its sound | yours | I bought five apples. |

25 Semicolons

The semicolon is a stronger mark of punctuation than a comma, and it is used with two kinds of closely related equal elements:

- between independent clauses
- between items in a series when any of the items contains a comma.

25a Semicolons in compound sentences

Use the semicolon when joining independent clauses not joined by the seven connectors that require commas: *and, but, for, nor, or, so, yet.*

Here are two patterns for using semicolons:

- **Independent clause + semicolon + independent clause.**

    He often watched TV reruns; she preferred to read instead.

- **Independent clause + semicolon + joining word or phrase + comma + independent clause.**

    He often watched TV reruns; **however**, she preferred to read.

Transitional words or phrases are all the joining words other than *and, but, for, or,* or *nor* that can be used to connect two independent clauses.

also	finally	instead
besides	for example	nevertheless
consequently	however	still
even so	in addition	therefore

A semicolon can be used instead of a comma with two independent clauses joined by *and, but, for, nor, or, so,* or *yet* when one of the clauses contains a comma.

- **Independent clause with commas + semicolon + independent clause.**

    Senator Dowson, who was accused of bribery, has resigned; he
    (independent clause #1 with commas)

    has refused to discuss his resignation with reporters.
    (independent clause #2)

25b Semicolons in a series

For clarity, use semicolons to separate a series of items in which one or more of the items contain commas. Semicolons are also preferred if items in the series are especially long.

- Items with their own commas:

  > Among her favorite movies were old Cary Grant pictures, such as *Arsenic and Old Lace*; any of Woody Allen's films; and children's classics, including *The Sound of Music* and *The Wizard of Oz*.

- Long items in a series:

  > When planning the trip, she considered the length of travel time between cities where stops would be made; the number of people likely to get on at each stop; and the times when the bus would arrive at major cities where connections would be made with other buses.

25c Semicolons with quotation marks

Place semicolons after quotation marks.

> Her answer to my question was "I'll have to think about that"; she clearly had no answers.

25d Unnecessary semicolons

Don't use a semicolon between a clause and a phrase or between an independent clause and a dependent clause.

Unnecessary semicolon: They wanted to see historical buildings; especially the court-house. *(should be a comma)*

Unnecessary semicolon: He tried to improve his tennis serve; because that was the weakest part of his game. *(should be no punctuation)*

Don't use a semicolon in place of a dash, comma, or colon.

Incorrect semicolon: The office needed more equipment; a laptop, an iPad, and a paper shredder. *(should be a colon, not a semicolon)*

26 Quotation Marks

26a Quotation marks with direct and indirect quotations

Quotation marks with prose quotations

Direct quotations:	the exact words said by someone you heard or read and are recopying. Enclose exact quotations in quotation marks.
Indirect quotations:	not someone's exact words but a rephrasing or summary of those words. Don't use quotation marks for indirect quotations.

If a quotation is longer than four lines, set it off as a block quotation by indenting one-half inch from the left margin. Use the same spacing between lines as in the rest of your paper, and don't use quotation marks.

- Direct quotation of a whole sentence: Use a capital letter to start the first word of the quotation.

   Mr. and Mrs. Yoder, farm owners, said, "We refuse to use that pesticide because it might pollute the nearby wells."

- Direct quotation of part of a sentence: Don't use a capital letter to start the first word of the quotation.

   Mr. and Mrs. Yoder stated that they "refuse to use that pesticide" because of possible water pollution.

- Indirect quotation: Don't use quotation marks.

   According to their statement, the Yoders will not use the pesticide because of potential water pollution.

- Quotation within a quotation: Use single quotation marks (' at the beginning and ' at the end) for a quotation inside another quotation.

   The agriculture reporter explained, "When I talked to the Yoders last week, they said, 'We refuse to use that pesticide.'"

If you leave some words out of a quotation, use an ellipsis (three spaced periods; see 27h) to indicate omitted words. If you need to insert something within a quotation, use brackets [ ] to enclose the addition. (See 27g.)

Quotation marks in poetry

When you quote a single line of poetry, write it like other short quotations. Separate two lines of poetry with a slash (/) at the end of the first line. Leave a space before and after the slash. If the quotation is three lines or longer, set it off, indented one-half inch, like a longer quotation, and do not use quotation marks.

Quotation marks in dialogue

Write each person's speech, however short, as a separate paragraph. Use commas to set off *he said* or *she said*. Closely related bits of narrative can be included in the paragraph. If someone's speech goes on for several paragraphs, use quotation marks at the beginning of each paragraph but not at the end of any paragraph except the last one.

26b Quotation marks for minor titles and parts of wholes

Use quotation marks for the titles of parts of larger works (titles of book chapters, magazine articles, website articles, blog entries, unpublished dissertations, lectures, and episodes of television and radio series) and for short or minor works (songs, short stories, essays, short poems, other literary works that are shorter than book length, and titles of photographs).

> "The Star-Spangled Banner"
> "The Drone Queen" (an episode of *Homeland*)

Use italics for larger, more complete works (*Hamlet*). Don't use quotation marks or italics for the titles of most religious texts (the Bible) or legal documents. (See 29a.)

26c Quotation marks for words

Use quotation marks or italics for words used as words rather than for their meaning.

> The word "accept" is often confused with "except." (or)
> The word *accept* is often confused with *except.*

26d Quotation marks with other punctuation

- Put commas and periods inside quotation marks. When a reference follows a short quotation, put the period after the reference.

  "Adonais," a poem by Percy Bysshe Shelley, memorializes John Keats.
  . . . after the stunning success" (252).

- Put a colon or semicolon after the quotation marks.

  . . . until tomorrow";

- Put a dash, a question mark, or an exclamation point inside the quotation marks when these punctuation marks are part of the quotation and outside the quotation marks when the marks apply to the whole sentence.

  He asked, "Do you need this book?"
  Does Dr. Lim tell all her students, "You must work harder"?

26e Unnecessary quotation marks

Don't put quotation marks around the titles of your essays, common nicknames, bits of humor, technical terms, and well-known expressions.

27 Other Punctuation

27a Hyphens

Hyphens have a variety of uses:

- **For compound words:**
  Some compound words are one word:
  weekend   granddaughter   hometown

  Some compounds are two words:
  high school   executive director   turn off

  Some compounds are joined by hyphens:
  father-in-law   president-elect   clear-cut

Fractions and numbers from twenty-one to ninety-nine that are spelled out have hyphens.

one-half　　　　thirty-six　　　　nine-tenths

For new words or compounds you are forming, check your dictionary. But not all hyphenated words appear there, especially new ones, and usage varies between dictionaries for some compounds.

e-mail (*or*) email　　witch-hunt (*or*) witch hunt
wave-length (*or*) wavelength (*or*) wave length

For hyphenated words in a series, use hyphens as follows:

five- and six-page essays

(Leave an extra space after the hyphens in all hyphenated words except the last one.)

- **For two-word units:**
  Use a hyphen when two or more words before a noun work together as a single unit to describe the noun. When these words come after the noun, they are not hyphenated.

  He needed up-to-date statistics. (*or*) He needed statistics that were up to date.

  They repaired the six-inch pipe. (*or*) They repaired the pipe that was six inches long.

  Do not use a hyphen with adverbs ending in -*ly*.

  That was a widely known fact.

- **For prefixes, suffixes, and letters joined to a word:**
  Use hyphens between words and prefixes *self-, all-,* and *ex-*.

  self-contained　　all-encompassing　　ex-president

  For other prefixes, such as *anti-, pro-,* and *co-*, use the dictionary as a guide.

  co-op　　　　antibacterial　　　　pro-choice

  Use a hyphen to join a prefix to a capitalized word or with figures and numbers.

  anti-American　　non-Catholic　　　　pre-1998

  Use a hyphen when you add the suffix -*elect*.

  president-elect

  Use a hyphen to avoid doubling vowels and tripling consonants and to avoid ambiguity.

  anti-intellectual　bell-like　re-cover　re-creation

- **To divide words between syllables when the last part of the word appears on the next line:**

  Every spring the nation's capital is flooded with tour-
  ists snapping pictures of the cherry blossoms.

- **When dividing words at the end of a line:**

  - Don't divide one-syllable words.

  - Don't leave one or two letters at the end of a line.

  - Don't put fewer than three letters on the next line.

  - Don't divide the last word in a paragraph or on a page.

  - Divide compound words between the parts of the compound. If a word contains a hyphen, break only at the hyphen.

- **When splitting website addresses that continue onto the next line:**

  - Don't insert an extra hyphen at the end of a line.

  - In MLA format, break the line after a slash or *http://*.

  - In APA format, break before a slash or other punctuation but after *http://*.

27b Colons

Use colons as follows:

- **To announce items at the end of the sentence**
  The company sold only electronics they could service: computers, printers, and television sets.

- **To separate independent clauses**
  Use a colon instead of a semicolon to separate two independent clauses when the second clause restates or amplifies the first.
  The town council voted not to pave the gravel roads: it did not have the funds for road improvement.

- **To announce long quotations**
  Use a colon to announce a long quotation (more than one sentence) or a quotation not introduced by words such as *said* or *stated*.
  The candidate offered only one reason to vote for her: "I will not raise parking meter rates."

- **In salutations and between elements**
  Dear Dr. Philippa: 6:12 a.m.   Genesis 1:8

- **With quotation marks**
  Put colons after closing quotation marks.
  "Don't argue with your boss": that's her motto for office harmony.

- **Unnecessary colons**

  Don't use a colon after a verb or phrases like *such as* or *consisted of.*

Unnecessary colon:	The two best players were: Timon Lasmon and Maynor Field.
Revised:	The two best players were Timon Lasmon and Maynor Field.
Unnecessary colon:	The camping equipment consisted of: tents, lanterns, and matches.
Revised:	The camping equipment consisted of tents, lanterns, and matches.

27c End punctuation

Periods

- Use periods at the ends of sentences that are statements, mild commands, indirect questions, or polite questions to which answers aren't expected.

    Electric cars are growing in popularity. (*statement*)

    Turn off your cell phones during class. (*mild command*)

    Would you please let me know when you're done. (*polite question*)

- Use a period with abbreviations, but don't use a second period if the abbreviation is at the end of the sentence.

    R.S.V.P.   U.S.A.   Mr.   8 a.m.

- A period is not needed after names of agencies, common abbreviations, names of well-known companies, and U.S. Postal Service state abbreviations.

    NATO   NBA   CIA   YMCA   IBM   DNA   TX

- Put periods that follow quotations inside the quotation marks. But if there is a reference to a source, put the period after the reference.

    She said, "I'm going to Alaska next week."
    Neman notes that "the claim is unfounded" (6).

Question marks

- Use a question mark after a direct question but not after an indirect one.

    Did anyone find my flash drive? (*direct question*)

    Jules wonders if he should buy a new iPhone. (*indirect question*)

- Place a question mark inside quotation marks if the quotation is a question. Place the question mark outside quotation marks if the whole sentence is a question.

Drora asked, "Is she on time?"
Did Eli really say, "I'm in love"?

- Question marks may be used between parts of a series.

  Would you like to see a movie? go shopping? eat at a
  restaurant?

- Use a question mark to indicate doubt about the correctness of a date, number, or other piece of information. But
  do not use it to indicate sarcasm.

  The ship landed in Greenland about 1521 (?) but did not keep
  a record of where it was.

  Not polite: Matti's sense of humor (?) evaded me.

  Revised: Matti's sense of humor evaded me.

Exclamation points

- Use the exclamation point after a strong command or a
  statement said with great emphasis or with strong feel-
  ing. But don't overuse the exclamation point.

  Correct: I'm absolutely delighted!
  Unnecessary: Wow! What a great party! I enjoyed every
     minute of it! The food was delicious, and
     the music was fantastic!

- Enclose the exclamation point within the quotation
  marks only if it belongs to the quotation.

  As he came in, he exclaimed, "I've won the lottery!"

27d Dashes

The dash is informal but can be used to add emphasis or
clarity, to mark an interruption or shift in tone, or to introduce a list. If you use a word processor without the dash,
use two hyphens to indicate the dash with no space before
or after the hyphens.

  The cat looked at me so sweetly—with a dead rat in its mouth.

27e Slashes

Use the slash to mark the end of a line of poetry and to
indicate acceptable alternatives. For poetry, leave a space
before and after the slash. For alternatives, leave no space.
The slash is also used in website addresses.

He repeated Milton's lines: "The mind is its own place, and in itself / Can make a Heaven of Hell, a Hell of Heaven."

pass/fail   and/or   http://www.whitehouse.gov

27f Parentheses

Use parentheses to enclose supplementary or less important material added as further explanation or example or to enclose figures or letters in a numbered list.

The newest officers of the club (those elected in May) were installed at the ceremony.

They had three items on the agenda: (1) the budget, (2) parking permits, and (3) election procedures.

27g Brackets

Use brackets to add your comments or additional explanation within a quotation and to replace parentheses within parentheses. The Latin word *sic* in brackets means you copied the original quotation exactly as it appeared, but you think there's an error.

We agreed with Fellner's claim that "this great team [the Chicago Bears] will go to the Super Bowl next year."

The lawyer explained, "We discussed the matter in a fiendly [*sic*] manner."

27h Omitted words (ellipsis)

Use an ellipsis (a series of three periods, with one space before and after each period) to indicate that you are omitting words or part of a sentence from the source you are quoting. If you omit a whole sentence or paragraph, add a fourth period with no space after the last word preceding the ellipsis.

"modern methods . . . with no damage."

"the National Forest System . . ." (Smith 9).

"federal lands. . . . They were designated for preservation."

If you omit words immediately after a punctuation mark (such as a comma) in the original, include that mark in your sentence.

"because of this use of the forest, . . ."

V

Mechanics

Contents

Question and Correct

28 Capitalization

28a Proper nouns and common nouns

Capitalize proper nouns, which are words that name one particular thing, most often a person or place rather than a general type or group of things. Listed here are categories of words that should be capitalized. If you are not sure about a particular word, check your dictionary.

Proper noun	Common noun
James Joyce	man
Thanksgiving	holiday
University of Maine	state university
Apple	computer
May	month

- Persons
  - Vincent Baglia   Rifka Kaplan   Masuto Tatami
- Places, including geographical regions
  - Milwaukee   Alberta   Northeast
- Peoples and their languages
  - French   Swahili   Portuguese
- Religions and their followers
  - Buddhist   Judaism   Christianity
- Members of national, political, racial, social, civic, and athletic groups
  - Democrat   African American   Green Bay Packers
  - Danes   Friends of the Library   Olympics Committee
- Institutions and organizations
  - Girl Scouts   Library of Congress   Lions Club
- Historical documents
  - Declaration of Independence   Magna Carta
- Periods and events, but not centuries
  - Middle Ages   World War II   twentieth century
- Days, months, and holidays, but not seasons
  - Tuesday   Thanksgiving   winter
- Trademarks
  - Coca-Cola   Toyota   Google
- Holy books and words denoting the Supreme Being (pronouns referring to God may be capitalized or lowercased)
  - Talmud   Bible   Lord

- Words and abbreviations derived from specific names, but not the names of things that have lost that specific association and now refer to general types

  | Stalinism | Freudian | NBC |
  | french fries | pasteurize | italics |

- Place words, such as *street, park,* and *city,* that are part of specific names

  | New York City | Wall Street | Zion National Park |

- Titles that precede people's names, but not titles that follow names

  | Governor Chris Christie | Aunt Sue | President Barack Obama |
  | Chris Christie, governor | Sue, my aunt | Barack Obama, president |

- Words that indicate family relationships when used as a substitute for a specific name

  | Here is a gift for | Li Chen sent a gift to his |
  | Mother. | mother. |

- Titles of books, magazines, essays, websites, blogs, movies, plays, and other works, but not articles (*a, an, the*), short prepositions (*to, by, on, in*), or short joining words (*and, but, or*) unless they are the first or last word. With hyphenated words, capitalize the first and all other important words.

  | *The Taming of the Shrew* | *The Indo-European Languages* |
  | *The Ground Beneath Her Feet* | *A Brother-in-Law's Lament* |

- The pronoun *I* and the interjection *O,* but not the word *oh*

  "Sail on, sail on, O ship of state," I said as the canoe sank.

- Words placed after a prefix that are normally capitalized

  | un-American | anti-Semitic | pro-Israel |

28b Capitals in sentences, quotations, and lists

- Capitalize the first word of every sentence.

- Capitalize the first word of a comment in parentheses if the comment is a complete sentence. Use lowercase if the comment is not a full sentence.

  The American Olympic ski team (which receives some government support) spent six months training for the elimination trials, whereas the German team trained for over two years. (Like most European nations, Germany provides financial support for its team.)

- Do not capitalize the first word in a series of questions in which the questions are not full sentences.

  What did the interviewer want from the rock star? details of her personal life? news about her next project?

- Capitalize the first word of directly quoted speech, but not a continuation of an interrupted direct quotation or a quoted phrase or clause that is integrated into the sentence.

    She answered, "Everyone will know the truth."

    "Everyone," she answered, "will know the truth."

    When Bataglio declined the nomination, he explained that he "would try again another year."

- Capitalize the first word in a list after a colon if each item in the list is a complete sentence or if each item is displayed on a line of its own.

    The popularity of walking as an alternative to jogging has led to various improvements: (1) better designs for walking shoes, (2) an expanding market for walking sticks, and (3) a rapid growth in the number of manufacturers selling walking shoes.

    (or)

    The popularity of walking as an alternative to jogging has led to various improvements:

    1. Better designs for walking shoes
    2. An expanding market for walking sticks
    3. A rapid growth in the number of manufacturers selling walking shoes

29 Italics

Use italics for titles of long works in word-processed documents. When you are writing by hand, use underlining (a printer's mark to indicate words to set in italics) for the kinds of titles and names indicated in this section.

29a Titles

- Use italics for titles and names of long or complete works, including the following:

Books	*Moby Dick*
Magazines	*Entertainment Weekly*
Newspapers	*The Washington Post*
Works of art (visual and performance)	*Swan Lake*

Pamphlets	*Saving Energy in Your Home*
Television, radio, website, and streaming series, but not individual episodes	*House of Cards*
Films and videos	*The Artist*
Long plays	*Macbeth*
Long musical works	*Canon in D*
Long poems	*In Memoriam*
Software	*Adobe InDesign*
Recordings	*Born This Way*
Websites (not individual webpages)	*The Onion*
Ships, airplanes, and trains	*Orient Express*

- Do not use italics or quotation marks for references to the Bible and other religious works, legal documents, the Internet, and titles of websites used as verbs.

Genesis	Bible	Upanishads
Torah	U.S. Constitution	Declaration of Independence
Internet	Google	Facebook

29b Other uses of italics

- Foreign words and phrases and scientific names of plants and animals
  de rigueur   *Felis domesticus*

- Trademarked names used as words
  Some words, such as *Kleenex*, are brand names for products.

- Letters used as examples or terms
  In English, the letters *ph* and *f* often have the same sound.

- Words being emphasized
  It *never* snows here at this time of year.

  (Use italics for emphasis sparingly.)

Do not use italics for the following:

- Words of foreign origin that are now part of English
alumni	cliché	manga
blitz	chutzpah	karaoke

- Titles of your own papers

30 Numbers

Style manuals for different fields and companies vary. The suggestions for writing numbers given here are generally useful as a guide for academic writing.

- Spell out numbers that can be expressed in one or two words, and use figures for other numbers.

Words	Figures
eight pounds	284 days
six dollars	$49.99
thirty-seven years	8,962 bushels

- Use a combination of figures and words for numbers that are close together to make the combination clear.

    The club celebrated the birthdays of six 90-year-olds born in the city.

Use figures for the following:

- Days and years

September 18, 2013	(or)	18 September 2013
A.D. 1066		
in 1931–1932	(or)	in 1931–32
the 1990's	(or)	the 1990s

- Time of day

8:00 A.M. (or) a.m.	(or)	eight o'clock in the morning
4:30 P.M. (or) p.m.	(or)	half past four in the afternoon

- Addresses

15 Tenth Street		
350 West 114 Street	(or)	350 West 114th Street
Prescott, AZ 86301		

- Identification numbers

Room 88	Channel 603
Interstate 95	Elizabeth II

- Page and division of books and plays

page 30	Book I
Act 3, sc. 2	Ch. 3

- Decimals and percentages

6.1 average	13½ percent
0.057 metric ton	

- Numbers in series and statistics
  two apples, six oranges, and three bananas
  115 feet by 90 feet
  Be consistent, whichever form you choose.

- Large round numbers

$14 billion	(or)	fourteen billion dollars
11.5 million	(or)	11,500,000

- Repeated numbers (in legal or commercial writing)
  Notice must be given at least ninety (90) days in advance.

Do not use figures for the following:

- Numbers that can be expressed in one or two words
  in his forties   the twenty-first century

- Dates when the year is omitted
  June sixth

- Numbers beginning sentences
  Ninety-five percent of our students are from South Carolina.

31 Abbreviations

In writing government, business, social science, science, and engineering documents, abbreviations are used frequently. However, for writing in the humanities, only a limited number of abbreviations are generally used.

31a   Abbreviating titles

- *Mr., Mrs.*, and *Ms.* are abbreviated when used as titles before a name.
  Mr. Toyagama   Ms. Patuk   Mrs. Begay

- *Dr.* and *St.* ("Saint") are abbreviated only when they immediately precede a name; they are written out when they appear after the name.
  Dr. Marlen Chafo   Marlen Chafo, doctor of neurology

- *Prof., Sen., Gen., Capt.*, and similar abbreviated titles can be used when they appear in front of a full name or before initials and a last name but not when they appear before the last name only.
  Gen. R. G. Brindo   General Brindo

- *Sr., Jr., J.D., Ph.D., M.F.A., C.P.A.*, and other abbreviated academic titles and professional degrees can be used after the name.

  Leslie O'Brien, Ph.D.   Kim Takamota, C.P.A.

- *Bros., Co.*, and similar abbreviations are used only if they are part of the exact name.

  Bass & Co.   Warner Bros.

31b   Abbreviating places

In general, spell out names of states, countries, continents, streets, rivers, and so on. But there are a few exceptions:

- Use the abbreviation *D.C.* in Washington, D.C.

- Use *U.S.* only as an adjective, not as a noun.

  U.S. training bases   training bases in the United States

- If you include a full address in a sentence, use the postal abbreviation for the state.

  For further information, write to us at 100 Peachtree Street, Atlanta, GA 30300, for a copy of our free catalog.

  The company's headquarters, on Peachtree Street in Atlanta, Georgia, will soon be moved.

31c   Abbreviating numbers

- Write out numbers that can be expressed in one or two words.

  eighteen   fifty-six   345

- The dollar sign is generally acceptable when the written-out phrase would be three words or more.

  $29 million   thirty dollars

- For temperatures, use figures, the degree symbol, and F (for Fahrenheit) or C (for Celsius).

  10°F   25°C

31d   Abbreviating measurements

Spell out units of measurement, such as *acre, meter, foot,* and *percent*, but use abbreviations for measurements in tables, graphs, and figures.

31e   Abbreviating dates

Spell out months and days of the week.

  January   Tuesday

The abbreviations B.C., B.C.E. (before the common era), and C.E. (common era) are placed after the year, but A.D. is placed before. With dates and times, the following are acceptable:

57 B.C.	57 B.C.E.	329 C.E.	A.D. 329
A.M., P.M. (or) a.m., p.m.		EST (or) E.S.T.	

31f Abbreviating names of familiar organizations or other entities

Use abbreviations for names of organizations, agencies, countries, and things usually referred to by their initials.

IBM	NAACP	NASA	NOW
PTA	UNICEF	the former USSR	DVD

If you are using the initials for a term that may not be familiar to your readers, spell it out the first time and give the initials in parentheses. From then on, you can use the initials.

The study of children's long-term memory (LTM) has been difficult because of the lack of a universally accepted definition of childhood LTM.

31g Abbreviating Latin expressions and documentation terms

Some Latin expressions always appear as abbreviations.

Abbreviation	Meaning
cf.	compare
e.g.	for example
i.e.	that is
et al.	and others
etc.	and so forth
vs. (or) v.	versus

The following abbreviations are appropriate for bibliographies and footnotes, as well as in informal writing, but, for formal writing, use the full phrase instead. The format for abbreviations may vary among style manuals, so use the abbreviations appropriate for the style you are following.

Abbreviation	Meaning
ed., eds.	editor (or) edited by, editors
n.d.	no date of publication given
n.p.	no place of publication given
n. pag.	no page number given
p., pp.	page, pages
vol., vols.	volume, volumes

32 Spelling

English spelling is difficult because it contains many words from other languages that have different spelling conventions. In addition, English has several ways to spell some sounds. But correct spelling is important, partly to be sure your words are understood correctly and partly because you don't want to signal your reader that are you are careless or not very knowledgeable.

TRY THIS

Improving Your Spelling

Following these strategies can help you improve your spelling.

- **Learn some common spelling rules.** Read the useful spelling rules in 32b.
- **Look up words in the dictionary.** If you are unsure of a spelling, try looking it up in a print or online dictionary. Many word-processing programs, such as Microsoft Word, also have built-in dictionaries.
- **Make up associations that will help you remember tricky words.** For example, you could try remembering that *dessert* is the sweet treat you'd like seconds of. So it has an extra *s*. And *desert*, with one *s*, is the one that refers to barren sandy places.

32a Proofreading

Proofreading means reading your work slowly and carefully to catch misspellings and typographical errors. This is best done after you have finished writing and are preparing to turn your paper over to your readers.

TRY THIS

Proofreading for Spelling Errors

Try these strategies to catch your spelling errors:

- **Slow down.** Proofreading requires slowing down your reading rate to see all the letters in each word.
- **Zoom in.** If you proofread on your computer, set the display at 125 percent or more so that you can clearly see each word.

- **Focus on each word.** One way to slow yourself down is to point a pencil or pen at each word as you say it aloud or quietly to yourself.

- **Read backward.** Move backward through each line from right to left. In this way, you won't be listening for meaning or checking for grammatical correctness.

FAQ

Won't a spell-checker catch all of my spelling errors?

Spell-checkers are useful tools, particularly as a final proofreading step in combination with other strategies. However, they can't catch all spelling errors:

- **Sound-alike words (homonyms).** Spell-checkers cannot always distinguish between words that sound alike, such as *there* and *their* or *its* and *it's.*

- **Substitution of one word for another.** For example, if you meant to write *own* and typed *one* instead, the spell-checker is not likely to catch the error.

- **Many proper nouns.** Some well-known proper nouns, such as *Washington,* may be in the spell-checker dictionary, but many others will not be.

- **Misspellings the spell-checker can't match to an appropriate word.** If you misspell words, the spell-checker may highlight the error, but it might not be able to suggest the correct spelling. If this happens, use a dictionary to find the word.

- **Missing words.** If you forget to type a word, the spell-checker will not flag it for you.

32b Some spelling guidelines

ie/ei

Write *i* before *e* / except after *c* / or when sounded like "*ay*" / as in *neighbor* and *weigh.* This rhyme reminds you to write *ie* except under two conditions:

- When the two letters follow a *c.*

- When the two letters sound like *ay* (as in *day*).

Some *ie* Words		Some *ei* Words	
believe	field	ceiling	eight
chief	yield	receive	deceive

- The following common words are exceptions to this rule:

conscience	either	height	neither	seize	sufficient
counterfeit	foreign	leisure	science	species	weird

Doubling consonants

- **One-syllable words:** If the word ends with a single short vowel and a consonant, double that last consonant when adding a suffix beginning with a vowel.

| shop | shopped | shopping | shopper |
| wet | wetted | wetting | wettest |

- **Two-syllable words:** For words with two or more syllables that end with a vowel and a consonant, double the consonant when (1) you are adding a suffix beginning with a vowel and (2) the last syllable of the word is accented.

| occur | occurred | occurring | occurrence |
| regret | regretted | regretting | regrettable |

Final silent *-e*

Drop the final silent *-e* when you add a suffix beginning with a vowel. But keep the final *-e* when the suffix begins with a consonant.

| line | lining | care | careful |
| smile | smiling | like | likely |

Words such as *true/truly* and *argue/argument* are exceptions to this rule.

Plurals

- Most plurals are formed by adding *-s*. But add *-es* when words end in *s, sh, ch, x,* or *z* because another syllable is needed to make the ending easy to pronounce.

one ankle	two ankles
one box	two boxes
one wish	two wishes

- With phrases and hyphenated words, pluralize the last word unless another word is more important.

one systems analyst	two systems analysts
one sister-in-law	two sisters-in-law
one attorney general	other attorneys general

- For words ending in a consonant plus *-y*, change the *-y* to *-i* and add *-es*. For proper nouns, keep the *-y*.

one company	four companies
a monkey	two monkeys
Mr. Henry	the Henrys

- For some words, form the plural by changing the base word. Other words have the same form for singular and plural. And other words, taken from other languages, form the plurals in the same way as the original language.

one child	several children
one woman	two women
one deer	nine deer
one medium	some media

FAQ

Are apostrophes needed when making single words into plurals?

Apostrophes are used to show possession (like *Sara's book*) or in contractions (such as *didn't* or *would've*), not for making words plural. For most plurals, just add *s*. See Chapter 24 for more information about the correct use of apostrophes.

two bikes	NOT: two bikes'
four oranges	NOT: four orange's

32c Sound-alike words (homonyms)

Word	Meaning	Example
accept:	to agree/receive	I have to accept the facts.
except:	other than	I called everyone except him.
affect:	to influence	Pollen affects my allergies.
effect:	a result	Sneezing is the effect.
anyone:	any person at all	This problem would make anyone angry.
any one:	specific person or thing in a group	Any one of those children could have taken the ball.
than:	used to compare	He is smarter than I.
then:	indicates time	Then I read a book.
their:	shows possession	The boys flew their kites.
there:	indicates location	They found it over there.
they're:	they are	They're happy now.
to	preposition	We are going to the movies.
two	number	He has two dogs.
too	very or also	This cake is too sweet.
your:	shows possession	Your suit looks great.
you're:	you are	You're ready for your interview.

VI

Multilingual Speakers

Contents

Question and Correct

	SECTION	PAGE
LEARNING OBJECTIVE: Understanding the style of American academic English		
✦ What are some characteristics of American style in writing?	33a	113
✦ How is American-style writing organized?	33a	113
✦ Are conciseness and a clearly announced topic important for American audiences?	33a	113
✦ Is it important in American writing to cite sources?	33a	113
✦ What does *World Englishes* refer to?	33c	115
✦ What are some websites that can help speakers of other languages learn American English?	33d	116
LEARNING OBJECTIVE: Learning about verb tenses, helping verbs, modal verbs, phrasal verbs, gerunds, and infinitives		
✦ What are the verb tenses in English, and how are they used?	34a	117
✦ How do helping verbs such as *be*, *do*, and *have* combine with main verbs?	34b	119

33 American Style in Writing/ESL Resources

33a American style

If your first language is not English, you may have writing style preferences that are different from American style and questions about English grammar and usage. Your style preferences and customs will depend on what language(s) you are most familiar with, but in general, consider the following differences between the languages you know and academic style in American English.

	Language Styles of Other Cultures	American Academic Language and Style
Conciseness	In some cultures, writers try for a style with a variety of words and phrases. Ideas can be repeated in various ways.	Effective academic and public writing style in American English is concise and avoids unnecessary words.
Introduction of topic	In some languages, the topic is not immediately announced or stated at all. Instead, suggestions lead readers to develop the main ideas themselves.	In American English, there is a strong preference for announcing the topic in the opening paragraph or near the beginning of the paper.
Organization	Digressions, or moving off the main topic into related matters, are encouraged in some cultures because they add to the richness of ideas.	In American English, there is a preference for staying on the topic and not moving away, or digressing, from it.

(continued)

	Language Styles of Other Cultures	American Academic Language and Style
Pattern of reasoning	Writers in some cultures prefer inductive reasoning, moving from specifics to the more general conclusion.	American academic writing is usually deductive, beginning with general ideas and moving to more specific reasons or details.
Citation of sources	In some cultures, there is less attention to citing sources, ideas, or the exact words used by others. Ideas of great scholars, for example, can be used without citation because it is assumed that readers know the sources.	In American academic writing, writers are expected to cite all sources of information that are not generally known by most people. A writer who fails to credit the words or ideas of others is in danger of being viewed as a plagiarist.

For writers from some other cultures, the American academic preference for organizing a paper from general to specific (deductive) may require a different way of thinking. This is because writing in some cultures moves toward the general thesis or main point of an argument by the end of the document. This is described as writing inductively.

33b American English grammar versus the grammar of other languages

If English is not your first language, you will notice that American English grammar may differ from your first or other languages in many ways. Some ways that American English grammar may be different from the grammar of other languages:

- **Sentence order.** American English sentences generally move from subject to verb to object. But sentences that are questions have the helping part of the verb first. (See Chapter 16.)

Subject	→	verb	→	object (if there is an object)
Martina	→	likes	→	strong coffee.

Part of verb	→	subject	→	rest of verb	→	object
Does	→	Martina	→	like	→	strong coffee?

- **Show time in verbs.** Verbs in American English show time (see 16b).

  Parth **drives** his car to campus.
  (*present tense*)

  Parth **drove** his car to campus.
  (*past tense*)

- **Show number in verbs.** Verbs in American English show whether the subject is singular or plural (see 16b).

  The battery **needs** to be recharged.
  (*singular verb*)

  The batteries **need** to be recharged.
  (*plural verb*)

- **Show gender in pronouns** (see Chapter 17).

  She washed **her** car.   **He** washed **his** car.
  (*female*)   (*female*)   (*male*)   (*male*)

- **Place adjectives before nouns** (see 18a).

  The **long road** wound into the **dark forest**.
  (*adjective*)(*noun*)   (*adjective*)(*noun*)

33c American English and World Englishes

American academic English is the English explained in this book, but it is only one form of spoken and written English. Other varieties of English used around the globe are referred to as World Englishes. No variety of English is better or more correct than another; each is appropriate for the circumstances and purposes for which it is being used. These varieties are just different forms of a language widely used around the world and may vary in pronunciation, vocabulary, spelling, punctuation, and grammatical rules.

You will want to write in grammatically correct and stylistically appropriate American English when you are studying in American schools and communicating with Americans. But when you are communicating with other World English speakers and writers, the World English you use is acceptable for social and sometimes business purposes.

33d Resources for learning English as another language

Some websites where you can find useful resources for learning English as another language include the following:

dictionary.cambridge.org

The site offers definitions in American, British, business, and learner's dictionaries, plus listings of dictionaries useful for people learning English as another language.

owl.english.purdue.edu

Purdue University's Online Writing Lab page includes links to handouts on ESL issues as well as other resources.

www.openculture.com

Open Culture offers links to educational language resources, including audio podcasts and online videos.

www.eslcafe.com

Dave Sperling's ESL Café provides discussion forums, help with pronunciation and slang, idioms, grammar lessons, quizzes, and other aids.

www.1-language.com

1-Language.com offers free English courses; an audio listening center; English courses for those who speak Chinese, German, or French; and other resources.

www.englishforum.com

Aardvark's English Forum includes dictionaries, interactive exercises, resources for teachers, world weather and news, and links to other useful sites.

34 Verbs

Unlike sentences in some other languages, verbs are required in English sentences because they indicate time and person (see 16b–e for information about verb forms, voice, and mood). The basic building blocks of English sentences are the subject and verb (see Chapter 16) and, when appropriate, the direct object. The order for sentences that are not questions is subject → verb → object. Sentences that are questions have helping verbs before the subject, and sentences that are commands do not state the subject because it is understood as *you*.

Standard order: Amit bought a new car.   The snow is falling.

Question: Did Amit buy a new car?   Is the snow falling?

Command: Change the TV channel.   Please give me the book.

*(The subject **you** is understood.)*

34a   Verb tenses

Progressive tenses: Use a form of *be* plus the *-ing* form of the verb, such as *going* or *running:*

She **is going** to the concert tonight.

They **are waiting** for me.

Perfect tenses: Use a form of *have* plus the past participle, such as *walked* or *gone.*

They **have finished** the project.

Juna **has answered** my question.

Present tense

Simple present:

- present actions or conditions

    She **feels** happy.   He **pays** the bill.

- a general action or literary truth

    The sun **sets** later during the summer.

    Ice cream **is** sweet.

- habitual actions

    I **take** my dog to the park every morning.

    They **are always** polite.

- future time

    The concert **begins** at 7:00 p.m. this evening.

    Next year I **will graduate.**

Present progressive: activity in progress, not finished, or continuing

He **is studying** Swedish.   It **is raining** out.

Present perfect: actions that began in the past and lead up to and include the present

She **has lived** in Alaska for two years.

That building **has been** there for more than one hundred years.

Present perfect progressive: action that began in the past, continues to the present, and may continue into the future

They **have been building** that parking garage for six months.

The politician **has been planning** his campaign for months.

Past tense

- **Simple past:** completed actions or conditions

  They **ate** breakfast in the cafeteria.

  He **woke up** early.

- **Past progressive:** past action that took place over a period of time or was interrupted by another action

  He **was swimming** when the storm began.

- **Past perfect:** action or event completed before another event in the past

  No one **had heard** about the crisis when the newscast began.

- **Past perfect progressive:** ongoing condition in the past that has ended

  I **had been** majoring in engineering, but now I'm studying economics.

Future tense

- **Simple future:** actions or events in the future

  The store **will open** at 9:00 a.m.

  The letter **will arrive** tomorrow.

- **Future progressive:** future action that will continue for some time

  I **will be working** on that project next week.

- **Future perfect:** action that will be completed by or before a specified time in the future

  Next summer, they **will have been** here for twenty years.

- **Future perfect progressive:** ongoing action or condition until a specific time in the future

  By tomorrow, I **will have been waiting** for the delivery for one month.

34b   Helping verbs with main verbs

Helping or auxiliary verbs combine with other verbs.

Forms of Helping Verbs

be	am	is	are	were +*ing* form of verb
have	have	has	had	
do	do	does	did	

34c   Modal verbs

Modal verbs are helping verbs that indicate possibility, uncertainty, necessity, or advisability. Use the base form of the verb after the modal.

| can | may | must | should | would |
| could | might | shall | will | ought to |

Your car battery **can die** if you leave your headlights on all night.

May I **take** this?   She **ought to buy** that purse.

34d   Two-word (phrasal) verbs

Some verbs are followed by a second (and sometimes a third) word that combine to indicate the meaning. Many dictionaries will indicate the meanings of these phrasal verbs.

look over ("examine")   She **looked over** the contract.
look up ("search for")   I need to **look up** that phone number.

The second word of some of these verbs can be separated from the main verb by a noun or pronoun. For other verbs, the second word cannot be separated from the main verb.

Manuel told the team to *count* **him** *in. (separable)*
The team could *count on* **him** to help. *(cannot be separated)*

Please *look* **this** *over. (separable)*
He *got over* **his cold**. *(cannot be separated)*

34e   Verbs with *-ing* and *to* + verb form

Some verbs combine only with the *-ing* form of the verb (the gerund), some combine only with the *to* + verb form (the infinitive), and some can be followed by either form.

Verbs Followed Only by -*ing* Forms (Gerunds)

admit	enjoy	recall
appreciate	finish	recommend
deny	keep	risk
dislike	practice	suggest

He *admits spending* that money.

I *enjoy eating* chocolate.

She *risked losing* her scholarship.

Verbs Followed Only by *to* + Verb Forms (Infinitives)

agree	have	plan
ask	mean	promise
claim	need	wait
decide	offer	wish

We *agree to send* an answer soon.

She *decided to buy* a new cell phone.

They *planned to go* on vacation.

Who *needs to leave* now?

Verbs That Can Be Followed by Either Form

begin	like	remember
continue	love	start
hate	prefer	try

They *begin to sing*.   (*or*)   They *begin singing*.

I *tried to fix* the car.   (*or*)   I *tried fixing* the car.

35 Nouns (Count and Noncount)

Proper and common nouns

Proper nouns name specific places, things, and people. They begin with capital letters; all other names are **common nouns** and are not capitalized.

Count and noncount nouns

Common nouns are of two types: count and noncount nouns. **Count nouns** name things that can be counted because those things can be divided into separate and distinct units. Count nouns have plurals and usually refer to things that can be seen, heard, touched, tasted, or smelled.

Count Nouns

book	one book, two books
chair	a chair, several chairs
child	the child, six children

Noncount nouns name things that cannot be counted because they are abstractions or things that cannot be cut into parts. Noncount nouns do not have plurals and may have a collective meaning. They are used with singular verbs and pronouns. They are never used with *a* or *an*, but they can be used with *some*.

Noncount Nouns

air	humor	oil	fun
furniture	literature	weather	freedom

The names of many foods and materials are noncount nouns.

bread	corn	electricity	wood
coffee	spaghetti	steel	cotton

To indicate the amount for a noncount noun, use a count noun first. If you use *some*, use a singular verb.

a pound of coffee	a loaf of bread	some milk
an ear of corn	a gallon of oil	a cup of sugar

36 Articles (*A, An,* and *The*)

A/An

A and *an* identify a noun in a general or indefinite way and refer to any member of a group. *A* and *an*, which mean "one among many," are generally used with singular count nouns (see Chapter 35).

She likes to read **a** book before going to sleep

> *(This sentence does not specify which book but refers to any book.)*

He ordered **an** egg for breakfast.   I need **a** pen to sign this.

The

The identifies a particular or specific noun in a group or a noun already identified in a previous phrase or sentence. *The* may be used with singular or plural nouns.

She read **the** book that I gave her.

> *(This sentence identifies a specific book.)*

A new model of computer was introduced yesterday. **The** model will cost much less than **the** older model.

> *(**A** introduces the noun the first time it is mentioned, and then **the** is used afterward whenever the noun is mentioned.)*

Some uses of *the*

- Use *the* when an essential phrase or clause follows the noun.
  The man who is standing at the door is my cousin.

- Use *the* when the noun refers to a class as a whole.
  The ferret is a popular pet.
  The French drink a lot of wine.

- Use *the* with names that combine proper and common nouns.
  the British Commonwealth   **the** Gobi Desert   **the** University of Illinois

- Use *the* when names are plurals.
  the Netherlands   **the** Balkans   **the** Smiths

- Use *the* with names that refer to rivers, oceans, seas, points on the globe, deserts, forests, gulfs, and peninsulas.
  the Nile   **the** Pacific Ocean   **the** Persian Gulf

- Use *the* with superlatives.
  the best reporter   **the** most expensive car   **the** largest window

No articles

Articles are not used with names of streets, cities, states, most countries, continents, lakes, parks, mountains, languages, sports, holidays, universities and colleges without *of* in the name, and academic subjects.

He traveled to Botswana. She applied to Brandeis University.

She is studying Mandarin. My major is political science.

37 Prepositions

Prepositions in English show relationships between words. The following guide will help you choose among *on, at, in, of, for*, and *with* to indicate time, place, and logical relationships.

Prepositions of time

on Use with days (**on** Monday).

at Use with hours of the day (**at** 9:00 p.m.) and with *noon, night, midnight*, and *dawn* (**at** midnight).

in Use with other parts of the day: *morning, afternoon, evening* (**in** the morning); use with months, years, seasons (**in** the winter).

They are getting married **on** Sunday **at** four o'clock **in** the afternoon.

Prepositions of place

on Indicates a surface on which something rests
She put curtains **on** the windows.
He wrote it **on** paper.

at Indicates a point in relation to another object
I'll meet you **at** Second Avenue and Main Street.

in Indicates an object is inside the boundaries of an area or volume
She is **in** the bank. The car is **in** the garage.

Prepositions to show logical relationships

of Shows relationship between a part (or parts) and the whole
One **of** her teachers gave a quiz.
Six **of** the balls were red.

of	Shows material or content
	They gave me a basket **of** food.
	He memorized a list **of** words.
for	Shows purpose
	We bought seeds **for** our garden.
	I reached **for** the phone.
with	Shows the means used
	He dug the hole **with** a shovel.
	She paid the bill **with** her credit card.
with	Shows cause or origin
	Matt was sick **with** the flu.
	He traveled **with** no plan in mind.
with	Shows possession
	The car **with** the Indiana license plate is mine.
	Please continue **with** your project.

38 Omitted and Repeated Words

38a Omitted words

Subjects and verbs can be omitted in some languages but are necessary and must appear in English sentences. The only exception in English is the command, which has an understood subject: "Move those chairs here." (The understood subject here is "you.")

Subjects

Include a subject in the main clause and all other clauses. *There* and *it* may sometimes serve as subject words. The subject is left out only when expressing a command (*Put that box here, please.*).

Certainly, _{there} are many confusing rules in English spelling.

_{It} is about ten miles from here to the shopping mall.

Verbs

Verbs such as *am, is*, and *are* and other helping verbs are needed in English and cannot be omitted.

is
Nurit ^ studying to be a computer programmer.

has
She ^ been studying ancient Mayan ruins in Mexico for many summers.

38b   Repeated words

In some languages, the subject can be repeated as a pronoun before the verb. In English, the subject is included only once.

The plane that was ready for takeoff ~~it~~ stopped on the runway.

> (**Plane** *is the subject of the verb* **stopped**, *and* **it** *is an unnecessary repetition of the subject.*)

When relative pronouns such as *who, which*, and *that* or relative adverbs such as *where* or *when* are the object of the verb, no additional word is needed.

The woman tried on the hat that I left ~~it~~ on the seat.

> (**That** *is the object of the verb* **left**, *and* **it** *is an unnecessary repetition.*)

The city where I live ~~there~~ has two soccer fields.

> (**Where** *is the object of the verb* **live**, *and* **there** *is an unnecessary repetition.*)

39   Idioms

An **idiom** is an expression that means something beyond the literal meaning of the words. An idiom such as *kick the bucket* (meaning "die") cannot be understood by examining the meanings of the individual words. Many idioms are used only in informal English. Dictionaries of American English, such as the *Cambridge International Dictionary of Idioms* (dictionary.cambridge.org) define many commonly used phrases.

bottom line	the last figure on a financial balance sheet, the result or final outcome or ultimate truth
hold water	be proved, be correct
on one's toes	eager, alert
on the house	something that is free
on the table	open for discussion
throw in the towel	give up and stop trying, quit in defeat
see the light	understand something clearly at last, realize one's mistake
under the weather	feel sick

The meanings of two-word (phrasal) verbs (see 34d) also change according to the prepositions that follow the verbs. Note the difference in the meanings of the two-word (phrasal) verbs *look after*, *look over*, and *look for:*

look after   take care of
Could you **look after** my dog while I am away on vacation?

look over   examine something (briefly)
I'll **look over** the report you gave me.

look for   to seek or search
I'll **look for** some bargains when I am shopping.

VII

Research

Contents

Question and Correct

40 Finding a Topic

40a Selecting a topic

Selecting a topic is one of the most important decisions you will make in the research process. You'll want to find a topic that is interesting, fits the guidelines of your assignment, and can be researched effectively with the resources and time available to you.

TRY THIS

To Select a Topic

- **Read newspapers, magazines, and online news sites.** Issues discussed in the news can often serve as effective paper topics.
- **Use Internet search engines and library databases.** Type in search terms for a topic interesting to you. (See 41b and 41c.)
- **Check reference guides.** Browse through the *Library of Congress Subject Headings* and the *Readers' Guide to Periodical Literature*.

40b Focusing your topic

After you identify a general topic, the next step is to make it more specific and manageable. As you define your topic, ask yourself: Is it too broad? too narrow? too obvious? If so, then you can work on revising the topic to make it more manageable and fit the guidelines of your assignment.

TRY THIS

Thinking About the Guidelines for Your Assignment

- How much time will you have to complete the research?
- Is there a number or type of sources required for this assignment?
- How long will your project need to be?

- Does your assignment specify a purpose for your writing? Is it to inform? to persuade? to educate? to call to action?
- Who is the intended audience for your writing project? Is it your peers? a group of readers who resist your idea? a person or group who has the power to make the changes you suggest?

Narrowing topics that are too broad

As you begin, consider whether your initial idea is too general and might need to be narrowed down. To narrow your topic, think of it as a tree whose branches are possible subtopics. For example, suppose you are writing an argumentative paper on fracking, a method of drawing natural gas and oil out of the shale rock beneath the ground. What might be some branches or subtopics?

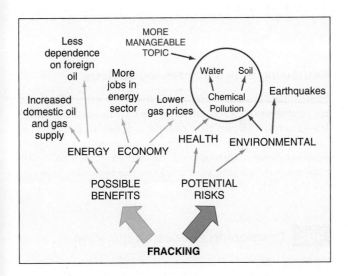

Broadening topics that are too narrow

Sometimes a topic is too narrow, especially when very little or only specialized information exists on the topic. If you're focused on a problem that affects only you or someone you know, how you can broaden your topic to find an approach that affects more people?

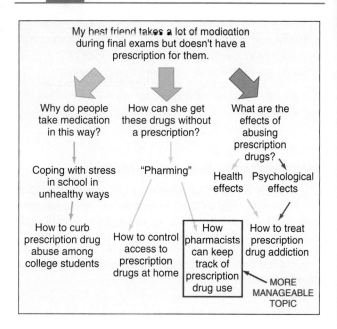

My best friend takes a lot of medication during final exams but doesn't have a prescription for them.

Why do people take medication in this way?

How can she get these drugs without a prescription?

What are the effects of abusing prescription drugs?

Coping with stress in school in unhealthy ways

"Pharming"

Health effects

Psychological effects

How to curb prescription drug abuse among college students

How to control access to prescription drugs at home

How pharmacists can keep track of prescription drug use

How to treat prescription drug addiction

MORE MANAGEABLE TOPIC

Rethinking topics that are too obvious

Some topics are not arguable because they are obvious and not controversial, such as "obesity is harmful to our health." It's generally known that obesity is a health problem, so instead, revise your topic. Perhaps you want to investigate whether obese adults should pay increased health insurance rates. Changing your angle on the topic can help you to offer a fresh perspective.

40c Developing a research question

When you start your research, think about the questions to ask yourself, the journalist's *who, what, when, where, why,* and *how.* The questions you ask will help to determine the information to look for. And your answers will help you form your thesis.

After completing your research and reviewing your sources, you should have enough information to create a research question about your topic. A research question is the main question you will answer in your paper. Your answer will be the thesis, or main point, of your paper.

TRY THIS

To Develop an Effective Research Question
- **Why** is this issue important?
- **Who** is affected by this issue?
- **What** is at stake for each group affected by this issue?
- **Who** has the power to do something about this issue?
- **Where?** Is this a local or national issue? an issue about a specific place?
- **When and how** did this issue arise?

These sample research questions focus the writer's investigation into specific aspects of each topic.

Research Question: Fracking	Research Question: Prescription Drug Abuse
Should oil companies be legally required to disclose all chemicals they use for fracking?	How can patients' access to prescription medications be effectively checked to prevent abuse?

40d Formulating your thesis statement

After completing your research and reviewing the information you've collected, you can begin to formulate a tentative thesis statement. Your thesis statement will answer your research question, communicate the main idea of your paper, and help you create a working outline. The thesis states your position or the point you are arguing and researching. It shows what you, as a knowledgeable writer, have learned about your topic. Your thesis may need to be revised further as you revise your paper.

These two thesis statements communicate the writer's conclusions about each topic.

Thesis Statement: Fracking	Thesis Statement: Prescription Drug Abuse
Congress should pass legislation requiring oil companies to reveal all chemicals used in their fracking operations.	With greater education and cooperation, the chain of drug distributors, including insurance companies, prescribers, and pharmacists, can make the biggest impact in alleviating prescription drug abuse.

A good thesis statement will provide the main idea of the essay as well as suggest your purpose for writing (such as *to explain, to persuade,* or *to interpret*). See 1d for more about thesis statements.

Research Question Format	Sample Research Question	Sample Thesis Statement
INFORMATIVE		
Why is it important to know [type of information]?	Why should people learn how to use a defibrillator?	Knowing how to use a defibrillator can help you save a life.
POSITION		
Should [person or organization] [take action]?	Should colleges permit students to carry handguns on campus?	Colleges should not permit students to carry handguns on campus.
Is [policy] helpful/useful/productive for [specific aspect] of [group]?	Is the use of drones a productive way to manage international conflict?	The use of drones is not a productive method for handling international conflict.
PROBLEM/SOLUTION		
What action will solve/improve/reduce [problem]?	What action will reduce voting difficulties at polling stations?	Legalizing weekend voting would reduce difficulties at polling stations.
How can [problem] be improved for/by [person or group]?	How can schools help reduce cyberbullying among high school students?	States should grant schools legal authority to step in when cyberbullying happens in high schools.
CAUSE-AND-EFFECT		
What is the [cause/effect] behind/for [problem/situation/result]?	What is causing the increasing number of measles cases in the United States?	Parents opposed to childhood vaccinations have contributed to the increase in measles in the United States.

Research Question Format	Sample Research Question	Sample Thesis Statement
LITERATURE/INTERPRETIVE		
What message does [author/ director] make through the portrayal of [conflict/ problem/character] in [title]?	What message does Christopher Nolan send through his characterization of The Joker in *The Dark Knight*?	Nolan shows through his characterization of The Joker that introducing chaos into civilized society is far more dangerous than any actions taken by a single madman.

41 Searching for Information

41a Choosing primary and secondary sources

Primary sources are original or firsthand materials. Primary sources include the following:

- Words written or spoken by the original author, such as essays, novels, editorials, or autobiographies (but not, for example, biographies *about* that person), speeches, e-mails, blogs, or posts on social networking sites

- Surveys, studies, or interviews you conduct

- Any creative works by the original author (poems, plays, web pages, art forms such as photos and sculptures)

- Accounts of events by people who were present

Primary sources may be more accurate because they have not been distorted by others. Primary sources are not always unbiased, however, because some people present pictures of themselves and their accomplishments that may not be objective.

Secondary sources are secondhand accounts, information, or reports about primary sources written or delivered by people who weren't direct participants in the events or issues being examined. Typical secondary sources include the following:

- News articles about events

- Reviews

- Biographies

- Documentaries

- Scholarly articles

- Encyclopedia entries

- Other material interpreted or studied by others

Although reading secondary sources may save time, they are *interpretations* and may be biased, inaccurate, or incomplete. Use secondary sources to examine views about your topic and support conclusions you reach based on primary sources.

41b Searching libraries and library databases

Libraries have the types of scholarly resources your instructor will probably want you to use for your research.

General reference sources

The library's reference section contains a variety of scholarly sources, including:

- Encyclopedias, including those for specific areas of study

- Dictionaries

- Biographies

- Almanacs, such as the *World Almanac* and *Book of Facts*

- Atlases

- Government publications

When you read an entry in a subject encyclopedia or other scholarly sources, you know you're reading information from authors who are selected because of their expertise.

Library indexes and catalogs

Your library will have book indexes such as *Books in Print,* periodical indexes such as the *Readers' Guide to Periodical Literature,* and other online indexes. Most library catalogs are online, so you can search the library's holdings by author, title, keyword, and subject heading.

Keyword Search	Subject Search
The search engine will look for the word in any part of the entry in the catalog (title, subtitle, abstract, etc.). When doing a keyword search, try synonyms for your topic or broader terms that might include it.	The subject heading has to exactly match the entry listed in the *Library of Congress Subject Headings* or the search headings named in the database you are using. Skimming through subject headings related to your topic can lead you in a helpful direction.

Library databases and subscription services

Many public and college libraries subscribe to periodical databases and other services that provide digital versions of articles from journals, magazines, and newspapers. Check your library's website or ask your reference librarians to find the database resources your library offers and information about accessing them.

Resources in library databases are a good place to start because they are considered scholarly or newsworthy, don't contain advertisements, have current information about issues and events, and have already been fact-checked and edited. Some companies, such as Pro-Quest, offer a wide range of specialized databases. Some of the most widely used library databases include the following:

- **Academic Search Complete** (EBSCOhost)—wide range of newspaper, magazine, and journal articles

- **InfoTrac College Edition**—extensive number of newspaper, magazine, and journal articles

- **JSTOR**—full-text articles from many academic journals

- **LexisNexis**—news articles, including transcripts of speeches, news programs, and other events

- **Project Muse**—full-text articles from academic journals

- **ProQuest Central**—full-text articles from academic journals, newspapers, and magazines as well as dissertations and theses

- **ScienceDirect**—science, technical, and medical articles

When searching a library database, you are likely to find a range of information:

- **Bibliographic citation.** This contains key information about sources, including the author's name, date of publication, article title, and source title.

- **Abstract.** This is a summary of the article or source.

- **Full-text article.** This option shows you the digitized text of articles originally published in other sources.

- **PDF file.** Short for "portable document format," a PDF file displays the article as it originally was published.

TRY THIS

To Conduct a Search on Library or Subscription Databases

- **Start with a search term or a keyword.** Would a subject search or keyword search be more helpful for finding information on your topic?

- **Search by subject.** When you search a broad subject, such as **globalization** or **cancer**, some databases will connect you to a list of subdivided topics that allow you to narrow your search.

- **Search by keyword.** If you have a more narrow or specific topic, such as the laws governing marijuana sales in Colorado, try searching a list of relevant keywords (**marijuana laws Colorado**) to find relevant hits in the title or full text of articles.

- **Use terms that refine your search.** Place quotation marks around search phrases to find sources containing that exact phrase. Use "OR" for choices between search terms and a minus sign to exclude certain items from your search.

- **Read the help section.** Read the directions for using the database's search engine to narrow your search.

- **Back up your research.** Download the articles you found and save them. Some databases also allow you to e-mail articles to yourself.

41c Searching the Internet

The Internet can be an extremely useful research tool. However, its resources may be best used in combination with other materials in your library. For current events topics, searching your library's databases can often be a better first step than starting with the Internet (see 41b).

Also, despite the ocean of information you can access online, your library is more likely to provide access to older books, collections of reference works, the content of some journals, and archives of old newspapers.

Search engines

Search engines locate websites based on keywords you enter into the engine's search function. Search engines can help you find materials from a vast variety of resources, such as images, news, videos, books, blogs, and more. Using the "Advanced Search" functions and search operators (special phrases and punctuation you type with your search terms) can help you narrow your results even further.

SEARCH OPERATOR	EXAMPLE	=	RESULTS
site:	site:.gov Kentucky Derby	=	results from only .gov sites
	site:cnn.com Kentucky Derby	=	results from only cnn.com
" "	"Kentucky Derby"	=	results from sites that contain the exact phrase "Kentucky Derby"
−	Kentucky −Derby	=	results from sites that contain "Kentucky" but not "Derby"
OR	Kentucky OR Derby	=	results from sites that contain "Kentucky" or "Derby," not both
+	+Kentucky Derby	=	results from sites that must mention "Kentucky" but may mention "Derby"

Google is a very powerful search engine and a good starting point for most searches. Bing, Ask, and Yahoo! are other popular search engines. Each search engine will turn up its own list of links based on its unique search formula. Also, many search engines include sponsored links (links that advertisers pay for) listed prominently on the first page of results. Google, Yahoo!, and others identify their paid links, but some search engines don't.

TRY THIS

To Use Internet Search Engines Effectively

- Use specific phrases instead of single words to define your search.
- Try a variety of keywords that apply to your topic.
- Search for phrases (as a unit) by enclosing them in quotation marks.
- Talk to a tutor in your writing center about possible search strategies for your topic.
- When you find a useful site, look for links to related, credible sites.
- Spell search terms correctly.
- Use search engine directories or categories, if available.

Using Directories Some search engines have materials arranged by general subjects in a directory. For example, in Yahoo!'s directory (http://dir.yahoo.com), you'll find broad categories such as "Health," "Science," and "Recreation & Sports." Within each subject, you can find related sites. For example, under "Health," you'll find subheadings including "Diseases and Conditions," "Nutrition," and "Pharmacy." These can be very helpful to browse through when you're looking for a topic for a paper or keywords to use in your search.

When you include material from the Internet, it is important to decide whether the information is credible before using it in your project. To determine whether your source is trustworthy, spend some time evaluating your sources (see Chapter 42).

OTHER TYPES OF INTERNET SOURCES	
Writers' Resources	Dictionaries, thesauruses, and online writing center sites
Online Databases and Directories	Sites listing multiple sources such as Google Scholar, ERIC (Educational Resources Information Center), and the Directory of Open Access Journals
Libraries and Subject Directories	The Library of Congress website and other library catalogs
Online Books (E-books)	Sites offering full-text books like Bartleby, Project Gutenberg, and Google Books
News Media	Websites for newspapers, magazines, radio news, and television news
Academic Journals	Scholarly research sites posting peer-reviewed articles
Government and Public Information	City, state, and federal websites. (USA.gov lists all government websites. The Government Publishing Office provides access to federal bills, reports, hearing testimonies, and more.)
Historical Sites	Archives and museums offering online resources about historical topics
Public Interest Group Sites	Charitable organizations or groups committed to a cause offering information on an issue affecting the public
Corporate Sites	Companies selling products or providing information about their operations and topics related to their business
Blogs	Sites with dated entries listed in reverse chronological order. (Blog types range from personal and informally written sites to serious independent journalism.)
Podcasts	Downloadable or streaming audio or video offering commentary on a range of topics
Multimedia	Photos, artwork, videos, songs, film clips, and more

41d Conducting firsthand research

Firsthand research involves investigating sources on your own. This can be done through taking notes on your own observations, conducting surveys, and interviewing people. These forms of information-gathering can add credibility and authority to your writing.

Observations

Conducting observations can help you gather information about your topic. You can learn a lot by watching a particular place and taking notes about what you see.

TRY THIS

To Conduct an Effective Observation

- **Ask permission, if necessary.** Permission is needed when observing a place with restricted access, such as an emergency room.
- **Record your observations.** Bring a pen or pencil, a notebook, a voice recorder, and/or a video camera.
- **Bring consent forms, if necessary.** Ask people you record to sign a consent form that grants you permission to record each person.
- **Answer basic questions.** Ask the journalistic questions first: *who, what, when, where, why,* and *how.*
- **Write detailed notes.** Note the time order of events, what people are doing, how people are interacting, and what is said.

Surveys

Conducting surveys can be another effective method of gathering information. A survey can provide you with quantitative information, or numerical data, about the attitudes or beliefs of a group of people about a specific topic. There are two basic types of survey questions: closed questions and open questions.

Closed Questions Closed questions have a limited number of answers. They are easier to count than open questions, making it easier to show the results in graphs or charts. Closed questions include the following types:

- **True/false or yes/no:** These are best for gathering respondents' opinions on specific issues.

- **Multiple choice:** These are useful for asking respondents about their actions or practices regarding a topic. You can ask people to select one or all responses that apply.

- **Likert scales:** These give readers a range of responses to choose from. Responses are selected from a numerical scale (e.g., 1 = most likely to 5 = least likely) or include descriptive phrases (e.g., strongly agree, agree, neutral, disagree, strongly disagree).

- **Rankings:** These types of questions ask readers to rate their preferences from strongest to weakest.

Open Questions Open questions ask for short-answer or narrative responses. This makes them harder than closed questions to count and represent in charts and graphs. But they can be helpful when you want individualized viewpoints on an issue. You can use quotations from responses to these open questions to support points in your paper.

Analyzing and Presenting Your Results Once you have your survey results, review them and think about their implications. Your readers expect that you are a credible researcher who has reviewed the data and presented the results fairly and accurately.

You can include pie charts or bar graphs to help your readers understand your results. Use pie charts to show the parts of a whole and bar graphs to show comparisons between items. See 4b for strategies for including visuals in your paper.

Interviews

Interviews are also a good method for gathering firsthand information. Talking with someone who is an authority or expert or has a specific connection to your topic may provide important information.

TRY THIS

To Conduct an Effective Interview

- **Do some searching before your interview.** Research your interview subject to learn about his or her background and expertise.
- **Be prepared with written questions.** Include open-ended questions that begin with *who, what, when, where, why,* and *how.*
- **Set up a time and place for your interview.** Contact your subject ahead of time to set up an interview.
- **Explain the purpose of your interview.** Let your interview subjects know that their words may be used in your paper or if your work will be published in a newspaper or online.

- **Bring a pen, pencil, notebook, and/or recorder.** Take notes during the interview so you can present your subject's words accurately.

- **Show you are an interested listener.** Maintain eye contact, sit up in your seat, and nod or respond to what the person says.

- **Use interview material responsibly.** When you include quoted or paraphrased material from your interview in your paper, present the person's viewpoints fairly and accurately.

42 Evaluating Sources

42a Getting started

To begin, ask yourself what type of information you are looking for and where you'll find appropriate sources for it.

- **What kind of information are you looking for?** Do you want facts? opinions? news reports? research studies? analyses? historical accounts? personal reflections? data? public records? scholarly essays reflecting on the topic? reviews?

- **Where would you find such information?** Which sources are most likely to be useful: the Internet? online library databases and subscription services? libraries with scholarly journals, books, and government publications? newspapers? community records? people on your campus or in your town?

For example, if you're searching for information on some current event, a reliable newspaper such as the *New York Times* will be a useful source, and it is available on the web and in a university or public library. If you need statistics on the U.S. population, government census documents on the web and in libraries are useful places to search. If you want to do research into local history, however, the archives and websites of local government offices and the local newspaper are better places to start.

Consider whether there are organizations that gather and publish the types of information you're seeking. For example, if you want information about local teen drinking and driving, a useful source would be a local office of Mothers Against Drunk Driving (MADD). If you want national or regional information, the MADD website is also likely to be helpful.

Ask yourself whether the sponsoring organization's goal for the site is to be objective, gain support for its viewpoint, or sell you something. For example, an energy consortium funded by a large oil company is not likely to be an unbiased source of information about the hazards of fracking.

42b Evaluating sources

As you start looking at your sources, do some investigating. Your goal is to get some sense of who the author is, what the author's organization or institution represents, and whether the article's content is credible and relevant to your research project.

Review the checklist on pages 146–147 to decide whether a source's viewpoint or knowledge of the topic is important to read or include in your research project.

FAQ

How can I learn more about the credibility of an author?

- Check a search engine and the Library of Congress catalog to see what else this person has written. Also look up the author's organization or institution.

- Review library databases for other articles by this person or sources in which the author has been cited.

- Read reviews of the author's other books, if available.

- Check a biography index or database to learn more about the author.

CHECKLIST FOR EVALUATING SOURCES

AUTHOR

- How reputable is the person listed as the author?
- What is the author's educational background?
- What has the author written in the past about this topic?
- Why is this person considered an expert or a reliable authority?
- If the author is an organization, what can you find out about it? How reputable is it?
- Did you see the person or organization listed in other sources that you've already determined to be trustworthy?
- What does the author want to accomplish?

AUTHOR'S AFFILIATION

- With which organization or company is the author associated? What is this group's reputation?
- What are this group's goals? Is there a bias or reason for the group to slant the truth in any way?
- Does the group monitor or review what is published under its name?
- Does the organization have a profit motive? Why might this group be trying to sell you something or convince you to accept its views?
- Do its members conduct objective, disinterested research? Are they trying to be sensational or grab attention to enhance their own popularity or ratings?

PUBLISHER, PRODUCER, OR SPONSOR

- Who published or produced the material?
- Is that publisher or sponsor reputable? (For example, a university press or a government agency is likely to be a reputable source that reviews what it publishes.)
- Is the group recognized as an authority?
- Is the publisher or group an appropariate one for this topic?
- Might the publisher be likely to have a particular bias? (For example, a brochure printed by a right-to-life group is not going to contain much objective material on abortion.)
- Does the source have a review or fact-checking process? (If a pharmaceutical company publishes data on a new drug it is developing, is there evidence of outside review of the data?)

CONTENT

Accuracy

- What reasons do you have to think the facts are accurate? Do they agree with other information you've read?
- Is the content fact, opinion, or propaganda?
- Is there a Works Cited or Reference List?
- Are there links or references to other credible sources?

Coverage

- Is the topic covered in adequate depth, or is it superficial?
- Is the source too specialized, popular, or brief to be useful?
- Is the coverage comprehensive, or is it limited to only one aspect of the topic?
- Does the source offer sufficient and credible evidence to back its claims?
- Are there broad or sweeping generalizations that overstate or simplify the matter?
- Does the author use a mix of primary and secondary sources?

Fairness and Objectivity

- If the author has a particular viewpoint, are differing views presented fairly and accurately?
- Is the language objective or emotional?
- Does the author acknowledge differing viewpoints?
- Are the various perspectives presented fairly?
- Do other articles in the same source promote a particular viewpoint?

Timeliness

- When was the source published? Is the information current enough to be useful? (For websites, look at the "last revised" date at the end of the page. If no date is available, check through the site for live links and updates.)
- How necessary is timeliness for your topic?

Relevance

- How closely related is the source to your topic? Is it relevant or merely related?
- Is the source too general, too specific, or too technical?

Audience

- Can you tell who the intended audience is?
- Is that audience appropriate for *your* purposes?

42c Evaluating online sources

Evaluating Internet sources is similar to evaluating sources found elsewhere, but there are some special matters to consider when deciding whether to use online sources. The Internet is a worldwide medium where anyone can post anything from anywhere. No monitors, evaluators, or fact-checking organizations regulate or review all of what is posted on the web. Although excellent sources of information exist online, sites can lead unsuspecting readers to biased, stolen, or false information.

TRY THIS

Understanding Domain Names

A website's *domain* consists of two or three letters that appear after the last dot in its URL. The domain can sometimes give you clues about the website's source or publisher.

.gov	government sites (These are usually dependable.)
.edu	educational institutions (These are dependable, though personal student websites may not be.)
.org	organizations (These include nonprofit or public service organizations that may have their own bias.)
.com, .biz, .net	commercial sites (Business websites are likely to have a profit motive. Individuals, however, may also post their personal websites and blogs on corporate servers.)
.uk, .de, .ca, .jp	foreign sites (.uk = England; .de = Germany, .ca = Canada, .jp = Japan; there are two-letter abbreviations for all countries of the world.)

In addition to asking the questions in 42b about evaluating an author's credibility and a source's content, do some additional searching when evaluating a website.

- **Find the site's home page.** Go to a site's home page by deleting all of the URL after the first slash and hitting "Enter."

- **Check the currency of the site.** Is there a date of origin and any sign the site has been maintained and revised in the recent past? If there are links to other sites, do they still work?

- **Determine whether the site is trying to sell you something.** Do you see a "shopping cart" or "checkout" link? If so, the site may be providing you information with the hope you will buy its products or services.

- **Check for ads.** Is there advertising (or pop-up windows) on the site? Does that interfere with the site's credibility? (Sites with .gov as the domain will not have advertising.)

- **Look for an "About Us" link on the site.** Be wary of sites that want to hide their sponsors or publishers.

- **Consider how you accessed the site.** Did you link to it from another reliable site? If you found the site through a search engine result, that means only that the site contains your search keywords; it says nothing about the site's trustworthiness or credibility.

43 Attributing Sources and Avoiding Plagiarism

43a Attributing sources

When we use primary and secondary sources in our writing, we show that we are aware of others who have knowledge about our topics. And we do that by indicating our sources in the text and citing them using a specific documentation format, such as MLA, APA, *Chicago Manual,* or CSE format. (See Chapters 45–48 for more information on these styles.) There are several reasons why we should attribute sources:

- **Attributing sources is ethical.** Recognizing our sources is part of the American academic writing process. We should "give credit where credit is due" and acknowledge that we used other sources to develop our own ideas and arguments.

- **Showing our use of sources is part of the learning process.** When we cite our sources, we assure readers (and instructors) that we are learning about our topic, developing critical thinking skills, and engaging with the ideas of others.

- **Documenting sources demonstrates our credibility as writers.** When we acknowledge our sources, we invite others to view our sources and see how we have developed our opinions and conclusions. This kind of transparency allows readers to see our thinking and development process, which in turn gives greater legitimacy to our ideas.

- **Citing sources shows respect for intellectual property.** Attributing our sources acknowledges other people's creativity and hard work. In a similar way, it would be unfair to us as writers if we had an interesting or important idea that was used by someone else in his or her work without acknowledging the real source.

- **Citing sources helps others.** Just as we read the work of others and find references to works we want to read or see, we too can be useful sources for others looking for information or ideas we found.

43b Avoiding plagiarism

Indicating sources properly also helps to avoid plagiarism. Plagiarism results when a writer fails to document a source and presents the words or ideas of someone else as the writer's own work. Plagiarism can occur in the following ways:

- Using someone's exact words without putting quotation marks around the words and without citing the source.

- Changing another person's words into your own words by paraphrasing or summarizing without citing the source.

- Stating ideas or research specifically attributed to another person or persons without citing the source.

- Claiming authorship of a paper written by someone else.

Why is avoiding plagiarism important?

- **Plagiarism is unethical.** When a writer uses someone else's words, information, or ideas and doesn't acknowledge using that work, that is considered an act of stealing, even if it happens because of carelessness or rushing too fast to write the paper.

- **Plagiarism means losing a learning opportunity.** Instructors assign research projects to help students learn how to use sources as well as gain knowledge about their topics. If we plagiarize instead of researching and citing our sources, we lose the opportunity to learn about our topics and the chance to practice critical thinking and research skills needed in college and the workplace.

- **Plagiarism diminishes credibility.** Drawing upon other people's ideas and words is appropriate when writing research papers. Our arguments are more compelling when we cite the opinions of experts. To be considered credible writers, we need to let readers know where we located those ideas and words. Blending our own ideas and language in conversation with information from other sources is an important goal of the research process.

- **Plagiarism may result in serious penalties.** Plagiarism is considered a violation of academic honesty and may result in a variety of penalties, including expulsion. After college, plagiarism can negatively affect careers and reputations. Plagiarists can be sued for copyright violations or for use of intellectual property without permission.

43c Distinguishing information requiring documentation vs. common knowledge

While most ideas borrowed from other sources require documentation, there are a few exceptions.

Information that requires documentation

The following types of source use require documentation:

- **Words taken directly from a source.** Enclose quotations in quotation marks and include an in-text citation. (See 44c.)

- **Specific ideas, findings, conclusions, and arguments taken from a source, even if you put them in your own words.** If you summarize or paraphrase information from a source, include an in-text citation. (See 44a and 44b.)

- **Statistics, figures, and the results of a study.** Unless you have conducted your own study and created your own set of statistics, you have probably used a source to get this data. Cite the source of the data.

Common knowledge: information that does not require documentation

Common knowledge is the body of general ideas we share with our readers, and it does not have to be documented. This may include the following:

- **Common historical facts.** For example, it is common knowledge that the Declaration of Independence was adopted in 1776 and that George Washington was the first U.S. president.

- **Common physical or scientific facts.** Most people know basic scientific facts such as the Earth is the third planet from the sun and water is composed of hydrogen and oxygen molecules.

- **Facts widely available in a variety of standard reference books.** Many reference books, for example, would note that Brazil is the largest country in South America and Great Britain has a parliamentary system of government.

- **Information that is widely shared and found in numerous sources without reference to any source.** For example, it has been widely reported in the news and in health sources that obesity is a major health problem in the United States. A statement about that does not need to be documented. However, if you are writing about the occurrence of obesity and find statistics for various segments of the population, cite your sources.

Common knowledge may also include more specific ideas or concepts, depending on the expertise of your audience. For example, if your audience is composed of educators, it's common knowledge among this group that U.S. schoolchildren aren't well acquainted with geography. However, if you cite test results documenting the extent of this problem or reference the ideas of a specific person about the causes of the problem, that is not common knowledge and needs documentation. If you are unsure of whether the information you are using is considered common knowledge, consult your instructor.

FAQ

Are there cultural differences about the documentation of sources?

In some cultures, documenting something, particularly from a well-known work of literature, can be interpreted as an insult because it implies that the reader is not familiar with that work. In American academic writing, however, it is very important to document sources. This may be a skill that is new or needs sharpening, but it is vitally important.

Other sources that do not require documentation include the following:

- **Studies and surveys you have conducted.** If you're reporting the results or data from your own study or survey, explain when and how the study or survey took place, but don't cite it unless it has been previously published in another source.

- **Your own opinions and narratives about yourself.** Because your name appears at the beginning of your paper, readers will consider the opinions and stories expressed in the paper as belonging to you unless you attribute them to someone else or another source.

43d   Checking work for plagiarism

Give yourself time to check your work to make sure you have attributed sources responsibly and have not inadvertently plagiarized any source materials. Follow these steps to check your work:

- Ask yourself whether your readers can properly identify which ideas and words are yours and which are from the sources you cite.

- Re-read what you wrote to see if you cited all ideas that aren't your own and aren't considered common knowledge.

- Check to ensure that all quotations are punctuated with quotation marks and contain in-text citations.

- Review paraphrased and summarized material to ensure language and sentence structures aren't too close to the original text.

- Check to see that all paraphrased and summarized material is acknowledged with in-text citations (see Chapter 44).

- Consider whether your paper predominantly reflects your words, phrases, and integration of ideas.

- Check to make sure your paper isn't a string of quotations from your sources.

- Check the sources in your Works Cited or References page to be sure they are cited in the body of the paper and vice versa.

Avoiding plagiarism: an example

Original source

Everyone knows that New York is full of foodies, but few realize that it is also full of farmers. City farmsteads are cropping up all over, and New York has more of them—and more on rooftops—than anywhere else. In addition to at least 7 rooftop enterprises, there are 17 ground-based farms in the Big Apple and 1,000-plus community gardens, far more than in any other American city.

Growing food in a city's dense core, urban farmers say, can turn back the diesel-chugging trucks hauling salad mix across the country, lower energy bills by replacing hot black-tar roofs with cool greenery, slim waistlines by supplying bodegas with fresh-picked tomatoes, and let children reared on concrete learn the joy of yanking a carrot from the soil.

Work Cited

Ferris, David. "Up on the Farm." *Sierra*, Nov.-Dec. 2012, pp. 52+.

Plagiarized passage

In New York, urban farms are cropping up all over. Urban farms can reduce the number of diesel trucks hauling salads across the country, and rooftop gardens can replace hot tar roofs with greenery. In addition, vegetables from these farms can slim waistlines. Children reared on concrete should learn the joys of yanking a carrot from the soil.

> *(This example illustrates plagiarism. A parenthetical citation is needed for all the material that is paraphrased from the original passage. The highlighted phrases are too close to the original text and should be paraphrased more completely. The last sentence needs to be quoted accurately, with quotation marks around the direct quote followed by a parenthetical citation.)*

Acceptable passage

According to *Sierra* writer David Ferris, New York leads America's cities in its number of urban farms and rooftop gardens (53). Advocates argue that urban farms save energy by reducing the amount of food transported across America's highways, thereby decreasing fossil fuel emissions (53). Rooftop gardens also save energy by insulating buildings, which lowers the cost of cooling them (54). In addition, locally grown food sources encourage city families to enjoy the pleasures of harvesting and eating healthy produce. As Ferris writes, these farms and gardens "let children reared on concrete learn the joy of yanking a carrot from the soil" (54).

> *(In the first four sentences, the main ideas of the original are communicated in the writer's own language and sentence structure. The last sentence is quoted accurately.*

References to the author and parenthetical citations indicate where the original ideas came from.)

43e Taking notes

As you develop your research projects, try to develop a system of keeping your notes organized. Think about how you are going to store, categorize, and process the materials you gather.

TRY THIS

Keeping Your Research Materials and Notes Organized

- Save articles from library databases or websites on a flash drive, on your computer's hard drive, in your e-mail account, or in a backup service such as Dropbox.
- Bookmark websites you may want to revisit later.
- Highlight passages in your notes that are quoted, paraphrased, or summarized from your original sources to avoid accidental problems with plagiarism.
- Divide your major topics into subtopics, and then save your research materials and notes in separate file folders labeled by subtopic.
- Save new files for each version of your draft with separate names ("Draft1-May1") to track revisions.
- Use your word processor's revision functions (such as "Track Changes" in Microsoft Word) to track the revisions you make in your drafts.

43f Writing an annotated bibliography

You may be asked to create an annotated bibliography as a step towards preparing your research project. Annotated bibliographies give you the opportunity to review, summarize, and organize your research materials on a particular topic. Each entry in an annotated bibliography contains three parts:

- **A bibliographic citation formatted in the documentation style required for your course.** See Chapters 45–48 for information on Works Cited and References citations.

- **An abstract (brief summary) of the source.** Fairly and objectively inform your readers of the main ideas in the work being discussed. Think about the situation or argument the author is addressing. What is the author's purpose? What are the key points stressed in the work? What conclusions does the author draw about the subject?

- **A short reflection about the significance of the source and its relevance for your research project.** Explain how the work will help you with your research project. How does the source expand your understanding of a topic? How and where might you use information from the work in your project?

Here is a sample entry from an MLA-formatted annotated bibliography developed for a paper about fracking.

Sheppard, Kate. "Loophole Allows Many Dangerous Chemicals in Fracking Fluids to Go Undisclosed: Report." *The Huffington Post*, 22 Oct. 2014, www.huffingtonpost.com/2014/10/22/fracking-chemicals-loophole_n_6030914.html.

> **Bibliographic citation**

Sheppard reviews the results of a report released by the Environmental Integrity Project (EIP), which discusses the implications of the 2005 loophole in the Safe Drinking Water Act of 1974. With this loophole, oil corporations engaged in fracking are permitted to insert some petroleum-based products underground without reporting their chemical composition to the public. Some fracking fluids legally used by drillers contain significant amounts of toxic chemicals, including benzene, which is a known cancer-causing agent. EIP Executive Director Eric Schaeffer believes Congress should pass legislation to prohibit use of these dangerous products for fracking. In addition, the EIP has requested that the Environmental Protection Agency mandate frackers to list chemicals they use on the FracFocus Chemical Disclosure Registry. For my research paper, this article will help me to define the gaps in current legislation and argue for new laws mandating public disclosure of all chemicals used in fracking fluid.

> **Abstract**

> **Reflection**

44 Integrating Sources

44a Summarizing

A summary is a brief restatement, using your own words, of the main ideas in a source. Unlike paraphrases (see 44b), summaries are shorter than the original source because they cover only the main points of the source.

FAQ

What are the characteristics of a summary?

- Summaries use fewer words than the source being summarized.
- Summaries include only the main points, omitting details, facts, examples, illustrations, direct quotations, and other specifics.
- Summaries are written in your own words, are not copied from your source, and use your own sentence structures.
- Summaries are objective and do not include your own interpretation or reflect your slant on the material.
- Summaries represent the viewpoint(s) of the author(s) fairly and accurately.
- Summaries must be cited in the documentation format (MLA, APA, *Chicago Manual*, CSE, etc.) you are using for your paper.

Summary: an example

Original Source: book excerpt

Most of us are already aware of the direct effect we have on our friends and family; our actions can make them happy or sad, healthy or sick, even rich or poor. But we rarely consider that everything we think, feel, do, or say can spread far beyond the people we know. Conversely, our friends and family serve as conduits for us to be influenced by hundreds or even thousands of other people. In a kind of social chain reaction, we can be deeply affected by events we do not witness that happen to people we do not know. It is as if we can feel the pulse of the social world around us and respond to its persistent rhythm. As part of a social network, we transcend ourselves, for good or ill, and become a part of something much larger. We are connected.

Christakis, Nicholas A., and James H. Fowler. *Connected: The Surprising Power of Social Networks and How They Shape Our Lives—How Your Friends' Friends' Friends Affect Everything You Feel, Think, and Do.* Back Bay Books, 2011.

Unacceptable Summary: too close to original language and sentence structure and missing a parenthetical citation

We are all part of a social chain reaction, where everything we think, feel, or do can affect our friends and family. We can also affect and are affected by hundreds or even thousands of people we do not know. As part of a social network, we are connected.

(The language and sentence structure of this example are too close to the original text and could be considered plagiarized. This example is also missing a parenthetical citation.)

Acceptable Summary

Researchers Nicholas A. Christakis and James H. Fowler argue that our individual emotions and behaviors inadvertently make an impression on other people. We are intertwined into the communities in which we live. Therefore, our emotions and behaviors have an impact on those closest to us, who in turn have an impact on those immediately around them. This process also works in the reverse, unconsciously shaping our own moods and decisions (30).

(The key idea of the original passage is communicated here in the writer's own language and sentence structure. A reference to the authors and a parenthetical citation indicate where the original idea came from.)

TRY THIS

Writing a Summary

1. Read the original source carefully and thoughtfully.
2. After the first reading, ask yourself what the author's major point is.
3. Go back and reread the source, making a few notes in the margin.
4. Look away from your source, and then, like a newscaster, panelist, or speaker reporting to a group, finish the sentence: "This person is saying that . . ."
5. Write down what you've just said.
6. Go back and reread both the source and your notes in the margins to check that you've correctly remembered and included the main points.
7. Revise your summary as needed.

Paraphrasing

A paraphrase restates information from a source, using your own words.

FAQ

What are the characteristics of a paraphrase?

- A paraphrase is approximately the same length as the passage from the original source and contains more detail than a summary would.

- Paraphrases use your own words, not those of the source, and are written in your own sentence structures.

- Paraphrases are objective and do not include your own opinions on the material.

- Paraphrases represent the viewpoint(s) of the author(s) fairly and accurately.

- Paraphrases must be cited in the documentation format (MLA, APA, *Chicago Manual*, CSE, etc.) you are using for your paper.

Paraphrase: an example

Original Source: magazine article excerpt

To ignite a pandemic, even the most lethal virus would need to meet three conditions: it would have to be one that humans hadn't confronted before, so that they lacked antibodies; it would have to kill them; and it would have to spread easily—through a cough, for instance, or a handshake. Bird flu meets the first two criteria but not the third.

Specter, Michael. "The Deadliest Virus." *The New Yorker*, 12 Mar. 2012, pp. 32–37.

Unacceptable Paraphrase: wording and sentence structure too close to the original source

To start a pandemic, a disease needs to meet three conditions. First, it would need to be new to humans so that they lacked antibodies to fight it off. Second, the disease would have to kill them. Third, it would need to spread easily through coughs or handshakes. Bird flu doesn't spread easily, but it meets the first two criteria (Specter 32).

(The language and sentence structure of this example are too close to the original text and could be considered plagiarized.)

Acceptable Paraphrase

H5N1, a new strain of avian influenza, proved fatal for many of those infected with it; their immune systems were unable to resist this mutation of the disease. However, because H5N1 did not effectively proliferate through airborne or surface contact, it did not reach the level of a worldwide epidemic (Specter 32).

(The main ideas of the original are communicated here in the writer's own language and sentence structures. A parenthetical citation indicates where the ideas originally came from.)

TRY THIS

Writing a Paraphrase

1. Read the original passage as many times as is needed to understand its full meaning.
2. As you read, take notes, using your own words, if that helps.
3. Put the original source aside and write a draft of your paraphrase, using your notes if needed.
4. Check your version against the original source by rereading the original to be sure you've included all the ideas from the source.
5. If you find a phrase worth quoting in your own writing, use quotation marks in the paraphrase to identify the words you're borrowing, and note the page number.

44c Quoting

A quotation records the exact words of a written or spoken source. Place quotation marks directly before and after the quoted words.

FAQ

What are the characteristics of quotations?

- Quotations are written exactly as they appear in the source.
- Quotations are enclosed by quotation marks.
- Quotations are introduced by text that indicates the speaker or writer of the quotation.
- Quotations must be cited in the documentation format (MLA, APA, *Chicago Manual*, CSE, etc.) you are using for your paper.

Quoting: an example

Original Source: article from a website

Some education experts say the opportunity to take advanced classes is critical to helping low-income students succeed later in life.

But opportunity doesn't always equal achievement. Our new analysis of data from the U.S. Department of Education shows that, in some states, Advanced Placement exam passing rates remain lower in schools with more poor students.

"You can't snap your fingers and change that overnight," said Kevin Welner, director of the National Education Policy Center at the University of Colorado. "Wealthy kids have much richer opportunities."

Work Cited

LaFleur, Jennifer. "At Some Schools, Achievement Lags Behind Opportunity." *ProPublica,* 24 Jan. 2013, www.propublica.org/article/new-data-analysis-at-some-schools-achievement-lags-behind-opportunity.

Unacceptable Quotations

Advanced Placement exam passing rates remain lower in schools with more poor students. Though more poor students can take Advanced Placement classes, they are not succeeding the way wealthy students do. Wealthy kids have much richer opportunities. This won't change overnight.

(The quoted material [highlighted] is not placed inside quotation marks, and no parenthetical citation is used to indicate the speakers of each quotation. The quotes are also not integrated into the paragraph. This is a plagiarized passage.)

Acceptable Quotations

Jennifer LaFleur, a journalist for *ProPublica,* reports that recent statistics from the U.S. Department of Education indicate that "Advanced Placement exam passing rates remain lower in schools with more poor students." More students from lower socioeconomic classes now have greater access to Advanced Placement classes, which education advocates claim are essential for future professional development. However, improving students' test scores will take time (LaFleur). According to National Education Policy Center Director Kevin Welner, "You can't snap your fingers and change that overnight. . . . Wealthy kids have much richer opportunities" (qtd. in LaFleur).

(The quotations are introduced effectively, and the words inside the quotation marks are taken exactly from the original source. The author of the article, LaFleur, is indicated within the sentence preceding

her quotation. The quote from Welner is cited as an indirect quotation, as indicated by "qtd. in" within the parentheses.)

Short quotations

Introduced with a comma. Use a comma to connect the signal phrase to the quotation. (See 44d for signal phrases.)

Psychologists Jean M. Twenge and W. Keith Campbell argue, "American culture encourages self-admiration with the belief that it will improve our lives" (13).

Introduced with a colon. Use a colon at the end of a full sentence.

Twenge and Campbell assert that narcissists do not have logical reasons to support their inflated self-perceptions: "Measured objectively, narcissists are just like everyone else. Nevertheless, narcissists see themselves as fundamentally superior—they are special, entitled, and unique" (19).

Introduced mid-sentence. Blend the quotation into your sentence so that your sentence remains grammatically correct.

Twenge and Campbell argue that Americans "have taken the desire for self-admiration too far—so far that our culture has blurred the distinction between self-esteem and narcissism in an extreme, self-destructive way" (17).

Long quotations (block quotations)

If the quotation is more than four typed lines, set it off by indenting one-half inch from the left margin in both MLA and APA style. Double-space the quotation, and don't use quotation marks.

Twenge and Campbell suggest that one of the causes behind the increase in narcissistic personality disorder among young adults may be overindulgent parenting:

> Some early psychodynamic theorists believed that narcissism resulted from cold, neglectful parents, but empirical data has not supported that conclusion very strongly except in some forms of vulnerable or covert narcissism. More modern behavioral theories argue that narcissism instead arises from inflated feedback—if you're told over and over that you are great, you'll probably think you are great. (80)

The MLA citation for this source would appear as follows:

Twenge, Jean M., and W. Keith Campbell. *The Narcissism Epidemic: Living in the Age of Entitlement.* Simon and Schuster, 2009.

FAQ

How do you know when to use a quote?

Quote when

- the writer's words are especially vivid, memorable, or expressive.
- an expert's explanation is so clear and concise that a paraphrase would be confusing or wordy.
- you want to emphasize the expertise or authority of your source.
- the words the source uses are important to the discussion.

TRY THIS

To Use Quotations Effectively

- Use quotations as evidence, support, or further explanation of what you have written. Quotations are not substitutes for stating your point in your own words.
- Use quotations sparingly. Too many quotations strung together with very little of your own writing makes a paper look like a scrapbook of pasted-together sources, not a thoughtful integration of what you know about a subject.
- Use quotations that illustrate the author's own viewpoint or style, or quote excerpts that would not be as effective if rewritten in different words. Effective quotations are succinct or particularly well phrased.
- Introduce quotations with words that signal the relationship of the quotation to the rest of your discussion (see 44d).

44d Using signal words and phrases

When you summarize, paraphrase, or quote from outside sources, identify each source and explain its connection to what you are writing about. You can do this by using signal words that tell the reader what to expect or how to interpret the material. These words can help integrate material smoothly into your writing.

TRY THIS

To Introduce Quoted, Paraphrased, or Summarized Words

Try using the following signal words:

acknowledges	condemns	points out
adds	considers	predicts
admits	contends	proposes
agrees	describes	reports
argues	disagrees	responds
asserts	explains	says
believes	finds	shows
claims	holds	speculates
comments	insists	suggests
concedes	notes	warns
concludes	observes	writes

FAQ

How can I integrate my sources smoothly into my paper?

- **Explain how the source material is connected to the rest of the paragraph.** Show your readers the connection between the reference and the point you are making. Introduce the material by showing a logical link, or add a follow-up comment that integrates a quotation into your paragraph.

- **Use the name of the source and, if appropriate, that person's credentials as an authority.** Name your source's job title or professional affiliation as you introduce quoted, paraphrased, or summarized material (According to **New York City Mayor** Bill de Blasio, ". . . .").

- **Use a verb to indicate the source's stance or attitude toward what is quoted, paraphrased, or summarized.**

  - Does the source think the statement is very important (Professor Mehta **stressed**, ". . . .")?

  - Does the source take a position on an issue (The senator **argued**, ". . . .")?

  - Does the source remain neutral about what is stated (The researcher **reported**, ". . . .")?

- **Use the appropriate verb tense.** When writing about literature and most other humanities subjects, use the present tense. Science writers generally use present tense verbs, except when writing about research that has been completed (When studying the effects of constant illumination on corn seedlings, Jenner **found** that ". . . .").
- **Include each source on your Works Cited or References page.** See Chapters 45–48 for examples of citation formats.

In the following two MLA-formatted examples, notice the difference in the way the writer's ideas and source material are integrated into the text.

Source Not Integrated into the Paragraph

Crowdfunding allows individuals to provide funds, as an investment or a loan, to help entrepreneurs finance a new project. Websites such as Kickstarter and Indiegogo have aided inventors, business owners, and artists with needed start-up cash (Liu). "Raising money is hard. Despite the proliferation of fundraising websites like Kickstarter and Indiegogo, the truth of the matter is that this newfangled crowdfunding still works best when you bring your own crowd" (Liu).

Work Cited

Liu, Jonathan H. "Getting Schooled about Crowdfunding." *Wired,* 17 Mar. 2013, www.wired.com/2013/03/getting-schooled-about-crowdfunding/.

(The quotation is abruptly dropped into the paragraph without an introduction. The writer does not show how Liu's statement relates to the ideas being discussed. Information in the quotation is also repeated.)

Revised Paragraph

Crowdfunding allows individuals to provide funds, as an investment or a loan, to help entrepreneurs finance a new project. Websites such as Kickstarter and Indiegogo have aided inventors, business owners, and artists with needed start-up cash (Liu). However, according to *Wired* writer Jonathan Liu, finding interested investors can still be a challenge: "[The] truth of the matter is that this newfangled crowdfunding still works best when you bring your own crowd" (Liu).

> *(This revision introduces the author before the quotation. The writer now shows how Liu's statement connects to the rest of the paragraph.)*

VIII

Documentation

Contents

Question and Correct

45 Documenting in MLA Style

For research papers in most of the humanities, use the format recommended by the **Modern Language Association (MLA)**. For more information about MLA format, check the MLA's website (style.mla.org) as well as the latest style manual:

Modern Language Association. *MLA Handbook.* 8th ed., MLA, 2016.

FAQ

What are the different parts of MLA citation format?

1. **Parenthetical references.** In your paper, use in-text citations to acknowledge words, ideas, and facts you've taken from outside sources. (See 45a.)
2. **Endnotes.** If you are adding material that would disrupt your paper if it were included in the text, include such notes at the end of the paper. But an endnote section is not required. (See 45b.)
3. **Works Cited list.** At the end of your paper, include a list of the sources from which you have quoted, summarized, or paraphrased. (See 45c.)

45a Parenthetical references

In-text citations, also referred to as "parenthetical references" because they are enclosed in parentheses, help your reader find the citation of the source in the Works Cited list at the end of the paper. Try to be brief, but not at the expense of clarity, and use signal words and phrases to introduce the citation (see 44d).

Examples of MLA In-Text Citations

1. One Author—Print or PDF Source 170
2. One Author—Web Source 170
3. Two Authors 171
4. Three or More Authors 171
5. No Author Listed—Print Source 171
6. No Author Listed—Web or Other Source 171
7. Work in an Anthology 171
8. Corporate or Organizational Author 171
9. Multivolume Work 171
10. Long Literary Work 172
11. Plays 172

12. Poems 172
13. Films 172
14. Time-Based Media Source 172
15. Biblical and Other Sacred Texts 173
16. Entire Work 173
17. Indirect Source 173
18. Two or More Sources 173
19. Two or More Sources by the Same Author 173
20. Web Source with Numbered Paragraphs 174
21. Lecture, Speech, or Presentation 174
22. E-Mail 174
23. Tweet 174

Source	Tips	In-Text Examples
1. One Author—Print or PDF Source	Include the author's name and page number.	One of the most commonly accepted theories is that "a dream is the fulfillment of a wish" (Freud 154). *(or)* According to famed psychoanalyst Sigmund Freud, "a dream is the fulfillment of a wish" (154).
2. One Author—Web Source	Include the author's name in the parenthetical citation or in the sentence.	For example, "Creativity is when you are trying to figure something out and something else keeps intruding" (Mullis). *(or)* According to Nobel-prize-winning chemist Kary Mullis, "Creativity is when you are trying to figure something out and something else keeps intruding."

Source	Tips	In-Text Examples
3. Two Authors	Name both authors in the citation or in the sentence. Add page numbers for print or PDF sources.	Carson and Lew argue that the statistics are inaccurate (112). *(or)* Some argue that these statistics are inaccurate (Carson and Lew 112).
4. Three or More Authors	Name the first author and *et al.* (meaning "and others"). Add page numbers for print or PDF sources.	Global Internet usage is expected to double within two years (Martin et al. 36).
5. No Author Listed— Print Source	Use a shortened form of the title that begins your Works Cited entry for the source.	Detailed nutritional information in food labels is proving to be a great advantage to diabetics ("New Labeling" 3).
6. No Author Listed— Web or Other Source	Include a shortened form of the title that begins your Works Cited entry for the source.	Community groups can effectively organize their members by using social networking platforms ("Environmental Activism").
7. Work in an Anthology	Name the author of the work, not the editor of the anthology.	When the author describes his first meeting with Narum, he uses images of light to show "the purity of the man's soul" (Aknov 262).
8. Corporate or Organizational Author	Name the corporate or organizational author in your sentence for smoother reading.	The United Nations Regional Flood Containment Commission has been studying weather patterns that contribute to flooding in Africa (4).
9. Multivolume Work	Include volume number and page number(s).	In his *History of the Civil War*, Jimmersen traces the economic influences that contributed to the decisions of several states to stay in the Union (3: 798-802).

Source	Tips	In-Text Examples
10. Long Literary Work	Give the page number, add a semicolon, and include other identifying information (e.g., chapter number).	In *The Prince*, Machiavelli argues that some find their greatest challenge in preserving their power: "Those who rise from private citizens to be princes merely by fortune have little trouble in rising but very much trouble in maintaining their position" (23; ch. 7).
11. Plays	Use act, scene, and line separated by periods.	Hamlet decides to test his uncle by staging a play: "The play's the thing / Wherein I'll catch the conscience of the King" (2.2.633-34).
12. Poems	Use *line* or *lines* in the first reference, and afterwards give only numbers. Use slashes (/) to separate lines of verse. Include a single space before and after slashes.	Eliot again reminds us of society's superficiality in "The Love Song of J. Alfred Prufrock": "There will be time, there will be time / To prepare a face to meet the faces that you meet" (lines 26-27).
13. Films	Include the film title (or a shortened version of it).	James Bond's backstory is finally revealed (*Skyfall*). (*or*) In *Skyfall*, James Bond's backstory is finally revealed.
14. Time-Based Media Source	Indicate the time in hours, minutes, and seconds.	Jordan Belfort begins his narration by stating, "The year I turned 26 as the head of my own brokerage firm, I made $49 million" (*Wolf of Wall Street* 00:01:52-55).

MLA

Source	Tips	In-Text Examples
15. Biblical and Other Sacred Texts	First reference: Include the shortened title of the edition (italicized), and the abbreviated title of the chapter, verse, and line numbers. Additional references: Omit the title of the edition.	The Bible emphasizes the seriousness of the passage to adulthood: "Banish anxiety from your mind, and put away pain from your body; for youth and the dawn of life are vanity" (*New Oxford Annotated Bible*, Eccles. 11.10). In his first letter, Paul echoes this sobering view of adulthood (1 Cor. 13.11-12).
16. Entire Work	Refer to the words (author or title) listed first in the Works Cited entry.	Lafmun was the first to argue that small infants respond to music.
17. Indirect Source	Cite the original source, if possible. If you use words from someone else, start with *qtd. in.*	Although Newman has established a high degree of accuracy for such tests, he reminds us that "no test like this is ever completely and totally accurate" (qtd. in Mazor 33).
18. Two or More Sources	Separate references with a semicolon.	Recent attempts to control the rapid destruction of Central American rainforests have met with little success (Kinderman 94; Costanza 22; Lazilo).
19. Two or More Sources by the Same Author	Include the author's name and a shortened form of the title. For a print or PDF source, add page numbers.	One current theory asserts that dreams express "profound aspects of personality" (Foulkes, *Sleep* 144). (*or*) Foulkes' investigation shows that young children's dreams are "rather simple and unemotional" ("Children's Dreams" 90).

MLA

Source	Tips	In-Text Examples
20. Web Source with Numbered Paragraphs	Add *par.* or *pars.* and the paragraph number or numbers used.	A number of popular romantic comedies from the late 1990s suggest that women can only succeed at maintaining their femininity by paying less attention to their careers (Negra, par. 6).
21. Lecture, Speech, or Presentation	Use the speaker's name in the text or a citation.	According to Carmen Tallis, Director of Financial Aid, a change in campus student loan policies is unlikely.
22. E-Mail	Use the sender's last name in the text or a citation.	The status of wild horses in national parks is currently under review (Draheim).
23. Tweet	Include the tweeter's name or handle in the text or a citation.	President Barack Obama stated, "In the midst of darkest tragedy, the decency and goodness of the American people shines through in these families" (@POTUS).

TRY THIS

To Format and Cite Quotations

Use signal words (see 44d) to introduce your quotation, and add a parenthetical reference directly after the quotation.

Short quotations

For short quotations (four or fewer typed lines), include the quotation within the body of the text. After the closing quotation marks in short quotations, include the parenthetical citation and add a period.

> Consumers would be wise to approach "the grocery store as a battlefield, dotted with landmines itching to go off" (Moss 347).

Long quotations

Set off long quotations (more than four typed lines) by indenting one-half inch from the left margin. Double-space the quotation, and do not use quotation marks. At the end of the quotation, put the parenthetical citation after the period.

Sugary, salty, and fatty foods are deliberately constructed to appeal to consumers:

> Their packaging is tailored to excite our kids. Their advertising uses every psychological trick to overcome any logical arguments we might have for passing the product by. Their taste is so powerful, we remember it from the last time we walked down the aisle and suc-cumbed, snatching them up. And above all else, their formulas are calculated and perfected by scientists who know very well what they are doing. (Moss 347)

No quotation marks

Indent 1/2"

The Works Cited entry for this example is as follows:

Moss, Michael. *Salt, Sugar, Fat: How the Food Giants Hooked Us*. Random House, 2013.

45b Notes

MLA-style papers may contain notes in which you provide additional comments about the text of your paper or give references to other relevant sources. Notes should be used only when they add information crucial for understanding the main text of your paper. Use the notes tool in your word processor (under "References" in Microsoft Word) to insert notes.

Notes should be numbered consecutively (1, 2, etc.) through the paper. Put a full-sized number, raised above the line, at the end of phrases, clauses, or sentences containing the material you are referencing, after the punctuation.

> Social scientists have concluded that each individual is connected to every other person through "six degrees of separation" (Gladwell 35).[1] According to Malcolm Gladwell, those whose acquaintances come from a wide variety of social groups are particularly influential in spreading social epidemics (48).[2]

Notes may be formatted in two different ways:

- **Endnotes.** All notes appear on a separate page after the text of your paper and before the Works Cited. Begin a new page with a one-inch margin and add the heading

"Notes." Double-space and begin listing your notes. Indent the first line of each note one-half inch.

- **Footnotes.** If the reference tools in your word-processing program are accurate, use them to insert footnotes on the bottoms of relevant pages in your paper.

For each note, indent five spaces, insert the note number and a period, and begin the note. Double-space, and if the note continues on the next line, begin that line at the left-hand margin. In your note, refer to the author and, if the reference is specific, add the page number(s) of the comment.

Notes

1. With the expansion of social media, the number of degrees between people may be even less. A recent study shows all Facebook users are connected by an average of only 3.74 users. See "Facebook."

2. Some argue that the success of social epidemics relies less on the people who spread messages than the quality of the messages themselves. See Berger 13-14.

45c Works Cited list

The Works Cited list includes all sources you cite in your paper. Each Works Cited entry usually includes name(s) of author(s) (if listed), a title, publishing information, and the date of publication. This list allows your readers to find the sources you used within your paper.

Formatting guidelines

- **Place the Works Cited at the end of your paper.** The Works Cited page begins after your endnotes (if you have any).
- **Title your page.** Center the heading "Works Cited" (without italics or quotation marks) at the top of the page.
- **Include only the sources you have cited in your paper.** Do not include materials you read but did not specifically include in the paper.
- **Alphabetize your entries.** Arrange sources alphabetically by the first word of each entry. Ignore articles such as *A*, *An*, and *The* when alphabetizing your list.
- **Use a hanging-indent format.** The first line of each entry should begin at the left margin. All following lines of that entry should be indented one-half inch.
- **Double-space all entries.** Leave a blank line between the title and your first entry.

The key to MLA Works Cited entries is to provide enough information so your readers can retrieve your sources. The *MLA Handbook* notes that there can be more than one way to cite a source, but following the template below can help you to determine what is important to include for each entry.

CONTAINER 1

1) Author.

2) Title of Source.

3) Title of Container,

4) Other Contributors,

5) Version,

6) Number,

7) Publisher,

8) Publication Date,

9) Location.

CONTAINER 2

3) Title of Container,

4) Other Contributors,

5) Version,

6) Number,

7) Publisher,

8) Publication Date,

9) Location.

The Quick Guide on pp. 182-185 and the examples in this chapter can help you to follow the template and create your own Works Cited entries.

Most entries will begin with the Author, which is generally defined as the person(s) or group(s) who created the source you used. This will be followed by the Title of the Source that you used. This could be a short work (enclosed in quotation marks), such as an article, song, or poem, or a long work (italicized), such as a book, play, or film.

After this, consider the container that holds the source you used. A container could be a book, periodical, website, or other long work. In some cases, your work will be located in a second container, such as a library database. You will want to provide detailed information about these containers so that your readers can retrieve your source.

Sometimes, the container will simply include information about the source you used. For example, if you were citing a book, after the Author and Title of the Book, you would include information about the Publisher and the Publication Date.

Book

CONTAINER 1		
1) Author.	Groff, Lauren.
2) Title of Source.	*Fates and Furies.*
3) Title of Container,	
4) Other Contributors,	
5) Version,	
6) Number,	
7) Publisher,	Riverhead Books,
8) Publication Date,	2015.
9) Location.	

Groff, Lauren. *Fates and Furies.* Riverhead Books, 2015.

Other times, your source will be located within a container. For example, if you used an article from a magazine, you would first list the Author and the Title of the Source. The magazine is the container for the article you used. So next, you would include the Title of the Container (here, the magazine), the Publication Date, and the Location (or pages) in which you found the article.

Magazine Article

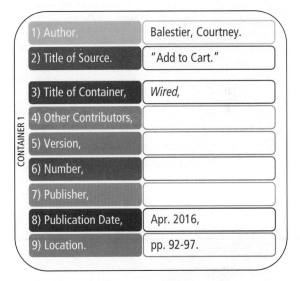

1) Author.	Balestier, Courtney.
2) Title of Source.	"Add to Cart."
3) Title of Container,	*Wired,*
4) Other Contributors,	
5) Version,	
6) Number,	
7) Publisher,	
8) Publication Date,	Apr. 2016,
9) Location.	pp. 92-97.

CONTAINER 1

Balestier, Courtney. "Add to Cart." *Wired,* Apr. 2016, pp. 92-97.

This template allows you to create Works Cited entries for many different types of sources, including apps, movies, television shows, and more. Check page 180 for some examples.

You may also find that your source is located in a second container. For example, imagine that you located a journal article on a library database. The journal would serve as the first container, and the library database would serve as the second container. After listing all of the relevant information for the journal article, you would include

MLA

App

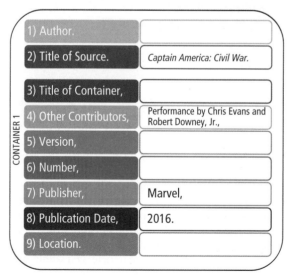

1) Author.	
2) Title of Source.	*Framed.*
3) Title of Container,	
4) Other Contributors,	
5) Version,	Version 1.0.0,
6) Number,	
7) Publisher,	Loveshack Entertainment,
8) Publication Date,	13 Nov. 2014.
9) Location.	

Framed. Version 1.0.0, Loveshack Entertainment, 13 Nov. 2014.

Film

1) Author.	
2) Title of Source.	*Captain America: Civil War.*
3) Title of Container,	
4) Other Contributors,	Performance by Chris Evans and Robert Downey, Jr.,
5) Version,	
6) Number,	
7) Publisher,	Marvel,
8) Publication Date,	2016.
9) Location.	

Captain America: Civil War. Performance by Chris Evans and Robert Downey, Jr., Marvel, 2016.

a second **Title of the Container (here, the database title)** and the **Location (here, a digital object identifier [DOI] number)**.

Journal Article from a Database

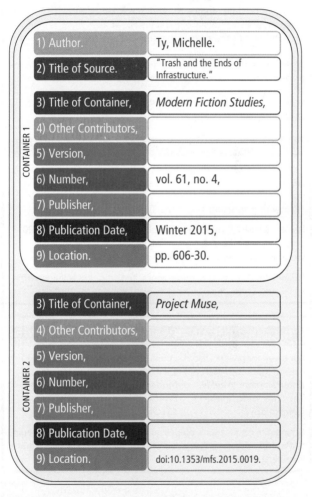

Ty, Michelle. "Trash and the Ends of Infrastructure." *Modern Fiction Studies,* vol. 61, no. 4, Winter 2015, pp. 606-30. *Project Muse,* doi:10.1353/mfs.2015.0019.

QUICK GUIDE: How Do I Format an MLA Works-Cited Entry?

1) AUTHOR.

One author: **Cole, James H.**
Two authors: **Cole, James H., and Sue F. Lin.**
Three or more authors: **Cole, James H., et al.**
No author: Start the entry with the title of the source.

When focusing on a person or group who had a central role in the project other than creating the core content, add a descriptive label:
Metz, Dan E., editor.   **Bola, Sara R., et al., translators.**
Gosling, Ryan, performer.

2) TITLE OF SOURCE.

For short works that are contained in longer works (articles, pages on Web sites, short stories, poems, songs, etc.): Use quotation marks.
"Protecting Yourself."   **"The Tyger."**   **"Hello."**

For long works (books, comic books, websites, TV shows, films, plays, apps, works of art, etc.): Use italics.
Great Expectations.   *Game of Thrones.*   *Hamlet.*

* Capitalize conjunctions, prepositions, and articles only if they begin a title, end a title, or follow a colon. Also capitalize prepositions that form parts of verbs.

3) TITLE OF CONTAINER,

For these long works (books, comic book series, websites, journals, magazines, newspapers, TV series, apps, etc.): Use italics.
Entertainment Weekly,   *Modern Fiction Studies,*
The New York Times,   *Pretty Little Liars,*
Comixology,   *JSTOR,*

* Capitalize conjunctions, prepositions, and articles only if they begin a title, end a title, or follow a colon. Also capitalize prepositions that form parts of verbs.

4) OTHER CONTRIBUTORS,

Identify their role with a descriptive phrase preceding their names:
directed by Alejandro G. Iñárritu,   edited by Cornel West,
performance by Viola Davis,   narrated by Kate Winslet,

5) VERSION,

To indicate a later or changed edition of a book, add a label:
3rd ed.,   expanded ed.,   updated ed.,

To indicate a number or special version of a media source, add a label:
version 2.5,   unabridged version,   director's cut,

6) NUMBER,

For a volume of a book, add a label: **vol. 3,**

For periodicals, use "vol." for the volume number and "no." for the issue number: **vol. 45, no. 6,**

For comic books numbered just by issue number: **no. 5,**

For television series episodes, add a label: **season 5, episode 8,**

7) PUBLISHER,

To find the publisher of a book, look at the title page and the copyright page. List the name of the publisher mainly responsible for the work. Omit words like "Co." and "Inc.":
Vintage Books,   Little, Brown,   Random House,

Use "UP" for "University Press": **Oxford UP   U of Mississippi P,**

For films and television series, name the company mainly responsible for it: **Columbia,**

For websites, list the publisher if the name is different than the name of the site:

Screencrush Network,   Capitol Records,

Omit the publisher for periodicals and works published by the author or editor. Also omit website publishers that are the same name of the website and the names of web design or production programs (like *WordPress* or *Adobe Muse*).

8) PUBLICATION DATE,

Abbreviate names of months except for May, June, and July.

Year: **2016,**

Month(s) and year: **Oct. 2016,   Sept.-Oct. 2016,**

Exact date: **4 Oct. 2016,**

Exact date and time (like for a tweet): **4 Oct. 2016, 11:25 p.m.,**

MLA

9) LOCATION.

Page(s)

Use a p. for a single page and pp. for multiple pages. Omit second hundredth digit when within the same 100 pages:
p. 8.   **pp. 8–10.**   **pp. 308–10.**

Use section letter and page number for newspapers: **p. A1.   p. 5D.**

For sources that have pages that are not consecutive, list the first page and a plus sign: **pp. 54+.**   **pp. A1+.**

DOI

Many journal articles, book chapters, and technical reports are now identified by DOI (Digital Object Identifier) numbers. A DOI is a unique code assigned to that publication and remains stable, even if a URL for the source changes. If the publication has been assigned a DOI, include it directly at the end of your entry. If you access the publication online, list the DOI (when available). **doi:10.1002/jbt.20384.**

If a DOI is not available, use a URL instead.

URL

For online sources, omit the *http://* or *https://* and list the whole URL. Break the lines after punctuation, if needed—ideally after a slash—and add a period at the end: **www.nytimes.com/2016/05/01/world/asia/nepals-earthquake-recovery-remains-in-disarray-a-year-later.html.**

For databases and other password-protected sites, use a stable URL, or permalink, if a DOI is not available.

Media Source

For material on DVD or Blu-ray, list the disc number: **disc 2.**

Physical Location

For sources that you experienced firsthand in a place, like a theater or a museum, name the place and the city. Omit the city if it is included in the name of the place.

Walker Art Museum, Minneapolis.   Milwaukee Art Museum.

In addition to these elements, there are several optional elements that can help your reader understand the type of source you used and find its location. There are examples for many of these elements in the sample Works Cited entries on pp. 187-198, but some of the most commonly used ones are listed below.

OPTIONAL ELEMENTS.

Date of Original Publication

If the original date of the work you accessed is different than that of the source you used, add a date immediately after the source title.

1785.

Date of Access

If you are using a source likely to be updated, or if the source does not have a date, you can indicate the date of access at the end of the entry.

Accessed 15 June 2016.

Descriptive Tags

Add a descriptive tag at the end of the entry for sources that are of an unforeseen or nonstandard medium.

Map.   Cartoon.   Transcript.

Examples of MLA Works Cited Entries

BOOKS AND PARTS OF BOOKS

1. Book with One Author 187
2. Book with Two Authors 188
3. Book with Three or More Authors 189
4. Book by a Corporate or Organizational Author 189
5. Book Accessed Online 189
6. E-Book Downloaded for E-Book Reader 189
7. Book Published Before 1900 189

MLA

Examples of MLA Works Cited

Please note that all entries should be double-spaced on your Works Cited page.

Books and parts of books

FAQ

What is the basic citation format for a book?

Author(s). *Book Title*. Publisher, Publication Date.

1. **Book with One Author** To cite books accessed online, see entry 5.

> Robinson, Marilynne. *Lila*. Farrar, Straus and Giroux, 2014.

MLA—Citing a Book

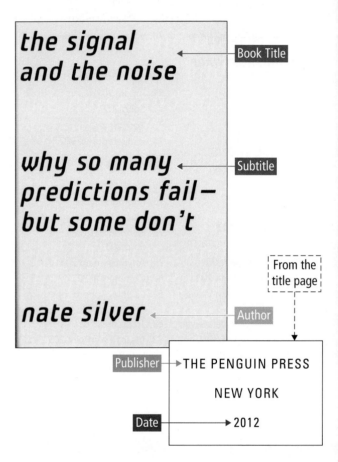

Works Cited Entry:

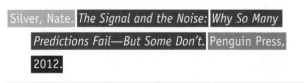

Silver, Nate. *The Signal and the Noise: Why So Many Predictions Fail—But Some Don't.* Penguin Press, 2012.

2. **Book with Two Authors** Reverse the name of the first author only.

> Bell, Stephen, and Andrew Hindmoor. *Masters of the Universe, Slaves of the Market.* Harvard UP, 2015.

3. **Book with Three or More Authors** List only the first author's name and add *et al.* (for "and others").

> Herman, David, et al. *Narrative Theory: Core Concepts and Critical Debates*. Ohio State UP, 2012.

4. **Book by a Corporate or Organizational Author**

> Mayo Clinic. *The Essential Diabetes Book*. 2nd ed., Time, 2014.

5. **Book Accessed Online**

> Fitzgerald, F. Scott. *This Side of Paradise*. Scribner Books, 1920. *Bartleby*, 1999, www.bartleby.com/115.

6. **E-Book Downloaded for Electronic Book Reader** Name the edition type (Kindle, iBooks, etc.) after the title.

> Hawkins, Paula. *The Girl on the Train*. Kindle ed., River-head Books, 2015.

7. **Book Published Before 1900** You may include the city of publication instead of the publisher's name.

> Swinburne, Algernon Charles. *Poems and Ballads*. London, 1889.

8. **Republished Work** State the original publication date after the title.

> Braddon, Mary Elizabeth. *Lady Audley's Secret*. 1862. Oxford UP, 2012.

9. **More Than One Work by the Same Author** Use the author's name in the first entry only. From then on, type three hyphens and a period, and then begin the next title. Alphabetize by title.

> Ishiguro, Kazuo. *The Buried Giant*. Alfred A. Knopf, 2015.
> ---. *Nocturnes: Five Stories of Music and Nightfall*. Faber and Faber, 2009.

10. **Anthology/Collected Works** An *anthology* is a book that contains several smaller works. If the anthology contains works from several authors, list the editor or editors first, followed by the word *editor* or *editors*. If the anthology contains works by a single author, list the author first and include the editor or editors after the title. Use the words *edited by* followed by the name(s) of the editor or editors.

Middleton, Thomas. *Thomas Middleton: The Collected Works*. Edited by Gary Taylor and John Lavagnino, Oxford UP, 2010.

Aslan, Reza, editor. *Tablet and Pen: Literary Landscapes from the Modern Middle East*. Norton, 2011.

11. **Work in an Anthology/Collected Works** State the author and title of the work first, and then give the title and other information about the anthology, including the pages on which the selection appears. Include the original publication date after the title of the work if it is different from the publication date of the anthology or collected works.

> Hurston, Zora Neale. "Sweat." 1926. *Literature: An Introduction to Fiction, Poetry, and Drama*, edited by X. J. Kennedy and Dana Gioia, 12th ed., Pearson, 2013, pp. 562-71.

> Mori, Kyoki. "Between the Forest and the Well: Notes on Death." *The Inevitable: Contemporary Writers Confront Death*, edited by David Shields and Bradford Morrow, Norton, 2011, pp. 33-49.

12. **Two or More Works in the Same Anthology/Collected Works** Include a complete entry for the collection and then cross-reference the works to that collection. In the cross-reference, include the author and title of the work, the last name of the editor of the collection, and the page numbers. For previously published material, you may include the original date of publication after the title of the work.

> Forrester, Andrew. "The Unknown Weapon." 1864. Sims, pp. 33-102.

> Sims, Michael, editor. *The Penguin Book of Victorian Women in Crime*. Penguin Books, 2011.

> Wilkins, Mary E. "The Long Arm." 1895. Sims, pp. 133-64.

13. **Article Reprinted in a Book** You may choose to include the original publication information at the end of the entry.

> Doherty, Brian. "Comics Tragedy: Is the Superhero Invulnerable?" *Best American Comics Criticism*, edited by Ben Schwartz, Fantagraphics, 2010, pp. 24-33. Originally published in *Reason*, May 2001, pp. 49-55.

14. **Article in a Scholarly Collection** List the author and article you used first.

> Tew, Philip. "After the First Decade: Revisiting the Work of Zadie Smith." *Postmodern Literature and Race,* edited by Len Platt and Sara Upstone, Cambridge UP, 2015, pp. 247-63.

15. **Second or Later Edition**

> Backman, Clifford R. *Cultures of the West: A History.* 2nd ed., Oxford UP, 2015.

16. **Work That Names a Translator** Use the abbreviation *Trans.* (for "Translated by").

> Descombes, Vincent. *Puzzling Identities.* Translated by Stephen Adam Schwartz, Harvard UP, 2016.

17. **Work That Has More Than One Volume**

> Hemingway, Ernest. *The Letters of Ernest Hemingway: 1907-1922.* Edited by Sandra Spanier and Robert W. Trogdon, vol. 1, Cambridge UP, 2011. 3 vols.

18. **Comic Book** If the comic book is part of a separately titled series, italicize both the comic book and series titles.

> Coates, Ta-Nehisi, et al. *Black Panther.* No. 1, Marvel Comics, 2016.

> Tomine, Adrian. *Summer Blonde. Optic Nerve,* no. 7, Drawn and Quarterly Publications, June 2000.

19. **Graphic Novel**

> Hart, Tom. *Rosalie Lightning.* St. Martin's Press, 2016.

20. **Illustrated Book**

> Bryant, Jen. *The Right Word: Roget and His Thesaurus.* Illustrated by Melissa Sweet, William B. Eerdmans Publishing, 2014.

21. **Introduction, Foreword, Preface, or Afterword** Start the entry with the author of the part you are citing. If the author of the part is not the author of the book, use the word *by* and give the book author's full name. If the author of the part and the book are the same, use *by* and the author's last name only.

Hirsch, E. D., Jr. Preface. *The Making of Americans: Democracy and Our Schools,* by Hirsch, Yale UP, 2009, pp. ix-xii.

Bird, Jeremy. Foreword. *Groundbreakers: How Obama's 2.2 Million Volunteers Transformed Campaigning in America,* by Elizabeth McKenna and Hahrie Han, Oxford UP, 2015, pp. vii-x.

22. **Work with a Title Within a Title** If a title that is normally italicized appears within another title, do not italicize it or use quotation marks.

Frankel, Glenn. The Searchers: *The Making of an American Legend.* Bloomsbury, 2013.

23. **Work in a Series** Add the series name and number at the end.

Verhoeven, Harry. *Water, Civilisation, and Power in Sudan: The Political Economy of Military-Islamist State Building.* Cambridge UP, 2015. African Studies 131.

24. **Biblical and Other Sacred Texts**

The Bible. Introduction and notes by Robert Carroll and Stephen Prickett, Authorized King James Version, Oxford UP, 2008.

The Jewish Study Bible: Tanakh Translation, Torah, Nevi'im, Kethuvim. Translated by the Jewish Publication Society, edited by Adele Berlin et al., Oxford UP, 2004.

25. **Article in a Dictionary, Encyclopedia, Reference Book, or Database** If the entry is attributed to a specific author, treat it like an article in a book or a page on a website.

Costello, Brannon. "Chaykin, Howard." *Encyclopedia of Comic Books and Graphic Novels,* edited by M. Keith Booker, vol. 1, Greenwood Publishing, 2010, pp. 95-96.

"Malapropism." *Merriam-Webster Online,* 2015, www.merriam-webster.com/dictionary/malapropism.

26. **Pamphlet** Cite a pamphlet like a book.

Starbucks Coffee Company. *Recycling and Reducing the Environmental Impact of Our Cups.* Starbucks, 2010.

Government publications

27. **Government Publication**

> Chilton, Bart. *Ponzimonium: How Scam Artists Are Rip-
> ping Off America.* United States, Commodity Futures
> Trading Commission, 2012.

> United States, Congress, Congressional Budget Office.
> *Updated Budget Projections: 2016-2026.* CBO, Mar.
> 2016.

28. **Article on a Government Website** List an author if one
    is named. For Web articles that do not list a date or
    are likely to be updated, MLA recommends adding an
    access date at the end of the entry.

> "Current Situation." *Flu.gov,* United States, Department
> of Health and Human Services, www.flu.gov/
> pandemic/current-situation/index.html. Accessed
> 8 May 2016.

> "Pollinators in Trouble." *National Park Service,* United
> States, Department of the Interior, www.nps.gov/
> subjects/pollinators/pollinators-in-trouble.htm.
> Accessed 14 Apr. 2016.

29. **Congressional Bill** Include the Congressional num-
    ber and session as well as the document type and
    number.

> United States, Congress, Senate. *Violence Against Women
> Reauthorization Act of 2013.* Government Printing
> Office, 2013. 113th Congress, 1st session, Senate
> Bill 47.

30. **Congressional Hearing**

> United States, Congress, House. Committee on Appro-
> priations, Subcommittee on Homeland Security.
> *Department of Homeland Security Appropriations for
> 2016.* Washington, Government Publishing Office,
> 2016. 114th Congress, 1st session, House Bill 83.

Journal articles

31. **Scholarly Journal Article**

> Schreiber, Michele. "Tiny Life: Technology and Masculinity
> in the Films of David Fincher." *Journal of Film and
> Video,* vol. 68, no. 1, Spring 2016, pp. 3-18.

MLA

FAQ

How do I cite a journal article from a library database or subscription service?

Author(s). "Title of Article." *Title of Journal,* vol. #, no. #, year, p. or pp. #. Title of Database, URL or DOI.

(INDENT 0.5")

32. **Journal Article Located in a Library Database or Subscription Service**

> Walkowitz, Rebecca L. "Ishiguro's Floating Worlds." *ELH,*
> vol. 68, no. 4, Winter 2001, pp. 1049-76. *JSTOR,*
> www.jstor.org/stable/30032004.

If your source has a DOI, include it instead of the URL at the end of the entry.

> Kotsonas, Antonis. "Politics of Periodization and the
> Archaeology of Early Greece." *American Journal of
> Archaeology,* vol. 120, no. 2, Apr. 2016, pp. 239-70.
> *JSTOR,* doi:10.3764/aja.120.2.0239.

33. **Article in an Online Journal**

> Dolgert, Stefan. "Empire's Walking Dead: The Zombie
> Apocalypse as Capitalist Theodicy." *Borderlands,*
> vol. 13, no. 4, 2014, www.borderlands.net.au/
> vol13no2_2014/dolgert_zombie.pdf.

Magazine articles

FAQ

How do I cite a magazine article?

Author(s). "Title of Article." *Title of Magazine,* day Mo. year, p. or pp. #.

(INDENT 0.5")

34. **Monthly or Bimonthly Magazine Article**

> Kelly, Kevin. "Hypervision." *Wired,* May 2016, pp. 74+.

> Miller, Jeremy. "Droughtlandia." *Pacific Standard,* May-
> June 2016, pp. 56-63.

MLA—Citing a Journal Article from a Database

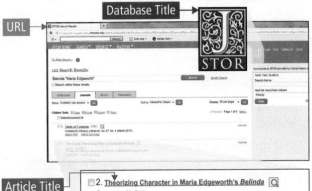

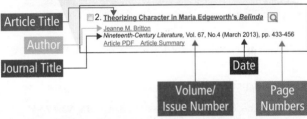

Works Cited Entry:

Britton, Jeanne M. "Theorizing Character in Maria Edgeworth's *Belinda*." *Nineteenth Century Literature,* vol. 67, no. 4, Mar. 2013, pp. 433-56, *JSTOR,* http://www.jstor.org/stable/10.1525/ncl.2013.67.4.433.

---

35. **Weekly or Biweekly Magazine Article**

    Breznican, Anthony. "Winner Take All." *Entertainment Weekly,* 11 Mar. 2016, pp. 26-32.

36. **Magazine Article Located in a Library Database or Subscription Service**

    Ellis, Sian. "Beyond the Green Baize Door." *British Heritage,* Jan. 2016, pp. 30-35. *Academic Search Complete,* search.ebscohost.com/login.aspx?direct=true&db=a9h&AN=110230979&login.asp&site=ehost-live&scope=site.

37. **Article in an Online Magazine**

    Schulz, Kathryn. "The Really Big One." *The New Yorker,* 20 July 2015, www.newyorker.com/magazine/2015/07/20/the-really-big-one.

38. **Article on a Magazine App**

> Poulsen, Kevin. "Double Cross: The Ukranian Hacker Who Became the FBI's Best Weapon—and Worst Nightmare." *Wired,* May 2016. *Google Play Newsstand*, version 3.5.2.

Newspaper articles

How do I cite a newspaper article?

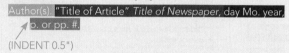

Author(s). "Title of Article." *Title of Newspaper,* day Mo. year, p. or pp. #.

(INDENT 0.5")

39. **Newspaper Article**

> Goode, Erica. "Social Workers in Blue." *The New York Times,* 26 Apr. 2016, pp. D1+.

40. **Newspaper Article Located in a Library Database or Subscription Service**

> Stobbe, Mike. "What to Know about the Tropical Zika Virus in Latin America." *South Florida Times,* 28 Jan. 2016, p. 4A. *Newspaper Source Plus,* search.ebscohost.com/login.aspx?direct=true&db= n5h&AN=113843653&login.asp&site=ehost-live& scope=site.

41. **Article in an Online Newspaper or Newswire**

> Stevens, Heidi. "New Study Says Spanking Doesn't Work, Makes Children's Behavior Worse." *Chicago Tribune,* 1 May 2016, www.chicagotribune.com/lifestyles/ stevens/ct-spanking-effects-study-balancing-0428- 20160428-column.html.

42. **Article on a Newspaper App**

> Rich, Motoko, et al. "Money, Race, and Success: How Your School District Compares." *The New York Times,* 29 Apr. 2016. *NYTimes for iPad*, version 3.15.

Other periodical sources

43. **Unsigned Article**

> "Hate Crimes: Study Finds Nearly 2 in 3 Incidences Go
> Unreported." *Wall Street Journal*, 22 Mar. 2013, p. A6.

44. **Editorial**

> "A Risky American Expansion in Syria." Editorial. *The New
> York Times,* 26 Apr. 2016, p. A20.

45. **Letter to the Editor**

> Neal, Jeff. Letter to the Editor. *The Wall Street Journal*, 26
> Apr. 2016, p. A12.

46. **Review of a Work**

> Sheffield, Rob. Review of *Lemonade*, by Beyoncé.
> *Rolling Stone,* 26 Apr. 2016, www.rollingstone.
> com/music/albumreviews/beyonce-lemonade-
> 20160425.

> Wood, James. "Stranger in Our Midst." Review of *The Little
> Red Chairs,* by Edna O'Brien. *The New Yorker,* 25
> Apr. 2016, pp. 96-98.

47. **Published Interview**

> Harington, Kit. "Dead Man Talking." Interviewed by James Hib-
> berd, *Entertainment Weekly,* 13 May 2016, pp. 14-23.

Websites and other online sources

48. **Entire Website**

> *CNN.* 2016, www.cnn.com.

> *International Spy Museum.* 2016, spymuseum.org.

FAQ

How do I cite a page or article from a website?

Author(s). "Title of Page or Article." *Title of Web Site*, Publisher
(if different from the Web site title) Date of publication,
revision, or update, URL or DOI.

(INDENT 0.5")

If you don't have a date of publication, revision, or update,
MLA recommends that you add a date of access at the end of
the entry: **Accessed 12 Aug. 2016.**

MLA—Page/Article on a Website

| Website Title | URL | Date |

Author | **Article Title**

From the bottom of the webpage

Site Publisher

Works Cited Entry:

Abrahamson, Jake. "Gust Junkies: Wind Sports Take
Off." *Sierra*, Mar. 2013, www.sierraclub.org/
sierra201303.wind-athletes/slide1-
paragliding.aspx.

---

49. **Page or Article on a Website**

> "Exquisitely Evil: 50 Years of Bond Villains." *International Spy Museum*, 2016, www.spymuseum.org/
> exhibition-experiences/exquisitely-evil/.
>
> Storrs, Carina. "How to Keep Away Mosquitos Carrying
> Zika, Dengue." *CNN*, 21 Jan. 2016, www.cnn.com/

2016/01/21/health/preventing-mosquito-borne-
viruses-zika-dengue-west-nile/index.html.

50. **Entire Page, Timeline, or Stream on a Social Networking Website**

> Timberlake, Justin. *Facebook: Justin Timberlake*.
> 8 May 2016, www.facebook.com/justintimberlake.

51. **Tweet**

> @POTUS (Barack Obama). "To my 5th grade teacher
> Ms. Mabel Hefty and the educators who inspire
> our young people every single day: Thank you."
> 3 May 2016, 11:12 a.m., twitter.com/POTUS/
> status/727561463993270272.

52. **Entire Blog**

> McBride, Bill. *Calculated Risk*. 2007-2016, www.
> calculatedriskblog.com.

53. **Post on a Blog**

> McBride, Bill. "Public and Private Sector Payroll Jobs:
> Carter, Reagan, Bush, Clinton, Bush, Obama."
> *Calculated Risk*, 6 May 2016, www.calculatedriskblog.
> com/2016/05/public-and-private-sector-payroll-jobs.
> html.

54. **Comment on a Blog**

> Firemane. Comment on "Public and Private Sector Payroll
> Jobs: Carter, Reagan, Bush, Clinton, Bush, Obama."
> *Calculated Risk*, 6 May 2016, 5:32 p.m., hoocoodanode.
> org/t/public-and-private-sector-payroll-jobs-carter-
> reagan-bush-clinton-bush-obama/10362/164.

Apps and software

55. **App**

> *Star Walk*, Version 7.2.0, Vito Technology, 2016.

56. **Article or Short Work on an App**

> "Hubble." *Star Walk*, version 7.2.0, Vito Technology, 2016.

57. **Video Game**

> *Civilization VI*. Firaxis, 2016.

Communications

50. **Letter or Memo** If a document is unpublished, you may indicate *Manuscript* or *Typescript* as a descriptive tag at the end of the entry.

> Blumen, Lado. Letter. Received by Lui Han, 14 Oct. 1998, Lado Blumen Papers, Minneapolis Museum of Art Library, Minneapolis. Manuscript.

> Johnson, Jeffrey. Letter. Received by Andrew James, 11 Jan. 2016. Typescript.

> Nafman, Theresa. Memo. Received by the Narragansett School Board, 3 May 2004, Narragansett High School, Boston. Typescript.

Cite a published letter like an article in an anthology.

> Shaw, George Bernard. "To Curt Otto." 20 Mar. 1920. *Bernard Shaw and His Publishers*, edited by Michel W. Pharand, U of Toronto P, 2009, pp. 129-30.

59. **E-Mail**

> Jones, Hannah. "Special Delivery." Received by April Krier, 3 Mar. 2016.

60. **Interview**

> Flannagan, Rebecca. Interviewed by Jennifer Kunka, 11 Mar. 2016, Florence.

Television, film, and video

61. **Television Series** You have the option to begin the entry with other contributors, such as the creator or performers, if they are most relevant to your discussion. Any of the following examples would be correct.

> *House of Cards*. Created by Beau Willimon, performance by Kevin Spacey, Netflix, 2013-16.

> Spacey, Kevin, performer. *House of Cards*. Created by Beau Willimon, Netflix, 2013-16.

> Willimon, Beau, creator. *House of Cards*. Performance by Kevin Spacey, Netflix, 2013-16.

62. **Television Episode** Insert names of contributors if they are relevant to your discussion.

> "Buckle Up." *Scandal*, created by Shonda Rhimes, performance by Kerri Washington, season 5, episode 19, ABC, 28 Apr. 2016.

"Home." *Game of Thrones*, season 6, episode 2, HBO, 1 May 2016.

63. **Television Episode Viewed Online**

"Genesis." *Arrow,* season 4, episode 20, CW, 4 May 2016. *Hulu,* www.hulu.com/watch/937553.

64. **Television Episode Viewed on DVD or Blu-ray**

"The Reichenbach Fall." *Sherlock*, performance by Benedict Cumberbatch and Martin Freeman, season 2, episode 3, BBC, 2012, disc 2.

65. **Television Program Viewed on an App**

"Inauguration." *Veep*, episode 10, season 5, HBO, 26 June 2016. *HBO NOW,* version 6.1.5785.

66. **Film** Add other contributors (director, performers) if you focus on them in your discussion.

Deadpool. Directed by Tim Miller, performance by Ryan Reynolds, 20th Century Fox, 2016.

67. **DVD or Blu-ray** Include the original release date after the title of the film if different from the date of the DVD or Blu-ray.

Star Wars: Episode VII—The Force Awakens. 2015. Directed by J. J. Abrams, performance by Harrison Ford, Lucasfilm, 2016.

68. **Film Viewed with an App**

Schumer, Amy, performer and screenwriter. *Trainwreck.* Universal Studios, 2015. *HBO GO*, version 1.6.1.

69. **Online Video** List the name or pseudonym of the person who posted the video recording, if available.

Slo Mo Guys. "Fire Tornado in Slow Motion 4k." *YouTube*, 22 Nov. 2015, www.youtube.com/watch?v=QwoghxwETng.

70. **Video Viewed with an App**

The Slo Mo Guys. "Fire Tornado in Slow Motion 4k." *YouTube*, 22 Nov. 2015. *YouTube*, Google, version 11.19.

MLA

Audio sources

71. **Album (digital or analog)**

> Beyoncé. *Lemonade*. Columbia Records, 2016. *SPIN*, 23 Apr. 2016, www.spin.com/2016/04/beyonce-new-album-lemonade-download-free-stream-tidal/. Accessed 23 Apr. 2016.

> Grande, Ariana. *Dangerous Woman*. Republic Records, 2016. *iTunes*, version 12.4.1.

> Prince. *The Very Best of Prince*. Rhino, 2001.

72. **Song** If you accessed the song on a Web site or with an app, list the point of access as a second container.

> Beyoncé. "Formation." *Lemonade*, Columbia Records, 2016.

> Grande, Ariana. "Dangerous Woman." *Dangerous Woman*, Republic Records, 2016. *iTunes*, version 12.4.1.

73. **Podcast**

> Koenig, Sarah. "The Captors." *Serial,* season 2, episode 4, 7 Jan. 2016, serialpodcast.org/season-two/4/the-captors.

74. **Radio Program**

> "Building a Smarter Team." *On Point*, narrated by Tom Ashbrook, National Public Radio, 27 Jan. 2015.

Other media

75. **Work of Art** If the artwork is in a book or on a Web site, treat that book or site as a container.

> Dalí, Salvador. *The Persistence of Memory*. 1931. Museum of Modern Art, New York.

> Lichtenstein, Roy. *Drowning Girl*. 1963. *Roy Lichtenstein*, by Janis Hendricksen, Taschen Books, 1988, p. 31.

76. **Photograph** Indicate the location and city where the photo is exhibited. Or if you accessed the photograph in a book or on a Web site, substitute publication information.

> Gursky, Andreas. *Times Square, New York*. 1997, Museum of Modern Art, New York.

> Smith, Sandra. Photograph of Times Square. 1 Jan. 2016, Smith Residence, Chicago.

77. Map

> "Chicago." *Google Maps,* 1 May 2016, www.google.com/
> maps/place/Chicago,+IL/.

> *Tennessee.* Map. Rand McNally, 2010.

78. Cartoon or Comic Strip

> Armstrong, Robb. "Jumpstart." *Morning News* [Florence],
> 12 Mar. 2012, p. A5.

> Kanin, Zachary. Cartoon. *New Yorker,* 26 Jan. 2015, p. 60.

79. Advertisement

> Toyota. Advertisement for Toyota Prius. *Wired,* Feb. 2015, p. 41.

80. Commercial

> Amazon. Commercial for Amazon Fire TV Stick. *CNN*, 24
> Jan. 2015.

> Apple. "The Kiss." *Apple.com*, 2016, www.apple.com/tv/films/.

81. Lecture, Speech, or Address

> McEwan, Ian. Address. 11 Apr. 2012, Law School Audito-
> rium, U of South Carolina, Columbia.

82. Transcript

> Lunden, Jeff. "Can Pop Musicals Bring New Audiences to
> Broadway?" *All Things Considered*, National Public
> Radio, 20 Apr. 2016, www.npr.org/templates/transcript/
> transcript.php?storyId=474857169. Transcript.

83. Class PowerPoint

> Jamberson, Jill. "Renaissance Art." 11 Feb. 2016, Oklahoma
> State U, Stillwater. Microsoft PowerPoint.

84. **Live Performance of a Play** Add other contributors
    (director, performers) if you focus on them in your
    discussion.

> Shakespeare, William. *Hamlet.* Directed by Lyndsey Turner,
> performance by Benedict Cumberbatch, 25 Aug. 2015,
> Barbican Centre, London.

85. Musical Composition

> Mozart, Wolfgang Amadeus. *The Magic Flute.* 1791. Faber
> and Faber, 2001.

45d Paper format

Follow the format shown here for the first page and the Works Cited page of an MLA-style research paper.

Paper Format Quick Guide – MLA	
Paper format	Set your top, bottom, left, and right margins at one inch. Justify your left margin but not the right unless your instructor requests it.
	Double-space all pages, headers, block quotes, and the Works Cited. Use a standard, easy-to-read font (such as Times New Roman, Cambria, Arial, or Calibri) that is 10- or 12-point size.
	Indent the first line of every paragraph ½ inch from the left margin. For long quotations, indent the passage ½ inch from the left margin.
Title and personal information	MLA-style papers do not require a separate title page. In the top left margin of your first page, create a double-spaced list. On separate lines, include your name, your instructor's name, the course number, and the date.
	Then double-space and type the title, centered on the page. Double-space the title if it extends to a second line. Capitalize all words in the title except for articles, conjunctions, and prepositions (unless they are the first word or follow a colon).
Header and page numbers	Beginning on page 1, create a header that is ½ inch from the top of the page and flush with the right margin. Include your last name, a space, and the page number: **Smith 1**
Headings and subheadings	Headings are short titles that break up sections and subsections in long reports and papers. Use consistent phrasing and font style for these.
Tables and figures	Insert tables and figures within the body of the text. Labels for tables appear directly above them. The label and the table title appear on separate lines (double-spaced).
	Table 1 **Circulation Statistics for Victorian Sensation Novels**
	For figures (including graphs, charts, photos, maps, etc.), create a brief label and place it directly below the figure:
	Fig. 7. Cruikshank's Illustration for *Oliver Twist*.
Works Cited	Insert a title called *Works Cited* and center it on the page. All entries should be double-spaced and organized alphabetically. Format entries in hanging indent style, meaning the second and following lines of an entry are indented ½ inch.

MLA

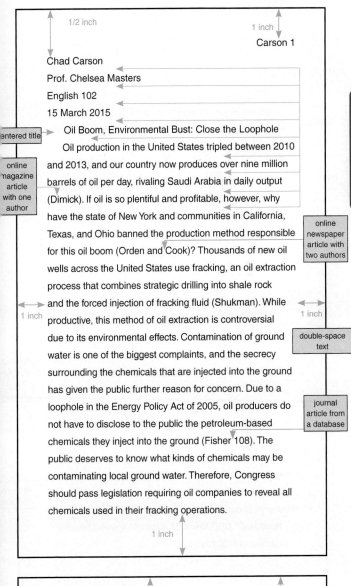

Carson 1

Chad Carson

Prof. Chelsea Masters

English 102

15 March 2015

centered title

Oil Boom, Environmental Bust: Close the Loophole

Oil production in the United States tripled between 2010 and 2013, and our country now produces over nine million barrels of oil per day, rivaling Saudi Arabia in daily output (Dimick). If oil is so plentiful and profitable, however, why have the state of New York and communities in California, Texas, and Ohio banned the production method responsible for this oil boom (Orden and Cook)? Thousands of new oil wells across the United States use fracking, an oil extraction process that combines strategic drilling into shale rock and the forced injection of fracking fluid (Shukman). While productive, this method of oil extraction is controversial due to its environmental effects. Contamination of ground water is one of the biggest complaints, and the secrecy surrounding the chemicals that are injected into the ground has given the public further reason for concern. Due to a loophole in the Energy Policy Act of 2005, oil producers do not have to disclose to the public the petroleum-based chemicals they inject into the ground (Fisher 108). The public deserves to know what kinds of chemicals may be contaminating local ground water. Therefore, Congress should pass legislation requiring oil companies to reveal all chemicals used in their fracking operations.

online magazine article with one author

online newspaper article with two authors

double-space text

journal article from a database

1 inch

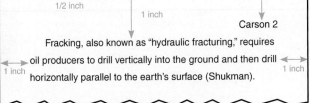

Carson 2

Fracking, also known as "hydraulic fracturing," requires oil producers to drill vertically into the ground and then drill horizontally parallel to the earth's surface (Shukman).

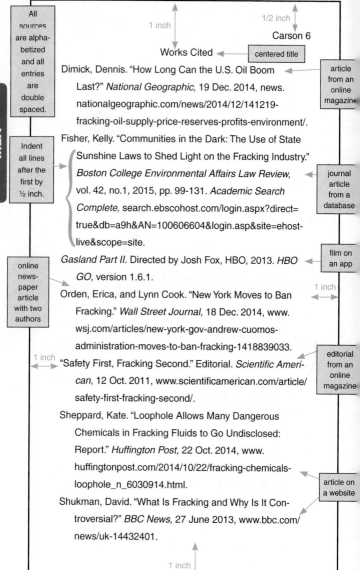

All sources are alphabetized and all entries are double spaced.

1 inch

1/2 inch

Carson 6

Works Cited ◄ centered title

Indent all lines after the first by ½ inch.

Dimick, Dennis. "How Long Can the U.S. Oil Boom Last?" *National Geographic,* 19 Dec. 2014, news. nationalgeographic.com/news/2014/12/141219-fracking-oil-supply-price-reserves-profits-environment/. ◄ article from an online magazine

Fisher, Kelly. "Communities in the Dark: The Use of State Sunshine Laws to Shed Light on the Fracking Industry." *Boston College Environmental Affairs Law Review,* vol. 42, no.1, 2015, pp. 99-131. *Academic Search Complete,* search.ebscohost.com/login.aspx?direct= true&db=a9h&AN=100606604&login.asp&site=ehost-live&scope=site. ◄ journal article from a database

Gasland Part II. Directed by Josh Fox, HBO, 2013. *HBO GO,* version 1.6.1. ◄ film on an app

online newspaper article with two authors

Orden, Erica, and Lynn Cook. "New York Moves to Ban Fracking." *Wall Street Journal,* 18 Dec. 2014, www. wsj.com/articles/new-york-gov-andrew-cuomos-administration-moves-to-ban-fracking-1418839033.

1 inch

"Safety First, Fracking Second." Editorial. *Scientific American,* 12 Oct. 2011, www.scientificamerican.com/article/safety-first-fracking-second/. ◄ editorial from an online magazine

Sheppard, Kate. "Loophole Allows Many Dangerous Chemicals in Fracking Fluids to Go Undisclosed: Report." *Huffington Post,* 22 Oct. 2014, www. huffingtonpost.com/2014/10/22/fracking-chemicals-loophole_n_6030914.html.

Shukman, David. "What Is Fracking and Why Is It Controversial?" *BBC News,* 27 June 2013, www.bbc.com/news/uk-14432401. ◄ article on a website

1 inch

46 Documenting in APA Style

The format prescribed by the **American Psychological Association (APA)** is used to document papers in fields such as psychology, sociology, business, education, nursing, social work, and criminology. For APA format, follow the guidelines offered here and consult the *Publication Manual of the American Psychological Association*, 6th ed. (Washington: APA, 2010) and the *APA Style Guide to Electronic References,* 6th ed. (Washington: APA, 2012). Check for further updates on the APA website (apastyle.apa.org), the *APA Style Blog* (blog.apastyle.org), and the APA Twitter feed.

APA

FAQ

What are the features of APA style?

- The paper begins with a brief abstract or summary.
- For in-text citations, give the author's last name and the source's year of publication. For quoted material, paraphrases, or other references to specific information in the original source, add a page (*p.*) number or paragraph (*para.*) number to guide readers to the original passage.
- A list of works mentioned in the paper is called References. In the References list at the end of the paper, give full publication information, alphabetized by author.
- Use authors' full last names but only initials for their first and middle names.
- In the References, capitalize only the first word and proper names in book and article titles, but capitalize all major words in journal titles. Italicize book and journal titles. Do not put article titles in quotation marks.
- Use the ampersand (&) instead of the word *and* with authors' names in parenthetical citations, tables, captions, and the References.

46a In-text citations

When you use APA format and refer to sources in your text, include the author's name, a comma, and then date of publication. For direct quotations or specific references to the original source, add another comma after the date. For print sources, include the page number, with *p.* (for page) before the number. For online or electronic sources, include the paragraph number, with *para.* (for paragraph) before the number.

Examples of APA In-Text Citations

FAQ

Are specific page or paragraph references needed for in-text citations?

In APA style, the author and year are typically included in in-text citations. When the reference provides a summary of a work's general conclusions, no page or paragraph reference is generally included.

> **This conclusion was supported by Seegars (2014) and Terrill and Toth (2015).**

However, quotations or specific references to the text should contain a page or paragraph number to guide readers to the original passage. For print sources, add *p.* and the page number. For online or electronic sources, add *para.* and the paragraph number.

> **Davis (2014) reported that response times would be affected by the number of available staff members (p. 14). McGee (2015), however, argued that response times would be more affected by the lack of available equipment (para. 6).**

Source	Tips	In-Text Examples
1. Direct Quote or Reference—Print or PDF Source	Include author name(s), date, and page number(s).	The effects are "likely to be pervasive and result in permanent damage" (Lin, 2013, p. 34). (*or*) Lin (2013) stated that the effects are "likely to be pervasive and result in permanent damage" (p. 34).
2. Direct Quote or Reference—Web Source	Include author names(s), date, and paragraph number(s).	With this change, new cases decreased by 30% within a year (Dill, 2015, para. 4). (*or*) Dill (2015) has noted that with this change, new cases have decreased by 30% within a year (para. 4).
3. Two Authors	Use *and* in the text, but use an ampersand (&) in parenthetical material, tables, and captions.	Perez and Raffia (2013) have argued that such interventions should be targeted and immediate. In addition, the procedure should be monitored for irregularities (Xi & Aziza, 2012).
4. Three, Four, or Five Authors	First reference: Include all authors. Use *and* in the text, but use an ampersand (&) in parenthetical material, tables, and captions. Later references: Use the first author's name and *et al.* (for "and others").	Shin, Hila, Lee, and Roma (2014) noted a trend in family members of veterans with PTSD. (*or*) A trend was noted in family members of veterans with PTSD (Shin, Hila, Lee, & Roma, 2014).

APA

Source	Tips	In-Text Examples
		Later in the paper: Shin et al. (2014) developed indicators to assess PTSD in family members of veterans.
5. Six or More Authors	Cite the first author, *et al.*, and the year for all references.	Wharton et al. (2010) noted a significant improvement in overall health.
6. Organization, Government Agency, or Group Author	Spell out the name, but if it is long, give the acronym in parentheses when the entire name first appears. Then use the acronym later in the paper.	When the National Institute of Mental Health (NIMH, 1992) prepared its initial report, small amounts of data were available.
		Later in the paper: NIMH (1992) reported no statistical changes.
7. Unlisted Author	Cite the first word or few words of the title in quotation marks and the year.	One recent article ("Bedbugs," 2011) documented an increase in insect infestations in hotels.
8. Authors with the Same Last Name	Include the authors' initials in text citations.	After J. L. Dean (2015) reviewed the initial study (C. A. Dean, 2011), a new report was issued.
9. Two or More Works in the Same Citation	Arrange the authors' names, separated with semicolons, in the order they appear in the References.	Several studies (Bao, 2011; Forster, 2009; Li & Yoon, 2013) reported similar behavior patterns in such cases.
10. Republished Work	List the original publication date and the date of the republished version.	The evolutionary development of species is a complex process (Darwin, 1859/2009).

Source	Tips	In-Text Examples
11. Chapter of a Source	Name the chapter in the reference.	Takai (2014, Chapter 9) investigated this phenomenon.
12. Section of a Webpage	Name the section heading and count the number of paragraphs following it.	No further study indicated any change in the results (Kimble, 2013, Conclusion section, para. 2).
13. E-Mails, Letters, IMs, and Unpublished Interviews	Personal communications are cited in-text only. Do not include them in the References.	According to P. P. Roy (personal communication, July 21, 2015), that outcome is likely.
14. Website— General Reference	To make a general reference to a website (but not a specific page), list the URL in the text.	Consult the website for the American Psychological Association (http://apastyle.apa.org) for updates.
15. Indirect Source	Try to locate the original source and cite it in your paper. If this is not possible, name the original source in the text and refer to the source you consulted in your in-text citation.	Goran's theory (as cited in Eames, 2009, p. 67) discusses the connections between criminality and social stimuli.

APA

TRY THIS

Introducing Sources and Formatting Quotations

When reporting the results of research, introduce sources with past-tense and past-perfect verbs:

Reynolds (2013) concluded that . . .

Johnson (2012) has noted that . . .

Quotations shorter than 40 words should be integrated into the text of your paragraphs. Those 40 words or longer should be set as block quotations, double-spaced, and indented ½ inch from the left with no quotation marks.

Some have argued that the public has been misled to believe that the fattiest foods in our diets are snacks and sweets:

> No quotation marks → In fact, the biggest deliverers of saturated fat—the type of fat doctors worry about—are cheese and red meat, and it is in producing and selling these two products that the food industry has shown its
>
> Indent 1/2 inch → greatest ability to influence public policy. (Moss, 2013, p. 213)

46b Footnotes

Footnotes are an optional feature of APA papers. When used, content footnotes add extra information not included in the main text of the paper; use them only if they strengthen the discussion. If you reproduce figures, tables, or other copyrighted materials in your paper, use footnotes to acknowledge you have permission to do so. Number footnotes consecutively with superscript numbers set above the line, such as [1] and [2]. Place notes at the bottom of pages on which they appear or list them together on a page following the References.

46c References list

On a new page, center References at the top of the page. Double-space all entries and alphabetize them by the author's last name; for several works by the same author, arrange them by year of publication with the earliest one first. For each entry, begin the first line at the left margin and indent all following lines five spaces (hanging-indent style).

Examples of APA References Entries

JOURNAL ARTICLES

APA

APA

Examples of APA References

All entries should be double-spaced on your References page.

Journal articles

1. **Journal Article—One Author**

> Goldstein, J. A. (2015). Orthopedic afflictions in the interventional laboratory: Tales from the working wounded. *Journal of the American College of Cardiology, 65,* 827–829. doi:10.1016/j.jacc.2014.12.020

2. **Journal Article—Two to Seven Authors**

> Luo, L. P., & Liu, L. (2014). Reflections on conducting evaluations for rural development interventions in China. *Evaluation and Program Planning, 47,* 1–8. doi:10.1016/j. evalprogplan.2014.06.004

> Vanwoerden, S., Kalpakci, A. H., & Sharp, C. (2015). Experiential avoidance mediates the link between maternal attachment style and theory of mind. *Comprehensive Psychiatry, 57,* 117–124. doi:10.1016/j. comppsych.2014.11.015

APA—Citing a Journal Article

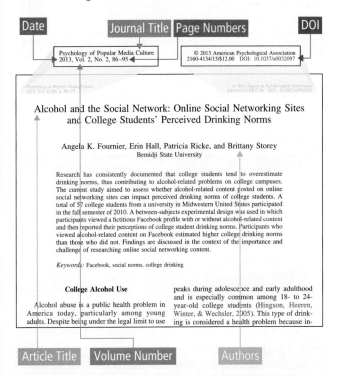

Date

Journal Title Page Numbers

DOI

Psychology of Popular Media Culture
2013, Vol. 2, No. 2, 86–95

© 2013 American Psychological Association
2160-4134/13/$12.00 DOI: 10.1037/a0032097

Alcohol and the Social Network: Online Social Networking Sites and College Students' Perceived Drinking Norms

Angela K. Fournier, Erin Hall, Patricia Ricke, and Brittany Storey
Bemidji State University

Research has consistently documented that college students tend to overestimate drinking norms, thus contributing to alcohol-related problems on college campuses. The current study aimed to assess whether alcohol-related content posted on online social networking sites can impact perceived drinking norms of college students. A total of 57 college students from a university in Midwestern United States participated in the fall semester of 2010. A between-subjects experimental design was used in which participants viewed a fictitious Facebook profile with or without alcohol-related content and then reported their perceptions of college student drinking norms. Participants who viewed alcohol-related content on Facebook estimated higher college drinking norms than those who did not. Findings are discussed in the context of the importance and challenge of researching online social networking content.

Keywords: Facebook, social norms, college drinking

College Alcohol Use

Alcohol abuse is a public health problem in America today, particularly among young adults. Despite being under the legal limit to use

peaks during adolescence and early adulthood and is especially common among 18- to 24-year-old college students (Hingson, Heeren, Winter, & Wechsler, 2005). This type of drinking is considered a health problem because in-

Article Title   Volume Number   Authors

APA

References Entry:

Fournier, A. K., Hall, E., Ricke, P., & Storey, B. (2013). Alcohol and the social network: Online social networking sites and college students' perceived drinking norms. *Psychology of Popular Media Culture,* 2, 86–95. doi:10.1037/a0032097

3. **Journal Article—More Than Seven Authors** List the first six authors followed by an ellipsis (three spaced periods) and the final author's name.

    Shikotra, A., Choy, D. F., Ohri, C. M., Doran, E., Butler, C., Hargadon, B., . . . Bradding, P. (2012). Increased expression of immunoreactive thymic stromal lymphopoietin in patients with severe asthma. *Journal of Allergy and Clinical Immunology, 129*, 104–111. doi:10.1016/j.jaci.2011.08.031

QUICK GUIDE: For an APA References page, how do I format . . .

AUTHORS' NAMES

One author: **Cole, J. H.**
Two authors: **Cole, J. H., & Lin, S. F.**
Three to seven authors: **Cole, J. H., Lin, S. F., & Bola, S. R.**
More than seven authors (list the first six authors, insert an ellipsis, and add the last author): **Cole, J. H., Lin, S. F., Bola, S. R., Metz, D. E., Phu, L. X., Hill, I. M., . . . Kim, T. N.**

DATES

Year: **(2015).**
Month and Year: **(2015, January).**
Exact Date: **(2015, January 8).**
No Date: **(n.d.)**
*Do not abbreviate months.

PAGE NUMBERS

8–14.
108–114.
2108–2114.

Use section letter and page number for newspapers: **p. A2.**

TITLES (Articles, Webpages, and Short Works)

Do not use quotation marks. Capitalize only the first word, the word after a colon, and proper nouns.
Protecting yourself from flu germs: A protocol for North Dakota.

TITLES (Books and Other Non-Periodicals)

Use italics. Capitalize only the first word, the word after a colon, and proper nouns.
The tipping point: How little things can make a big difference.

TITLES (Periodicals—Journals, Magazines, Newspapers)

Use italics. Capitalize all words except for conjunctions, articles, and prepositions, unless they appear after a colon or begin the title.
The Lancet   ***Scientific American***   ***The New York Times***

CITY OF PUBLICATION

List the city and state followed by a colon.   **Chicago, IL:**

VOLUME AND ISSUE NUMBERS

For journals, list just the volume number if the pagination continues from issue to issue. Volume numbers should be italicized: **25,**
Include the volume and issue number in your entry if each issue of the publication starts with page 1. Italicize the volume number. Enclose the issue number in parentheses and do not italicize it: **25(3),**

PUBLISHER

Give the full names of publishers, but omit *Co.* and *Inc.*
University of Chicago Press. **Farrar, Straus, and Giroux.**

DOIs

Many journal articles, books, and technical reports are now identified by DOI (Digital Object Identifier) numbers. A DOI is a unique code assigned to that publication. If there's a DOI number assigned, include it after the publication information. If you access the publication online, list the DOI instead of the URL. A DOI may appear in one of two formats. List the DOI as it appears in your publication: **http://dx.doi.org/10.1002/jbt.20384 doi:10.1002/jbt.20384**

RETRIEVAL INFORMATION

Retrieval information is needed for sources accessed online. A retrieval line generally includes "Retrieved from" and the URL. In some cases, a retrieval line is not necessary; in other cases, more information may be needed:

- **URL** Include a URL for works accessed online that do not have DOIs. Include just the home page URL (up to the first /) when accessing materials available by search or subscription.
  http://www.cnn.com/ **http://www.cdc.gov/**

  Give the full URL for pages on sites that are difficult to search. If you have to divide the URL onto two or more lines, break the address before slashes and punctuation marks (except within *http://*), and never add a hyphen. Do not use underlining, italics, angle brackets, or an end period.
- **Date of retrieval** Include the date you accessed the material only if the item is very likely to be updated or changed (see entry 49).
- **Databases** For materials located on widely available databases, including library subscription services, do not include a retrieval line. Include the names of databases in the retrieval line only if the source is rare, a print version is difficult to locate, or the material is available only on a small number of databases (see entries 6, 10, and 17).

4. **Article in a Journal Paginated Separately by Issue—No DOI** If each issue begins with 1, include the issue number in parentheses after the volume number.

> Brouwers, A., & Tomic, W. (2014). A longitudinal study of relationships between three burnout dimensions among secondary school teachers. *Sensoria: A Journal of Mind, Brain, and Culture, 10*(2): 23–33.

5. **Article from an Online Journal—No DOI** Add a retrieval line with the article's web address (URL). List just the home page URL if the site has a search function.

> Banwell, S. (2011). Women, violence, and gray zones: Resolving the paradox of the female victim-perpetrator. *Internet Journal of Criminology, 11.* Retrieved from http://www.internetjournalofcriminology.com

6. **Journal Article with No DOI from a Library Database or Subscription Service** Name the database *only* if the source is rare or is available on a small number of databases.

> Dowling, J. (2012). The very model of a better mousetrap. *American History, 46,* 56–61.

> Wright, W. K. (1916). Psychology and the war. *Psychological Bulletin, 13*(12), 462–466. Retrieved from PsycINFO database.

7. **Journal Article—Advance Online Publication** This type of article may not yet be formatted for final publication or have assigned volume and issue numbers. Add a label after the journal title.

> Hall, A., Miguel, A., & Weitzel, K. (2015). Providing feedback to learners in outpatient and ambulatory care practice settings. *Currents in Pharmacy Teaching and Learning.* Advance online publication. doi:10.1016/j.cptl.2014.12.007

Magazine articles

8. **Article in a Monthly or Bimonthly Magazine** Include the publication month after the year. Include the volume number in italics after the magazine title. If each issue of the magazine begins with page 1, add the issue number in parentheses after the volume number.

> Nash, J. M. (2013, January). Tunnel vision. *Smithsonian, 43*(9), 20–22.

9. **Article in a Weekly or Biweekly Magazine** Include the publication month and day after the year. Include the

volume number in italics after the magazine title. If each issue of the magazine begins with page 1, add the issue number in parentheses after the volume number.

> Pollan, M. (2015, February 9). The trip treatment. *The New Yorker, 90*(47), 36–47.

10. **Magazine Article from a Library Database or Subscription Service** Add a retrieval line that names the database *only* if the source is rare or available on a small number of databases.

> Scherer, M. (2014, June 2). Crude awakening. *Time, 183*(21): 14–15.

> Trollope, A. (1861). The civil service as a profession. *The Cornhill Magazine, 3*, 214–228. Retrieved from the Wellesley Index of Victorian Periodicals.

11. **Article in an Online Magazine** If a volume and issue number are available, add them after the magazine title.

> Moscaritolo, A. (2015, February 26). Only 40 percent of world's population has even gone online. *PCMag .com*. Retrieved from http://www.pcmag.com

12. **Magazine Article on an App** If a volume and issue number are available, add them after the magazine title.

> Hempel, J. (2015, February). Restart. In *Wired* [Mobile application software]. Retrieved from http://www.itunes.com

13. **Exclusive Online Magazine Content** Use this format for online content not available in the print version.

> Levy, S. (2010, February 22). How Google's algorithm rules the web [Online exclusive]. *Wired, 18*(3). Retrieved from http://www.wired.com/magazine/2010/02 /ff_google_algorithm/

Newspaper articles

14. **Article in a Newspaper** For newspaper articles, use *p.* (for a single page) or *pp.* (for multiple pages) before the page numbers. If the article appears on multiple disconnected pages, list each page number.

> Fink, S. (2015, March 1). At cusp of zero cases, ebola returned by sea. *The New York Times*, pp. A1, A12.

15. **Unsigned Article** Place the article title before the publication date.

> Ex-envoy to U.S. testifies in probe. (2012, January 10). *The Washington Post*, p. A8.

16. **Article in an Online Newspaper**

> Mann, L. (2015, February 23). Deadly kidney disease can
>   make a sneak attack. *Chicago Tribune*. Retrieved
>   from http://www.chicagotribune.com

17. **Newspaper Article from a Library Database or Subscription Service** Add a retrieval line that names the database *only* if the source is rare or available on a small number of databases.

> Schneider, C. (2014, October 1). First U.S. ebola case cited.
>   *Atlanta Journal-Constitution,* p. 1A.

> Smith, C. S. (1898, July 3). Wartime prosperity. *The New
>   York Times*, p. 18. Retrieved from The Historical New
>   York Times database.

18. **Newspaper Article on an App**

> Tuller, D. (2015, February 27). Study on chronic fatigue may
>   help with diagnoses. In *NYTimes for iPad* [Mobile appli-
>   cation software]. Retrieved from http://www.itunes.com

19. **Editorial**

> Protecting fragile nest eggs [Editorial]. (2015, March 1). *The
>   New York Times*, p. SR8.

20. **Letter to the Editor**

> Senders, W. (2013, January 9). All our choices are terrifying
>   [Letter to the editor]. *San Francisco Chronicle*, p. A9.

Other periodical sources

21. **Review of a Work** If the review is untitled, place the material in brackets directly after the date.

> Metzl, J. (2013). A bitter pill [Review of the motion picture
>   *Side Effects*]. *The Lancet, 381,* 1174. http://
>   dx.doi.org/10.1016/S0140-6736(13)60786-2

22. **Published Interview** List the interviewer as the author.

> Worth, J. (2006, November). Punk rock capitalism? *New
>   Internationalist, 395*, 16–17.

Books, parts of books, and reports

23. **Book with a DOI** If the book has been assigned a digital object identifier (DOI), omit the publication city and publisher and add the DOI after the book title.

APA—Citing a Book

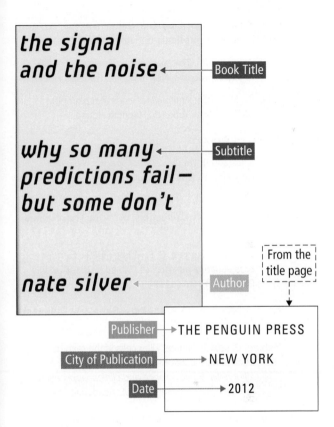

Book Title ← the signal and the noise

Subtitle ← why so many predictions fail—but some don't

Author ← nate silver

From the title page

Publisher → THE PENGUIN PRESS

City of Publication → NEW YORK

Date → 2012

APA

References Entry:

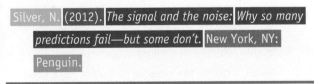

Silver, N. (2012). *The signal and the noise: Why so many predictions fail—but some don't.* New York, NY: Penguin.

Bianchi, D. W., Crombleholme, T. M., D'Alton, M. E., & Malone, F. (2010). *Fetology: Diagnosis and management of the fetal patient.* doi:10.1036/0071442014

24. **Book with No DOI**

Engel, S. (2015). *The hungry mind: The origins of curiosity in childhood.* Cambridge, MA: Harvard University Press.

25. **Book Accessed Online** If the book has a DOI, use the format for entry 23 instead.

James, W. (1907). *Pragmatism.* Retrieved from http://www.gutenberg.org

26. **More Than One Work by the Same Author** Arrange entries by year of publication, the earliest first.

Taleb, N. N. (2007). *The black swan: The impact of the highly improbable.* New York, NY: Random House.

Taleb, N. N. (2012). *Antifragile: Things that gain from disorder.* New York, NY: Random House.

27. **Republished Work**

Darwin, C. (2009). *On the origin of species* (W. Bynum, Ed.). New York, NY: Penguin. (Original work published 1859)

28. **Anthology, Scholarly Collection, or Work That Names an Editor**

Brettell, C. B., & Sargent, C. F. (Eds.). (2009). *Gender in cross-cultural perspective* (5th ed.). Upper Saddle River, NJ: Prentice Hall.

29. **Article or Chapter in an Anthology, Scholarly Collection, or Work**

Mehrad, B. (2010). Natural killer cells in the respiratory tract. In M. T. Lotze & A. W. Thomson (Eds.), *Natural killer cells: Basic science and clinical application* (pp. 321–329). Burlington, MA: Academic Press.

30. **Second or Later Edition** Place the number of the edition in parentheses after the book title.

Bauman, R. W. (2014). *Microbiology with diseases by body system* (4th ed.). Boston, MA: Benjamin Cummings.

31. **Work That Names a Translator**

Nesbø, J. (2013). *The redeemer* (D. Bartlett, Trans.). New York, NY: Knopf.

32. **Work by a Group or Corporate Author** List *Author* as the publisher if it is the same as the author of the work.

American Medical Association. (2014). *Principles of CPT coding* (8th ed). Chicago, IL: Author.

33. **Work That Has More Than One Volume**

Little, T. D. (2014). *Oxford handbook of quantitative methods* (Vols. 1–2). New York, NY: Oxford University Press.

34. **Introduction, Foreword, Preface, or Afterword** List the author of the section first. Include the page numbers after the title of the book.

> West, C. (2012). Foreword. In M. Alexander, *The new Jim Crow: Mass incarceration in the age of colorblindness* (pp. ix–xi). New York, NY: New Press.

35. **Biblical and Classical Works** The Bible, ancient Greek and Roman works, and other classical works are not listed in the References. Mention them within the text of your paper.

36. **Technical or Research Report** If there is a report number, include it in parentheses after the title. If there is a DOI number, include this instead of the retrieval line.

> Biddy, I., & Jones, S. (2013, March). *Catalytic upgrading of sugars to hydrocarbons technology pathway* (Report No. NREL/TP-5100-58055). Golden, CO: National Renewable Energy Laboratory.

37. **Technical or Research Report Accessed Online** If there is a report number, include it in parentheses after the title. If there is a DOI number, include this instead of the retrieval line.

> Cordova, A., Price, C. C., & Saltzman, E. (2013). A two-step procedure to estimate participation and premiums in multistate health plans (Report No. RR-202-DHHS). Retrieved from http://www.rand.org/

38. **Government Publication**

> Office of the President. (2014). *Budget of the United States government, fiscal year 2015.* Washington, DC: U.S. Government Printing Office.

39. **U.S. Government Report Available Online**

> U.S. Government Accountability Office. (2015, January). *Food safety: Additional actions needed to help FDA's foreign offices ensure safety of imported food.* (Publication No. GAO-15-183). Retrieved from http://www.gao.gov/

40. **Signed Article in a Dictionary, Encyclopedia, or Reference Book**

> Reibman, J. E. (2010). Fredric Wertham. In M. Keith Booker (Ed.), *Encyclopedia of comic books and graphic novels* (Vol. 2, pp. 683–685). Santa Barbara, CA: Greenwood.

41. **Unsigned Article in a Dictionary, Encyclopedia, or Reference Book** If using a multivolume work, add the volume number after the book title (see entry 33).

APA

Whizzbang. (2008). In *Webster's new college dictionary* (3rd ed., p. 1290). Boston, MA: Houghton Mifflin Harcourt.

42. **Online Dictionary, Encyclopedia, or Reference Book Article**

Biofuel. (2015). In *Encyclopaedia Britannica online*. Retrieved from http://www.britannica.com

43. **Print Brochure**

Starbucks Coffee Company. (2010). Recycling and reducing the environmental impact of our cups [Brochure]. Seattle, WA: Author.

44. **Online Brochure**

World Health Organization. (2011). Combat drug resistance [Brochure]. Retrieved from http://www.emro.who.int

45. **Published Dissertation Accessed from a Database** Add the dissertation file number at the end of the entry.

Senk, P. A. (2011). *A nursing domain model: Prevention of pressure ulcers* (Doctoral dissertation). Retrieved from ProQuest Dissertations and Theses. (UMI No. 3462814)

Websites and electronic communications

46. **Page on a Website** Add the date of access to the retrieval line only if the URL or content is likely to change. APA does not require the title of the website for citations of non-periodical sources. Include the website title (in italics) when it would help your reader find your web source, especially when the source has a different site author. Include only the URL if the site has a search function.

Reinberg, S. (2015, February 25). ADHD may raise odds for premature death. Retrieved from http://www.webmd .com

47. **Section of a Report Posted Online**

National Commission on the Causes of the Financial and Economic Crisis in the United States. (2011, January). Shadow banking. In *The Financial Crisis Inquiry Report* (chap. 2). Retrieved from http:// www.gpo.gov

APA—Page from a Government Website

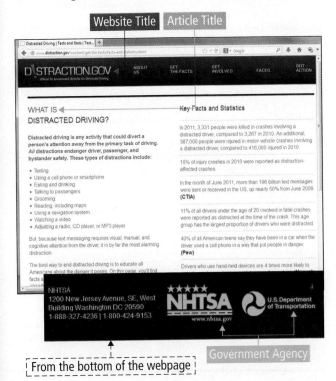

Website Title | Article Title

Government Agency

From the bottom of the webpage

References Entry:

U.S. Department of Transportation, National Highway
Traffic Safety Administration. (n.d.). What is
distracted driving? Retrieved from
http://www.distaction.gov

No date

URL

---

48. **Blog Posting**

> McBride, B. (2015, February 20). A comment on
> Greece. [Blog post]. Retrieved from http://
> www.calculatedriskblog.com

49. **Wiki Article** Wikis are websites that are written and edited
by many people. Assess the credibility of such sources
before including them in your work. Wikis are likely to be
updated, so include the retrieval date in your entry.

Effective demand. (2014, August 24). Retrieved January 2, 2015, from Wikipedia: http://en.wikipedia.org

50. **Tweet** Include the full tweet in your entry.

Obama, B. [POTUS]. (2015, June 19). In the midst of darkest tragedy, the decency and goodness of the American people shines through in these families. [Twitter post]. Retrieved from http://twitter.com/potus

51. **Facebook Status Update** Include the full post in your entry.

White House. (2015, July 9). Go stargazing with the Girl Scouts on the White House lawn! [Facebook update]. Retrieved from http://www.facebook.com/WhiteHouse

52. **E-Mail and Instant Messaging (IM)** Personal e-mail, instant messaging, and other electronic communications that are not archived are identified as personal communications in the paper and are not listed in the References. See example 13 in 46a.

Apps and computer software

53. **Computer Program or Software** Reference entries are unnecessary for most popular software programs. This citation format applies only to specialized software programs.

Stardock. (2011). WindowBlinds (Version 7.3) [Computer software]. Retrieved from http://www.stardock.com

54. **App** Follow the format for citing computer software.

Vito Technology. (2014). Star Walk (Version 7.0.4) [Mobile application software]. Retrieved from http://itunes.apple.com/

55. **Entry in an App**

Hubble. (2014). In Star Walk (Version 7.0.4) [Mobile application software]. Retrieved from http://itunes.apple.com

56. **Facebook App** Follow the format for citing computer software.

Spotify. (n.d.). Spotify [Facebook application]. Retrieved from https://www.facebook.com/appcenter/

Audio and visual sources

57. **Television Series** Start with the creator's name and then, in parentheses, the person's function (for example, *Producer*).

Wolf, D. (Creator/Executive producer). (1999–2015). *Law and order: Special victims unit* [Television series]. New York, NY: NBC.

58. **Episode from a Television Series**

Fellowes, J. (Creator/Writer), & Morshead, C. (Director). (2015, January 11). Episode 5.2 [Television series episode]. In R. Eaton, J. Fellowes, N. Marchant, G. Neame, & L. Trubridge (Executive producers), *Masterpiece classic: Downton Abbey*. Boston, MA: WGBH.

59. **Television Series Episode Online**

Smith, M. (Writer/Director/Producer). (2014, October 28). The rise of ISIS [Television series episode]. In D. Fanning (Executive producer), *Frontline*. Retrieved from http://www.pbs.org

60. **Motion Picture Released Theatrically**

Marsh, J. (Director), Bevan, T., Bruce, L., & Fellner, E. (Producers). (2014). *The theory of everything* [Motion picture]. United States: Working Title Films.

61. **DVD or Blu-ray** Insert the media type in brackets.

Fuller, S. (Writer/Director/Producer). (2010). *Shock corridor* [DVD]. United States: Criterion. (Original release date 1963)

62. **Online Video**

The Slo Mo Guys. (2014). Leaping slow motion doggy [Video file]. Retrieved from http://www.youtube.com

63. **Video Podcast**

Philadelphia Museum of Art. (2013). Great and mighty things [Video podcast]. Retrieved from http://www.itunes.com

64. **Audio Recording on CD**

Rivers, J. (Speaker). (2014, September 30). Diary of a mad diva [CD]. New York, NY: Penguin Random House Audio.

65. **Music Recording on CD or MP3** List the songwriter(s) first. If the songwriter and the performer are the same person, list the person's name only at the beginning of the entry.

Ronson, M., Lawrence, P., Bhasker, J., & Mars, B. (2014). Uptown funk [Recorded by M. Ronson feat. B. Mars]. On *Uptown special* [MP3 file]. New York, NY: RCA.

APA

Swift, T. (2014). Shake it off. On *1989* [CD]. Nashville, TN: Big Machine Records

66. **Audio Podcast**

Inskeep, S., Montagne, R., & Greene, D. (Hosts). (2015, February 18). Why penguins can't taste fish [Audio podcast]. *Morning Edition*. Retrieved from http://www.npr.org

Ryssdal, K. (Host). (2015, February 24). *Marketplace* [Audio podcast]. Available from iTunes.

67. **Radio Broadcast**

Shiffman, K. (Executive Producer). (2015, January 29). *On point with Tom Ashbrook* [Radio program]. Boston, MA: WBUR.

Other media

68. **Print Map**

Greater Atlanta [Map]. (2010). Skokie, IL: Rand McNally.

69. **Online Map**

San Diego [Map]. (2015). Retrieved from http://www.mapquest.com

70. **Print Advertisement**

Toyota. (2015, February). Prius [Advertisement]. *Wired, 23*(2), 41.

71. **Online Advertisement**

Apple. (2015). Apple Watch [Advertisement]. Retrieved from http://www.apple.com

72. **Commercial**

Amazon. (2015, January 24). Amazon Fire Stick [Advertisement]. New York, NY: CNN.

73. **Lecture Notes or Multimedia Slides**

Climate Prediction Center. (2015, February 9). *2014 Annual Ocean Review* [PowerPoint slides]. Retrieved from http://www.cpc.ncep.noaa.gov/

74. **Online Lecture, Speech, or Address**

Knight, R. (2014, February). *How our microbes make us who we are*. Lecture at TED 2014. Vancouver, Canada. Retrieved from http://www.ted.com

46d Paper format

Follow the format shown here for a title page, abstract, first page of the paper, and first page of the References list.

Paper Format Quick Guide—APA	
Paper format	Set your top, bottom, left, and right margins at one inch. Double-space all pages, headers, block quotes, notes, and the References. Use a standard, easy-to-read font (like Times New Roman, Cambria, Arial, or Calibri) that is 10- or 12-point size.
	Indent the first line of paragraphs and footnotes ½ inch or five spaces from the left margin. Indent long quotations ½ inch or five spaces from the left margin.
	Order your pages as follows: 1. Title page 2. Abstract 3. Text of paper 4. References (start on a separate page) 5. Footnotes (optional; list them together, starting on a separate page) 6. Appendices (optional; start each on a separate page) 7. Tables (optional; start each on a separate page) 8. Figures and figure captions (optional; place each figure with its caption on a separate page)
Title page and titles	Include a title page (all double-spaced) with the title centered between left and right margins and positioned in the upper half of the page. Include your name and college on separate lines.
	Capitalize all words in the title except for articles, conjunctions, and short prepositions (unless they are the first word or follow a colon).
Running head and page numbers	In the upper left margin of the header on the title page, begin a running head. This is an abbreviated version of the title that appears on each page of your document. On the first page, include *Running head*, followed by a colon, and an abbreviated version of the title in all capital letters. On all other pages, just include the abbreviated title.
	Page numbers should be placed in the header at the right margin, beginning with the title page.
Abstract	An abstract is a short summary about the major conclusions of your work. At the top of page 2, center the word *Abstract*. Then double-space and provide your summary.

Headings and subheadings	Headings and subheadings are short titles that define sections and subsections in long reports and papers. Only one level of heading is recommended for short papers, centered on each page in bold font, with each word (except short prepositions, articles, and conjunctions) capitalized. If multiple levels of headings are needed, follow this format as a guide.
	Level 1: **Bold, Centered Title**
	Level 2: **Bold Title on Left Margin**
	Level 3: **Indented title in bold.**
	Level 4: ***Indented title in bold and italics.***
	Level 5: *Indented title in italics.*
Tables and figures	Labels for tables appear directly above them. The label and the table title (italicized) appear on separate lines (double-spaced). **Table 1** ***Ninth-Grade Science Performance Scores among G-20 Nations*** For figures (including graphs, charts, photos, maps, etc.), create a brief label and place it directly below the figure. Italicize *Figure* and lowercase all words except the first and proper nouns: ***Figure 7*. Variance of ninth-grade science performance scores from 1965–2015.**
Footnotes	You may use your word-processing software to insert footnotes. In the text, insert a superscript number (small and raised above the text) to expand on content or indicate a source citation. You may include footnotes on the bottom of each page on which they appear. You may also choose to create a separate page after the References titled *Footnotes* (centered with no italics).
Bibliography	Insert a title called *References* and center it on the page. All entries should be double-spaced and organized alphabetically. Format entries in hanging indent style, meaning the second and following lines of an entry are indented ½ inch.

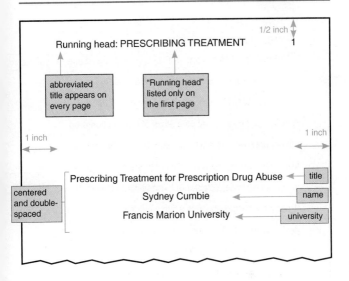

Running head: PRESCRIBING TREATMENT

1/2 inch
1

abbreviated title appears on every page

"Running head" listed only on the first page

1 inch

1 inch

Prescribing Treatment for Prescription Drug Abuse ← title

Sydney Cumbie ← name

Francis Marion University ← university

centered and double-spaced

APA

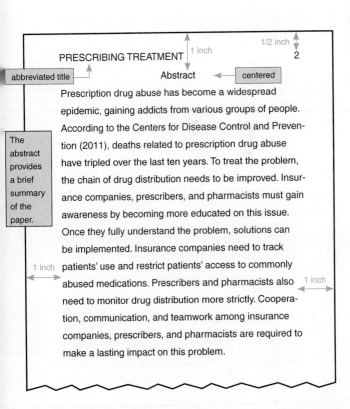

PRESCRIBING TREATMENT

1 inch

1/2 inch
2

abbreviated title

Abstract ← centered

Prescription drug abuse has become a widespread epidemic, gaining addicts from various groups of people. According to the Centers for Disease Control and Prevention (2011), deaths related to prescription drug abuse have tripled over the last ten years. To treat the problem, the chain of drug distribution needs to be improved. Insurance companies, prescribers, and pharmacists must gain awareness by becoming more educated on this issue. Once they fully understand the problem, solutions can be implemented. Insurance companies need to track patients' use and restrict patients' access to commonly abused medications. Prescribers and pharmacists also need to monitor drug distribution more strictly. Cooperation, communication, and teamwork among insurance companies, prescribers, and pharmacists are required to make a lasting impact on this problem.

The abstract provides a brief summary of the paper.

1 inch

1 inch

abbreviated title

3

Prescribing Treatment for Prescription Drug Abuse — centered

The Centers for Disease Control and Prevention (CDC, 2011) has reported that approximately forty Americans die each day as a result of prescription drug abuse, and over the past ten years, the number of deaths from prescription drugs has tripled (para. 1–3). According to Gil Kerlikowske, Director of National Drug Control Policy, "Prescription drug abuse is a silent epidemic that is stealing thousands of lives and tearing apart communities and families across America" (CDC, 2011, para. 4). Prescription drug addicts include people from a variety of groups, including teenagers, soldiers, Medicare patients, and newborn infants. With greater education and cooperation, the chain of drug distributors, including the insurance companies, prescribers, and pharmacists, can make the biggest impact in alleviating prescription drug abuse.

The National Institute on Drug Abuse (NIDA, 2011) defines prescription drug abuse as using a medication in a way that it is not recommended by a prescriber, taking medication not prescribed to the user, or taking prescribed drugs to get high (para. 1). Some of the most popular prescription drugs abused are Vicodin, OxyContin, Ritalin, Adderall, Valium, and Ambien (O'Connor, 2010, p. 40). The Mayo Clinic (2010) has defined a variety of causes for prescription drug abuse, including peer pressure, intoxication, relaxation, and experimentation (Causes, para. 1). Many abusers have also mistakenly believed that using prescription drugs is both legal and safer than illegal drugs, which is not true

PRESCRIBING TREATMENT   1 inch   1/2 inch
                                              8

References ← centered

abbreviated title

Anderson, C. (2011, April 19). US targets "pill mills,"

    prescription drug abuses. *Miami Herald*. Retrieved   double-space

    from http://www.miamiherald.com/

All sources are alphabetized and all entries are double-spaced.

Andrews, M. (2011, April 5). Some doctors ask patients to

    sign "pain contracts" to get prescriptions. *Kaiser Health*

    News. Retrieved from http://www.kaiserhealthnews.org/

Back, S. E., Lawson, K. M., Singleton, L. M., & Brady,

    K. T. (2011). Characteristics and correlates of men

    and women with prescription opioid dependence.

    Addictive Behaviors, 36, 829–834. doi://10.1016/j   journal article with a DOI

    .addbeh.2011.03.013

Centers for Disease Control and Prevention. (2011,

    November 1). Prescription painkiller overdoses at epi-   article on a website

    demic levels. Retrieved from http://www.cdc.gov/

Davis, H. L. (2011, March 23). Controlling pain without

    creating addicts. *Buffalo News*, p. A1.   article from a newspaper

Mayo Clinic. (2010, June 25). Prescription drug abuse.

    Retrieved from http://www.mayoclinic.com/

National Institute on Drug Abuse. (2011, May). Pre-

1 inch   scription drug abuse. Retrieved from http://   1 inch

    www.drugabuse.gov/

O'Connor, G. (2010). Doctors' role in the prescription

    abuse crisis. *Addiction Professional, 8*(4), 40–41.   article from journal with nonconsecutive pagination

Pear, R. (2011, October 3). Report on Medicare cites pre-

    scription drug abuse. *The New York Times*. Retrieved

    from http://www.nytimes.com/   newspaper article online

U.S. Drug Enforcement Administration. (2011, October 19).

    DEA to hold its third nationwide Prescription

    Drug Take-Back Day this month. Retrieved http://

    www.justice.gov/dea/

1 inch

APA

47 *Chicago Manual of Style* (CMOS)

In disciplines such as history and other humanities, the preferred style is that of *The Chicago Manual of Style* (16th ed., 2010), which is also explained in the *Student's Guide to Writing College Papers* (4th ed., 2010).

When you use CMOS style, you may use notes or endnotes to acknowledge sources in the text, or you may use in-text citations that refer the reader to a bibliography at the end of the paper.

47a In-text citations

When using *Chicago Manual* style, you can opt to use numbered notes or the author-date citation format.

Numbered notes

- **Numbering in the text.** Numbered notes indicate publication information and add explanations and other material that would otherwise interrupt the main text. Number citations consecutively with superscript numbers ([1]). Put the note number at the end of the sentence or end of a clause immediately following the punctuation mark. Don't insert a space between the punctuation mark and the superscript number.

  > Appropriate government regulation may be the key to turning resource-rich countries into successful, profitable economies for their citizens.[6] Peter Maass has noted that "countries dependent on resource exports . . . are susceptible to lower growth, higher corruption, less freedom, and more warfare."[7]

- **Placing notes.** List notes at the bottom of the page as footnotes or at the end of the essay as endnotes.

- **Spacing notes.** Single-space each note. Indent the first line of each note the same space that you indent paragraphs. Use your word-processing software to format this section of your paper.

- **Ordering the parts of notes.** Begin with the author's first and last names, add the title, and then include the publishing information and page numbers.

- **Punctuating notes.** Use commas between elements, and put publishing information within parentheses.

- **Formatting titles.** Capitalize titles of articles, books, and journals. Use quotation marks around titles of periodical articles and sections of books.

- **Using a bibliography page.** A bibliography page is usually added to a paper containing notes.

- **Adapting the style to the source material.** *Chicago Manual* style allows for some flexibility in creating bibliography entries, particularly for works accessed online. In bibliography and note entries, include all relevant source materials needed to retrieve the source.

Ordering Notes in a Paper The first time you cite a source, include the authors' full names, followed by a comma; the full title; publication information, enclosed in parentheses; a comma; and the page or pages being cited, omitting *p.* or *pp.* Later citations include authors' last names, a shortened version of the title, and page numbers.

Use *Ibid.* to refer to the work in the directly preceding note or, if the page is different, use *Ibid.* followed by a comma and the page number.

> 6. Paul Collier, *The Plundered Planet: Why We Must—and How We Can—Manage Nature for Global Prosperity* (New York: Oxford University Press, 2010), 5.
> 7. Peter Maass, *Crude World: The Violent Twilight of Oil* (New York: Knopf, 2009), 6.
> 8. Collier, *Plundered Planet*, 132–33.
> 9. Ibid., 122.
> 10. Maass, *Crude World*, 7.

Author-date citation format

The author-date citation format requires both in-text citations and a bibliography page. For in-text citations:

- Up to three authors are cited by last name. If there are four or more authors, list only the first author's last name, followed by *et al.*

- The date of publication is given next, with no intervening punctuation.

- If a page number is required, it is given following a comma.

(Newhouse and Zuzu 1889)   (Baez et al. 2013, 244)

(Patel 2015, 18)   As explained by Hill (2014, 67), . . .

CMOS

QUICK GUIDE: For CMOS Bibliography entries, how do I format . . .

AUTHORS' NAMES

One author: **Cole, James H.**
Two to ten: **Cole, James H., Sue F. Lin, Sara R. Bola, and Dan E. Metz.**
Eleven or more: List the first seven authors and add **et al.**

TITLES

For short works (articles, webpages, short stories, poems, songs), use quotation marks. **"Tracking Avian Flu"** **"The Story of an Hour"**
For long works (books, websites, databases, journals, magazines, newspapers), use italics. *LexisNexis* *The New York Times*
*Capitalize conjunctions, prepositions, and articles only if they begin a title, end a title, or follow a colon.

VOLUME AND ISSUE NUMBERS

For a book: **Vol. 2**
For a journal, list volume and issue number: **14, no. 3**

PAGE NUMBERS

18–34.

Omit second hundredth digit when within same 100 pages. **218–34.**

DATES

Year: **2013**
Month and Year: **January 2015**
Exact Date: **January 8, 2015**
Give an access date for websites: **accessed May 2015**

CITY OF PUBLICATION

List state if city is not known to readers or could be mistaken for other cities with the same name.
New York **Springfield, MA**

DOIs (DIGITAL OBJECT IDENTIFIERS)

A DOI number is a unique code a publisher assigns to a book, journal article, or other source. If a DOI number is available for your source, list it at the end of your entry:
10.1016/j.jcps.2012.07.003
List the DOI instead of a URL when possible.

URLs

If no DOI is available for your online source, include a URL (or website address) at the end of your entry. Give the homepage URLs for works listed in the bibliography and exact URLs for works listed in the notes. Break URL lines after http:// and colons; break them before all other punctuation.

CMOS

For online or electronic works without page numbers, indicate the section title (if available) under which the specific reference can be located:

> (Quinn 2015, under "Espionage")

47b Note and bibliography entries

In the following examples, *N* stands for note format and *B* stands for bibliography format. Notes and bibliography entries may be either single-spaced or double-spaced in manuscripts, but *The Student's Guide to Writing College Papers*, 4th ed., by Turabian et al., indicates that notes should be single-spaced and bibliography entries should be double-spaced in student papers, as shown.

Examples of CMOS-Style Notes and Bibliography

CMOS

References examples

In the following examples, *N* stands for note format and *B* stands for bibliography format.

Books, parts of books, and reports

1. **One Author**

N: 1. Louis P. Masur, *Lincoln's Last Speech: Wartime Reconstruction and the Crisis of Reunion* (New York: Oxford University Press, 2015), 62.

B: Masur, Louis P. *Lincoln's Last Speech: Wartime Reconstruction and the Crisis of Reunion*. New York: Oxford University Press, 2015.

2. **Two Authors**

N: 2. Alan L. Olmstead and Paul W. Rhode. *Arresting Contagion: Science, Policy, and Conflicts over Animal Disease Control* (Cambridge: Harvard University Press, 2015), 12.

B: Olmstead, Alan L., and Paul W. Rhode. *Arresting Contagion: Science, Policy, and Conflicts over Animal Disease Control*. Cambridge: Harvard University Press, 2015.

3. **Three Authors**

N: 3. Philippa Gregory, David Baldwin, and Michael Jones, *The Women of the Cousins' War: The Duchess, the Queen, and the King's Mother* (New York: Simon & Schuster, 2011), 20–21.

B: Gregory, Philippa, David Baldwin, and Michael Jones. *The Women of the Cousins' War: The Duchess, the Queen, and the King's Mother*. New York: Simon & Schuster, 2011.

4. **Four or More Authors** In the notes format, list the first author and add *et al.* or *and others* with no intervening punctuation.

N: 4. James A. Baker III et al., *The Iraq Study Group Report: The Way Forward—a New Approach* (New York: Vintage, 2006), 27.

In the bibliography format, list all authors for a work with between four and ten authors. If the work has 11 or more authors, list the first seven authors and add *et al.*

B: Baker, James A., III, Lee H. Hamilton, Lawrence S. Eagleburger, Vernon E. Jordan Jr., Edwin Meese III, Sandra Day O'Connor, Leon E. Panetta, William J. Perry, Charles S. Robb, and Alan K. Simpson. *The Iraq Study Group Report: The Way Forward—a New Approach*. New York: Vintage, 2006.

FAQ

What types of extra information do I need to cite online sources?

When citing sources you accessed online, additional information may be needed in your notes and bibliography entries.

Digital Object Identifier (DOI) Number—A DOI number is a unique code a publisher assigns to a book, journal article, or other source. If a DOI number is available for your source, list it at the end of your entry. (See entries 20 and 23.)

URL—If no DOI is available for your online source, include the full URL (or online address) at the end of your entry. (See entries 20 and 23.)

Date of Access—If your online source does not contain a date of publication or update, or if your instructor requests it, include the date you accessed your source. In notes entries, after the source title, include *accessed* and the date,

CMOS

followed by a comma. In bibliography entries, after the source title, include *Accessed* and the date, followed by a period.

5. **Online Book** List the book's Digital Object Identifier (DOI) number at the end of the entry. If no DOI is available, provide the book's URL at the end of the entry. For an older book that has been republished online, give the original year of publication, and then add the website title and year of online publication.

N: 5. William Caferro, *Contesting the Renaissance* (Malden, MA: Wiley/Blackwell, 2011), 62, doi:10.1002/9781444324501.

B: Caferro, William. *Contesting the Renaissance*. Malden, MA: Wiley/Blackwell, 2011. doi:10.1002/9781444324501.

6. **Book for an Electronic Reader** Name the edition type at the end.

N: 6. David Axelrod, *Believer: My Forty Years in Politics* (New York: Penguin, 2015), Kindle edition.

B: Axelrod, David. *Believer: My Forty Years in Politics*. New York: Penguin, 2015. Kindle edition.

7. **Book with an Editor**

N: 7. George Ritzer and Zeynep Atalay, eds., *Readings in Globalization: Key Concepts and Major Debates* (Malden, MA: Wiley-Blackwell, 2010), 1.

B: Ritzer, George, and Zeynep Atalay, eds. *Readings in Globalization: Key Concepts and Major Debates*. Malden, MA: Wiley-Blackwell, 2010.

8. **Second or Later Edition**

N: 8. Howard Spodek, *The World's History: Combined Volume,* 5th ed. (Boston: Pearson, 2014), 139–41.

B: Spodek, Howard. *The World's History: Combined Volume*. 5th ed. Boston: Pearson, 2014.

9. **Reprinted Book**

N: 9. Edith Wharton, *House of Mirth* (1905; repr., London: Vintage, 2011), 64–65.

B: Wharton, Edith. *House of Mirth*. 1905. Reprint, London: Vintage, 2011.

10. **Online Reprinted Book** For an older book edited for online reproduction, give the original year of publication, and then add the name of the website and year of online publication. Add a URL at the end.

N: 10. Edith Wharton, *The Age of Innocence* (1920; Bartleby, 2000), 64, http://www.bartleby.com/1005/.

B: Wharton, Edith. *The Age of Innocence*. Reprint of the 1920 New York edition, Bartleby, 2000. http://www.bartleby.com/1005/.

11. **Selection or Book Chapter in an Anthology/Scholarly Collection**

N: 11. Robert E. Wright, "Capitalism and the Rise of the Corporation Nation," in *Capitalism Takes Command: The Social Transformation of Nineteenth-Century America*, ed. Michael Zakim and Gary J. Kornbluth (Chicago: University of Chicago Press, 2012), 146.

B: Wright, Robert E. "Capitalism and the Rise of the Corporation Nation." In *Capitalism Takes Command: The Social Transformation of Nineteenth-Century America*, edited by Michael Zakim and Gary J. Kornbluth, 145–68. Chicago: University of Chicago Press, 2012.

12. **Multivolume Book** In the notes format, when citing a book without an individual volume title, omit the volume number after the book title. Instead, after the facts of publication, insert the volume number, followed by a colon, and the page numbers (e.g., 2:45–96).

N: 12. Spielvogel, Jackson J., *Western Civilization*, vol. 1, *To 1715*, 9th ed. (New York: Cengage, 2014), 134–35.

B: Spielvogel, Jackson J. *Western Civilization*. Vol. 1, *To 1715*. 9th ed. New York: Cengage, 2014.

13. **Online Government Document**

N: 13. Federal Trade Commission, *2014 Report on Ethanol Market Concentration* (Washington, DC: Federal Trade Commission, December 5, 2014), 3, http://www.ftc.gov/system /files/documents/reports/report-congress-ethanol-market -concentration/2014ethanolreport.pdf.

B: Federal Trade Commission. *2014 Report on Ethanol Market Concentration*. Washington, DC: Federal Trade Commission, December 5, 2014. http://www.ftc.gov/system /files/documents/reports/report-congress-ethanol-market -concentration/2014ethanolreport.pdf.

CMOS

14. **Article in a Reference Book** Don't include the volume or page number. Instead, cite the term in the reference book under which the information is contained. Use the abbreviation *s.v.* for *sub verbo*, meaning "under the word," and place the term in quotation marks. Well-known reference books are not listed in the bibliography.

N: 14. *Encyclopaedia Britannica*, 15th ed., s.v. "Parks, Rosa."

15. **Article in an Online Reference Book** Follow the example in entry 14 but omit the edition number. Add an access date and the URL.

N: 15. *Encyclopaedia Britannica Online*, s.v. "Parks, Rosa," accessed February 4, 2015, http://www.britannica.com /EBchecked/topic/444180/Rosa-Parks.

16. **Source Quoted from Another Source** Quotations from secondary sources should ordinarily be avoided. If, however, the original source is unavailable, list both sources in the entry.

N: 16. H. H. Dubs, "An Ancient Chinese Mystery Cult," *Harvard Theological Review* 35 (1942): 223, quoted in Susan Naquin, *Millenarian Rebellion in China: The Eight Trigrams Uprising of 1813* (New Haven, CT: Yale University Press, 1976), 288.

B: Dubs, H. H. "An Ancient Chinese Mystery Cult." *Harvard Theological Review* 35 (1942): 223. Quoted in Susan Naquin, *Millenarian Rebellion in China: The Eight Trigrams Uprising of 1813*. New Haven, CT: Yale University Press, 1976, 288.

17. **Biblical or Other Scriptural Reference** Scriptural references are usually cited in the notes or in the parenthetical citation. List book (abbreviated), chapter, and verse.

N: 17. Gen. 21:14–18.

Journal articles

18. **Article in a Journal**

N: 18. Gary C. Jacobson, "How Presidents Shape Their Party's Reputation and Prospects: New Evidence," *Presidential Studies Quarterly* 45, no. 1 (2015): 19. doi:10.1111/psq.12168.

B: Jacobson, Gary C. "How Presidents Shape Their Party's Reputation and Prospects: New Evidence." *Presidential Studies Quarterly* 45, no. 1 (2015): 1–28. doi:10.1111/psq.12168.

TRY THIS

Citing Articles Located in a Library Database or Subscription Service

Start your notes or bibliography entry by following the citation format for the print version of the source.

- Include an access date only if a publication date is not available. **accessed May 1, 2015**

- For sources available by subscription (as in a library database) or for material that does not contain a stable URL or DOI, name the database at the end of the entry, followed by a period. **LexisNexis. Newsbank.**

- If the source contains a stable URL or a Digital Object Identifier (DOI) number, list it instead of the URL that appears in your Internet browser.

  http://0-www.jstor.org.libcatalog.fmarion.edu/stable/30030042

  doi:10.1111/j.1540-5907.2010.00472.x

19. **Journal Article Located in a Library Database or Subscription Service** If the article has numbered pages (as in a PDF file), list them after the date. List the article's DOI number at the end of the entry. If no DOI is available, name the database in which you located the article.

N: 19. David Lewis, "High Times on the Silk Road: The Central Asian Paradox," *World Policy Journal* 27, no. 1 (2010), 39–49, Project Muse.

N: 20. Marc F. Plattner, "Is Democracy in Decline?" *Journal of Democracy* 25, no. 1 (2015), 6. doi:10.1353/jod.2015.0014.

B: Lewis, David. "High Times on the Silk Road: The Central Asian Paradox." *World Policy Journal* 27, no. 1 (2010): 39–49. Project Muse.

B: Plattner, Marc F. "Is Democracy in Decline?" *Journal of Democracy* 25, no. 1 (2015): 5–10. doi:10.1353/jod.2015.0014.

20. **Article from an Online Journal** If the article has numbered pages (as in a PDF file), list them after the date. List the article's DOI number at the end of the entry. If no DOI is available, provide the full URL for the article.

N: 21. Robert M. Haberle and Melinda A. Kahre, "Detecting Secular Climate Change on Mars," *MARS: The International Journal of Mars Science and Exploration* 5 (August 2010): 69, doi:10.1555/mars.2010.0003.

N: 22. Dinesh Joseph Wadiwel, "Cruel Indignities: Animality and Torture," *Borderlands* 13, no. 1 (May 2014): 6, http://www .borderlands.net.au/Vol13No1_2014/wadiwel_indignities.pdf.

B: Haberle, Robert M., and Melinda A. Kahre. "Detecting Secular Climate Change on Mars." *MARS: The International Journal of Mars Science and Exploration* 5 (August 2010): 68–75. doi:10.1555/mars.2010.0003.

B: Wadiwel, Dinesh Joseph. "Cruel Indignities: Animality and Torture." *Borderlands* 13, no. 1 (May 2014): 1–9. http://www .borderlands.net.au/Vol13No1_2014/wadiwel_indignities.pdf (accessed March 2, 2015).

Magazine articles

21. **Article in a Magazine** While referenced page numbers should be included in the notes entry, omit page numbers for the bibliographic entry.

N: 23. Alec MacGillis, "Testing Time," *New Yorker*, January 26, 2015, 45.

B: MacGillis, Alec. "Testing Time." *New Yorker*, January 26, 2015.

22. **Magazine Article Located in a Library Database or Subscription Service** If the magazine has numbered pages, provide a page reference in the notes. Otherwise, provide a reference to headings or numbered paragraphs, if available, in the notes. List the article's DOI number at the end of the entry. If no DOI is available, name the database title.

N: 24. Sandra Lawrence, "Hedgerows and Their Friends," *British Heritage*, March 2015, 56, Academic Search Complete.

B: Lawrence, Sandra. "Hedgerows and Their Friends." *British Heritage*, March 2015. Academic Search Complete.

23. **Article from an Online Magazine** If the magazine has numbered pages, provide a page reference in the notes. Otherwise, provide a reference to headings or numbered paragraphs, if available, in the notes. List the DOI number at the end of the entry. If no DOI is available, provide the full URL for the article.

N: 25. Mat Honan, "Never Buy a Phone Again," *Wired*, January 5, 2015, http://www.wired.com/2015/01 /phones-are-tablets/.

B: Honan, Mat. "Never Buy a Phone Again." *Wired*, January 5, 2015. http://www.wired.com/2015/01/phones-are-tablets/.

Newspaper articles

24. **Article in a Newspaper** No page numbers are listed. If you are citing a specific edition of the paper, you may add a comma after the year and list the edition (e.g., late edition, Southeast edition), followed by a period.

N: 26. Timothy Kudo, "How We Learned to Kill," *New York Times*, March 1, 2015.

B: Kudo, Timothy. "How We Learned to Kill." *New York Times*, March 1, 2015.

25. **Newspaper Article Located in a Library Database or Subscription Service**

N: 27. Tom Robbins, "A Brutal Beating Wakes Attica's Ghosts," *New York Times*, March 1, 2015, LexisNexis Academic.

B: Robbins, Tom. "A Brutal Beating Wakes Attica's Ghosts." *New York Times*, March 1, 2015. LexisNexis Academic.

26. **Article from an Online Newspaper**

N: 28. Kurtis Alexander, "California Poised to See Driest January on Record," *San Francisco Chronicle*, January 26, 2015, http://www.sfgate.com/bayarea/article/California-poised-to-see -driest-January-on-record-6041058.php.

B: Alexander, Kurtis. "California Poised to See Driest January on Record." *San Francisco Chronicle*, January 26, 2015. http:// www.sfgate.com/bayarea/article/California-poised-to-see -driest-January-on-record-6041058.php.

Other periodical sources

27. **Book Review**

N: 29. Evan Rhodes, review of *Fight Pictures: A History of Boxing and Early Cinema*, by Dan Streible, *Modernism/Modernity* 17, no. 1 (2010): 264–66.

B: Rhodes, Evan. Review of *Fight Pictures: A History of Boxing and Early Cinema*, by Dan Streible. *Modernism/Modernity* 17, no. 1 (2010): 264–66.

28. **Published Interview** List the interviewer after the title.

N: 30. Matt Damon and Michael Douglas, "Romancing the Rhinestone," interview by Adam Markovitz, *Entertainment Weekly,* March 15, 2013, 29.

B: Damon, Matt, and Michael Douglas. "Romancing the Rhinestone." Interview by Adam Markovitz. *Entertainment Weekly,* March 15, 2013.

CMOS

Websites and electronic communications

29. Page on a Website

N: 31. "Plants: Native Seed Gene Bank," *San Diego Zoo*, Zoological Society of San Diego, accessed January 5, 2015, http://www.sandiegozoo.org/CF/plants/seed_bank.html.

N: 32. Raymund Flandez, "Museum Condemns Desecration of Dachau Memorial Site," *United States Holocaust Memorial Museum*, November 4, 2014, http://www.ushmm.org/information/press/press-releases/museum-condemns-desecration-of-dachau-memorial-site.

B: *San Diego Zoo*. Zoological Society of San Diego. Accessed January 5, 2015. http://www.sandiegozoo.org/.

B: *United States Holocaust Memorial Museum*. November 4, 2014. http://www.ushmm.org/.

30. Blog Entry Start the entry with the name or pseudonym of the writer. Provide specific citation information for the notes, but only name the blog's home page in the bibliography.

N: 33. The Little Professor, "Authorial Intent," *The Little Professor* (blog), April 23, 2010, accessed May 2, 2010, http://littleprofessor.typepad.com/the_little_professor/2010/04/authorial-intent.html.

N: 34. McBride, Bill, "A Comment on Greece," *Calculated Risk* (blog), February 20, 2015, accessed February 27, 2015, http://www.calculatedriskblog.com/2015/02/a-comment-on-greece.html.

B: The Little Professor. *The Little Professor* (blog). http://littleprofessor.typepad.com.

B: McBride, Bill. *Calculated Risk* (blog). http://www.calculatedriskblog.com.

31. Comment on a Blog or Website Start the notes entry with the name or pseudonym of the commenter. Provide specific citation information for the notes, but only give the blog or website's home page in the bibliography.

N: 35. Zhiv, April 27, 2010 (7:08 p.m.), comment on Little Professor, "Authorial Intent," *The Little Professor* (blog), April 23, 2010, accessed May 2, 2010, http://littleprofessor.typepad.com/the_little_professor/2010/04/authorial-intent.html#comments.

N: 36. TheEconomist, February 20, 2015 (2:28 p.m.), comment on Bill McBride, "A Comment on Greece," *Calculated Risk* (blog), February 20, 2015, accessed February 27, 2015, http://www.hoocoodanode.org/node/21202.

CMOS

B: The Little Professor. *The Little Professor* (blog). http://littleprofessor.typepad.com.

B: McBride, Bill. *Calculated Risk* (blog). http://www.calculatedriskblog.com.

32. **Tweet** Information about tweets usually appears only in the notes or parenthetical citations, not in the bibliography.

N: 37. Cory Booker, Twitter post, March 5, 2012. 2:42 p.m., http://twitter.com/#!/corybooker.

33. **E-Mail Message or Posting to a Mailing List** E-mail messages and postings to mailing lists usually appear only in the notes or parenthetical citations.

N: 38. Dora Dodger-Gilbert, e-mail message to Veterinary Questions and Viewpoints mailing list, January 3, 2015.
39. Daniel Kaplan, e-mail message to author, February 23, 2015.

Apps

34. **App** The *Chicago Manual* does not yet provide explicit instructions for citing an app. These guidelines follow CMOS recommendations about multimedia sources.

N: 40. "Hubble," *Star Walk*, Version 7.0.4, iPad app, Vito Technology, 2014.

B: "Hubble." *Star Walk*. Version 7.0.4. iPad app. Vito Technology, 2014.

Audio and visual sources

35. **Television Episode**
N: 41. *Game of Thrones*, Episode no. 4.6, directed by Alik Sakharov and written by David Benioff, D. B. Weiss, and Bryan Cogman, HBO, May 11, 2014.

B: *Game of Thrones*. Episode no. 4.6. Directed by Alik Sakharov and written by David Benioff, D. B. Weiss, and Bryan Cogman. HBO. May 11, 2014.

36. **Television Interview**
N: 42. John Kerry, interview by Chuck Todd, *Meet the Press*, NBC, February 8, 2015.

B: Kerry, John. Interview by Chuck Todd. *Meet the Press*. NBC. February 8, 2015.

37. **Film on Videotape or DVD**

N: 43. *Lincoln,* directed by Steven Spielberg (2012; Glendale, CA: Dreamworks, 2013), DVD.

B: *Lincoln.* Directed by Steven Spielberg. 2012. Glendale, CA: Dreamworks, 2013. DVD.

38. **Online Video** Add the provider and file format at the end of the entry.

N: 44. Khalida Brohi, "How I Work to Protect Women from Honor Killings," October 2014, TED video, 18:13 (Posted October 2014), http://www.ted.com/talks/khalida_brohi_how_i _work_to_protect_women_from_honor_killings.

B: Brohi, Khalida. "How I Work to Protect Women from Honor Killings." Filmed October 2014. TED video, 18:13. Posted October 2014. http://www.ted.com/talks/khalida_brohi _how_i_work_to_protect_women_from_honor_killings.

39. **Sound Recording** Include the product number (often located on the spine of a CD) at the end of the entry.

N: 45. Johann Sebastian Bach, *Four Concerti for Various Instruments*, Orchestra of St. Luke's, dir. Michael Feldman, Musical Heritage Society, CD 512268T.

B: Bach, Johann Sebastian. *Four Concerti for Various Instruments.* Orchestra of St. Luke's, dir. Michael Feldman. Musical Heritage Society, CD 512268T.

40. **Podcast**

N: 46. Melvyn Bragg, Carolin Crawford, Yvonne Elsworth, and Louise Harra, "The Sun," *BBC Radio 4: In Our Time* (January 1, 2015), iTunes MP3.

N: 47. Ellie Goulding, *Lights* (New York: Interscope, 2011), iTunes MP3.

B: Bragg, Melvyn, Carolin Crawford, Yvonne Elsworth, and Louise Harra. "The Sun." *BBC Radio 4: In Our Time*. January 1, 2015. iTunes MP3.

B: Goulding, Ellie. *Lights*. New York: Interscope, 2011. iTunes MP3.

Other media

41. **Advertisement** List ads in the bibliography only if they are retrievable.

N: 48. Tempurpedic, "Love Birds," television advertisement, Carmichael Lynch, by Martin Granger, 2013.

B: Tempurpedic. "Love Birds." Television advertisement. Carmichael Lynch, directed by Martin Granger, 2013.

42. **Personal or Telephone Interview** In the author-date format, personal communications are acknowledged in the
text but not in the bibliography.

N: 49. John Sutton, interview by the author, May 12, 2015,
Florence, South Carolina.

47c Paper format

Follow the format shown here for a title page, first and
second pages of the paper, and the bibliography. Also refer
to the *Student's Guide to Writing College Papers* (4th ed.,
2010) for additional guidelines.

Paper Format Quick Guide—CMOS	
Paper format	Use 12-point serif font (like Times New Roman or Cambria) throughout your paper. Set margins between 1 and 1½ inches.
Title page and titles	Include a title page for papers with five or more pages. Place the title ⅓ down the page. Insert your name, class, instructor, and date ⅔ down the page. Center all lines.
	For papers with less than five pages, insert your title at the top center of the page. Insert four blank lines and then insert your name, class, instructor, and date. Insert four blank lines and begin the first paragraph.
	Capitalize all words in the title except for articles, conjunctions, and short prepositions (unless they are the first word, last word, or follow a colon). If you have a subtitle, include the title and a colon, and then place the subtitle on the line immediately below it.
Header and page numbers	If you have a title page, count the title page as page 0 and the first page of the paper as page 1. Begin the header on page 2. If you don't have a title page, begin the paper on page 1 and begin the header on page 2.
	Place the header on the right margin in 10-point font. Include your name, a hyphen, and the page number: **Smith-2**
Tables and figures	Insert tables and figures within the body of the text. For a table, create a brief label and place it directly above the table: **Table 1: Unemployment rates by state in 2015**

	For figures, create a brief label and place it directly below the figure. **Figure 7. Average per capita income for counties in Arkansas**
Notes	Use your word-processing software to insert the notes. In the text, insert a superscript number (small and raised above the text) to indicate a source citation.
	For footnotes, the note information should appear at the bottom of the page, single-spaced, and in 10-point font.
	If you use endnotes instead, create a new page before the bibliography and center *Endnotes* at the top. Single-space notes with a blank line between each.
Bibliography	Type *Bibliography* and center it on the page. Double-space and alphabetize entries in hanging-indent style.

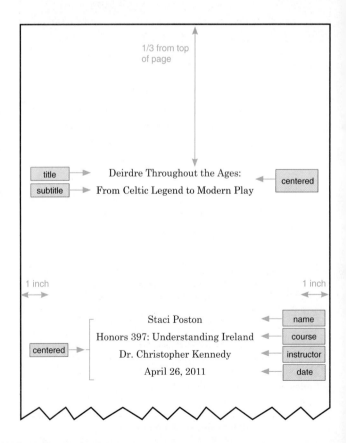

1/3 from top of page

title → Deirdre Throughout the Ages: ← centered
subtitle → From Celtic Legend to Modern Play

1 inch   1 inch

Staci Poston ← name
Honors 397: Understanding Ireland ← course
centered → Dr. Christopher Kennedy ← instructor
April 26, 2011 ← date

1 inch

Mythological stories contain universal themes and archetypes that recur throughout their telling and retelling. As Joseph Campbell explains, "The themes are timeless, and the inflection is to the culture."[1] The story of Deirdre, a well-known Irish legend, contains similarities to other stories and fairy tales because of this function of mythology. Besides existing in Irish history as far back as the Ulster Cycle, the story has continued to be reproduced and used by modern storytellers, such as playwright J. M. Synge's *Deirdre of the Sorrows* (1910). Though the ideas, themes, and archetypes remain constant, the story itself changes and adapts over time, depending on the context, culture, and medium in which it is told.

1 inch

1 inch

The legend of Deirdre is told in *The Tragic Death of the Sons of Usnech*, which is estimated to have been first composed in the 8th or 9th century. However, the oldest extant version of the legend is preserved in the *The Book of Leinster* (c. 1160), a part of the Ulster Cycle.[2] *The Book of Leinster* is a compilation of both sacred and secular Irish verse and prose from manuscripts and oral traditions that was written and completed in the mid-12th century.[3]

The original legend of Deirdre begins with a prophecy. At a feast, a druid named Cathbad tells Deirdre's parents of the beauty and danger that their child will have: "A fair woman is she, for whom heroes that fight / In their chariots for Ulster, to death shall be dight."[4] Though the men of Ulster protest this and request that the infant be killed, her father, Fedlimid, arranges for her to be raised in

CMOS

---

1. Joseph Campbell, *The Power of Myth*, ed. Betty Sue Flowers (New York: Anchor Books, 1988), 13.

2. *Encyclopaedia Britannica Online*, s.v. "Deirdre," accessed March 3, 2011, http://www.britannica.com/EBchecked/topic/156147/Deirdre.

3. *Encyclopaedia Britannica Online*, s.v. "The Book of Leinster," accessed March 3, 2011, http://www.britannica.com/EBchecked/topic/335440/The-Book-of-Leinster.

4. "Deirdre—or, The Exile of the Sons of Usnech," in *The Book of Leinster* (1160; Celtic Literature Collective, 2011), http://www.maryjones.us/ctexts/usnech.html.

1 inch

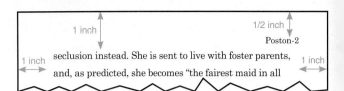

1 inch — 1 inch

1/2 inch

Poston-2

seclusion instead. She is sent to live with foster parents, and, as predicted, she becomes "the fairest maid in all

---

1 inch

1/2 inch

Poston-8

Bibliography ← centered

Campbell, Joseph. *The Power of Myth*. Edited by Betty Sue Flowers. New York: Anchor Books, 1988. ← double-space

"Deirdre—or, The Exile of the Sons of Usnech." *The Book of Leinster*. Reprint of the 1160 edition, Celtic Literature Collection, 2011. http://www.maryjones.us/ctexts/usnech.html.

Grene, Nicholas. *Synge: A Critical Study of the Plays*. Totowa, NJ: Rowman and Littlefield, 1975.

King, Mary C. *The Drama of J. M. Synge*. New York: Syracuse University Press, 1985.

Price, Alan. *Synge and Anglo-Irish Drama*. New York: Russell & Russell, 1972.

Ritschel, Nelson O'Ceallaigh. *Synge and Irish Nationalism: The Precursor to Revolution*. Westport, CT: Greenwood, 2002.

Synge, John Millington. *Deirdre of the Sorrows*. Reprint of the 1911 edition, Electronic Text Center, University of Virginia Library, 1999. http://etext.virginia.edu/toc/modeng/public/SynDeir.html.

Thornton, Weldon. *J. M. Synge and the Western Mind*. New York: Harper and Row, 1979.

1 inch — 1 inch

CMOS

48 Council of Science Editors (CSE) Style

Writers in the physical and life sciences follow Council of Science Editors (CSE) style, found in *Scientific Style and Format: The CSE Manual for Authors, Editors, and Publishers* (8th ed., 2014). The *CSE Manual* offers three documentation styles: *name-year*, *citation-sequence*, and *citation-name*.

48a In-text citations

1. **Name-Year Format** Authors' names and publication dates are included in parenthetical citations in the text, closely resembling *Chicago Manual* name-date style (see 47a).

   ### In-Text Citation

   H1N1 influenza, which comprises elements of human seasonal, porcine, and avian influenza viruses (Gatherer 2009), evolved quickly and spread rapidly. Studies on emerging zoonotic influenza strains (Charlton et al. 2009; Gatherer 2009) show that the development of rapid-testing diagnostic tools is essential for monitoring pandemics like H1N1 influenza.

   In the list of references at the end of the paper, list names alphabetically with the date after the name. Journal titles are abbreviated, without periods.

   ### Reference List Entries

   Charlton B, Crossley B, Hietala S. 2009. Conventional and future diagnostics for avian influenza. Comp Immunol Microbiol Infec Dis. 32(4):341–50.

   Gatherer D. 2009. The 2009 H1N1 influenza outbreak in its historical context. J Clin Virol. 45(3):174–78.

2. **Citation-Sequence Style** References may instead be cited by means of in-text superscript numbers (numbers set above the line, such as [1] and [2]) that refer to a list of numbered references at the end of the paper. The

CSE

references are numbered in the order in which they are cited in the text, and later references to the same work use the original number. When you have two or more sources cited at once, put the numbers in sequence, separated with commas but no spaces.

In-Text Citation

Studies of influenza viruses[1,4,9] show humans can become doubly infected with seasonal and zoonotic influenza strains. The mixture of strains can lead to new variants that require new testing procedures[1,2] and new vaccines[3–6] to detect and control pandemic outbreaks.

Reference List Entries

1. Gatherer, D. The 2009 H1N1 influenza outbreak in its historical context. J Clin Virol. 2009;45(3):174–78.

2. Charlton B, Crossley B, Hietala S. Conventional and future diagnostics for avian influenza. Comp Immunol Microbiol Infec Dis. 2009;32(4):341–50.

3. **Citation-Name Style** In this style, all sources are first listed on the References page in alphabetical order by authors' names and then assigned a number in sequence. These numbers correspond to in-text superscript numbers. Other than the change in numbering, the in-text and the reference list citation formats are the same as that used for the citation-sequence style.

48b References list

At the end of the paper, include a list titled "References" or "Cited References." The placement of the date depends on which style you use.

- **Name-year style.** Put the date after the author's name. Arrange the list alphabetically by last names. Do not indent any lines in the entries.

- **Citation-sequence and citation-name styles.** For books, put the date after the publisher's name. For periodicals, put the date after the periodical name. Arrange the list by number. Put the number at the left margin, followed by a period and a space and then the authors' names.

CSE

QUICK GUIDE: For CSE References, how do I format . . .

AUTHORS' NAMES

One author: **Cole JH.**
Two to authors: **Cole JH, Lin SF, Bola SR, Metz DE.**
More than ten authors: List the first ten authors and end with **et al.**

TITLES

Don't use italics or quotation marks. Capitalize only first words and proper nouns in article titles.   **Fracking: an overview.** **USA Today.**
Abbreviate journal and magazine titles. **J Mol Biol. JAMA. Sci Am.**

VOLUME AND ISSUE NUMBERS

List volume and issue number: **14(3)**

CITY OF PUBLICATION

List city and state. **Chicago (IL)**

DATES

Year: **2013**
Month and Year: **2013 Jan**
Exact Date: **2013 Jan 8**

PAGE NUMBERS

218–234.
List all pages if text is interrupted: **18–20, 22–34.**

PUBLISHERS

Give the full name: **Elsevier Science.**

URLs

For databases, give a stable URL and add **by subscription.**

Examples of CSE Format for a Reference List

BOOKS, PARTS OF BOOKS, AND REPORTS

JOURNAL ARTICLES

MAGAZINE ARTICLES

CSE

Note: In the following examples, NY stands for name-year format and CS/CN stands for citation-sequence and citation-name format. References should be single-spaced, with a blank line between each entry.

Books, parts of books, and reports

1. **Book**

CS/CN: 1. Calvo RA, Peters D. Positive computing: technology for wellbeing and human potential. Boston (MA): MIT Press; 2014.

NY: Calvo RA, Peters D. 2014. Positive computing: technology for wellbeing and human potential. Boston (MA): MIT Press.

2. **Anthology, Scholarly Collection, or Work That Names an Editor**

CS/CN: 2. So EL, Ryvlin P, editors. MRI-negative epilepsy. New York (NY): Cambridge University Press; 2015.

NY: So EL, Ryvlin P, editors. 2015. MRI-negative epilepsy. New York (NY): Cambridge University Press.

3. **Article in an Anthology, Scholarly Collection, or Work**

CS/CN: 3. Griffin PJ. Nuclear technologies. In: Marshall M, Oxley J, editors. Aspects of explosives detection. Amsterdam: Elsevier; 2009. p. 59–87.

NY: Griffin PJ. 2009. Nuclear technologies. In: Marshall M, Oxley J, editors. Aspects of explosives detection. Amsterdam: Elsevier; p. 59–87.

4. **Second or Later Edition** Add the edition after the book title: 11th ed. See entry 5.

5. **Organizational or Corporate Author** Begin the name-year entry with the group's acronym, placed in square brackets.

CS/CN: 5. Council of Science Editors, Style Manual Subcommittee. Scientific style and format: the CSE manual for authors, editors, and publishers. 8th ed. Chicago (IL): University of Chicago Press; 2014.

NY: [CSE] Council of Science Editors, Style Manual Subcommittee. 2014. Scientific style and format: the CSE manual for authors, editors, and publishers. 8th ed. Chicago (IL): University of Chicago Press.

6. **Book Accessed Online**

CS/CN: 6. Kansagara D, Gleitsmann K, Gillingham M, Freeman M, Quiñones A. Nutritional supplements for age-related macular degeneration: a systematic review [Internet]. Washington (DC): Dept of Veterans Affairs; 2012 [cited 2012 May 7]. Available from: http://www.ncbi.nlm.nih.gov /books/NBK84269/

NY: Kansagara D, Gleitsmann K, Gillingham M, Freeman M, Quiñones A. 2012. Nutritional supplements for age-related macular degeneration: a systematic review [Internet]. Washington (DC): Dept of Veterans Affairs; [cited 2012 May 7]. Available from: http://www.ncbi.nlm.nih.gov/books/NBK84269/

Journal articles

7. **Article in a Journal**

CS/CN: 7. Chaney RA, Rojas-Guyler L. Spatial patterns of adolescent drug use. App Geog. 2015;56(1);71–82.

NY: Chaney RA, Rojas-Guyler L. 2015. Spatial patterns of adolescent drug use. App Geog. 56(1);71–82.

8. **Journal Article Located in a Library Database or Subscription Service**

CS/CN: 8. Aryal P, Sansom MSP, Tucker SJ. Hydrophobic gating in ion channels. J Mol Biol. 2015 [accessed 2015 Feb 27];427(1):121–30. http://www.sciencedirect.com/ by subscription. doi:10.1016/j.jmb.2014.07.030.

NY: Aryal P, Sansom MSP, Tucker SJ. 2015. Hydrophobic gating in ion channels. J Mol Biol [accessed 2015 Feb

CSE

27];427(1):121–30. http://www.sciencedirect.com/ by subscription. doi:10.1016/j.jmb.2014.07.030.

9. Article in an Online Journal

CS/CN: 9. Oliveira A, Weiland I, Hsu TF. Food appraisal; discussing healthy diet and eating in elementary science. Elec J
of Sci Ed. 2015 [accessed 2015 Mar 1];19(2):1–24. http://
ejse.southwestern.edu/article/view/14195/9485.

NY: Oliveira A, Weiland I, Hsu TF. 2015. Food appraisal; discussing healthy diet and eating in elementary science. Elec
J of Sci Ed. [accessed 2015 Mar 1];19(2):1–24. http://
ejse.southwestern.edu/article/view/14195/9485.

Magazine articles

10. Article in a Magazine

CS/CN: 10. Castelvecchi D. The compass within. Sci Am. 2012
Jan;48–53.

NY: Castelvecchi D. 2012 Jan. The compass within. Sci
Am. 48–53.

11. Article in an Online Magazine

CS/CN: 11. Klemetti E. New volcano identified in central Columbia.
Wired. 2015 Feb 24 [accessed 2015 Feb 28]. http://www
.wired.com/2015/02/new-volcano-identified-central
-colombia/

NY: Klemetti E. 2015 Feb 24. New volcano identified in central
Columbia. Wired [accessed 2015 Feb 28]. http://www.wired
.com/2015/02/new-volcano-identified-central-colombia/

Newspaper articles

12. Article in a Newspaper Provide the page number and
column number of the beginning of the article.

CS/CN: 12. Freehill-Maye L. Moving outdoors to embrace the cold.
New York Times (National Ed.). 2015 Mar 1;Sect. TR:4
(col. 1–5).

NY: Freehill-Maye L. 2015 Mar 1. Moving outdoors to embrace the
cold. New York Times (National Ed.). Sect. TR:4 (col. 1–5).

13. Article in an Online Newspaper

CS/CN: 13. Alexander K. California poised to see driest January
on record. San Francisco Chronicle. 2015 Jan 26

[accessed 2015 Feb 1]. http://www.sfgate.com/bayarea
/article/California-poised-to-see-driest-January-on
-record-6041058.php

NY: Alexander K. 2015 Jan 26. California poised to see driest
January on record. San Francisco Chronicle [accessed 2015
Feb 1]. http://www.sfgate.com/bayarea/article/California
-poised-to-see-driest-January-on-record-6041058.php

14. **Unsigned Newspaper Article** Begin the entry with the
article title.

CS/CN: 14. Japan marks year since quake, tsunami disaster. Florence Morning News. 2012 Feb 17;Sect. A:4 (col. 2–4).

NY: Japan marks year since quake, tsunami disaster. 2012 Feb
17. Florence Morning News. Sect. A:4 (col. 2–4).

15. **Editorial** After the title, add [editorial].

CS/CN: 15. Reilly WK, Cayten MR. Preventing a Deepwater Horizon
redux [editorial]. Washington Post, 2012 Feb 19;Sect.
A:21 (col. 2–4).

NY: Reilly WK, Cayten MR. 2012 Feb 19. Preventing a Deepwater Horizon redux [editorial]. Washington Post. Sect. A:21
(col. 2–4).

Online, audio, and visual media

16. **Website Home Page**

CS/CN: 16. Southern California earthquake data center. Pasadena
(CA): Cal Tech; c1992–2015 [accessed 2015 Mar 15].
http://scedc.caltech.edu

NY: Southern California earthquake data center. c1992–2015.
Pasadena (CA): Cal Tech; [accessed 2015 Mar 15]. http://
scedc.caltech.edu

17. **Page or Article on a Website**

CS/CN: 17. Pew Research Center. Washington (DC): Pew Research
Center; c2012. Oil spill seen as ecological disaster;
2010 May 11 [accessed 2012 May 15]. http://pewresearch
.org/pubs/1590/poll-gulf-oil-disaster-obama-bp-support
-for-drilling

NY: Pew Research Center. c2012. Washington (DC): Pew Research Center. Oil spill seen as ecological disaster; 2010
May 11 [accessed 2012 May 15]. http://pewresearch.org
/pubs/1590/poll-gulf-oil-disaster-obama-bp-support-for-drilling

CSE

18. Blog

CS/CN: 10. McBride B. A comment on oil prices [blog]. Calculated Risk. 2015 Dec 15 [accessed 3 Jan 2015]. http://www.calculatedriskblog.com/2014/12/a-comment-on-oil-prices.html

NY: McBride B. 2015 Dec 15. A comment on oil prices [blog]. Calculated Risk. [accessed 3 Jan 2015]. http://www.calculated riskblog.com/2014/12/a-comment-on-oil-prices.html

19. Social Networking Site

CS/CN: 19. Mark Zuckerberg. Facebook [fan page, shared link]. 2015 Feb 25, 1:42 p.m. [accessed 27 Feb. 2015]. https://www.facebook.com/zuck.

NY: Mark Zuckerberg. 2015 Feb 25, 1:42 p.m. Facebook [fan page, shared link]. [accessed 27 Feb. 2015]. https://www.facebook.com/zuck.

20. Infographic

CS/CN: 20. Centers for Disease Control and Prevention. Is it flu or ebola? [infographic]. Atlanta(GA): CDC. 13 Nov 2014 [accessed 15 Feb 2015]. http://www.cdc.gov/vhf/ebola/pdf/is-it-flu-or-ebola.pdf.

NY: Centers for Disease Control and Prevention. 13 Nov 2014. Is it flu or ebola? [infographic]. Atlanta(GA): CDC. [accessed 15 Feb 2015]. http://www.cdc.gov/vhf/ebola/pdf/is-it-flu-or-ebola.pdf.

21. DVD, Blu-ray, or Videocassette

CS/CN: 21. Frontline: Inside Japan's nuclear meltdown [DVD]. Edge D, director; Fanning D, Sullivan M, executive producers. Arlington (VA): PBS; 2012. 1 DVD: 60 min., sound, color.

NY: Frontline: Inside Japan's nuclear meltdown [DVD]. 2012. Edge D, director; Fanning D, Sullivan M, executive producers. Arlington (VA): PBS. 1 DVD: 60 min., sound, color.

22. Online Video

CS/CN: 22. Big bang machine. [video]. NOVA. PBS. 2015 Jan 14, 53:10 min. [accessed 2015 Feb 28], http://www.pbs.org/wgbh/nova/physics/big-bang-machine.html

NY: Big bang machine [video]. 2015 Jan 14. NOVA. PBS. 53:10 minutes. [accessed 2015 Feb 28], http://www.pbs.org/wgbh/nova/physics/big-bang-machine.html

23. **Podcast**

CS/CN: 23. Flatow, I. Dawn of the cyborg bacteria [podcast]. Science Friday. Science Friday Initiative. 2015 Feb 27, 7:34 minutes. [accessed 2015 Feb 28]. http://www.sciencefriday.com/segment/02/27/2015/dawn-of-the-cyborg-bacteria.html

NY: Flatow, I. 2015 Feb 27. Dawn of the cyborg bacteria [podcast]. Science Friday. Science Friday Initiative. 7:34 minutes. [accessed 2015 Feb 28]. http://www.sciencefriday.com/segment/02/27/2015/dawn-of-the-cyborg-bacteria.html

24. **E-Mail and Instant Messaging (IM)** Personal e-mail, instant messaging, and other personal communications are identified in the body of the paper and are not listed in the References.

48c Paper format

The CSE Manual does not provide explicit directions for formatting student papers. The information provided here, however, follows CSE protocols for formatting written work.

Paper Format Quick Guide—CSE	
Paper format	Set paper margins of at least one inch on all sides. Double-space the main text of your paper, but single-space block quotations and your notes. Use single space for your bibliography entries, but leave a blank line between items.
Title page and titles	Include a title page. Place the title ⅓ down the page, and insert name, class, and date ⅔ down the page. Center all lines.
Header and page numbers	Place page numbers in a consistent location throughout your paper, either flush with the right margin, centered in the header, or centered in the footer.
Abstract, headings, and subheadings	Many CSE papers include an abstract, which is a short summary of your work. At the top of the second page, center the word *Abstract* and double-space summary.
	Use a consistent style for headings and subheadings. Following scientific style, the paper may include headings such as *Introduction*, *Methods*, *Results*, and *Discussion*.

Paper Format Quick Guide—CSE	
Tables and figures	Insert tables and figures within the body of the text. For a table, create a brief label and place it directly above the table: **Table 1: Average July temperature for Mexico, 1965–2015** For figures, create a brief label and place it directly below the figure: **Figure 7: Structure of a Multiple Vortex Tornado**
Notes	In the text, insert a superscript number (small and raised above the text) to indicate a source citation. For the citation-sequence style, number the references at the end of your paper in the order they appear in your paper. For the citation-name style, at the end of your paper, organize entries alphabetically and assign each a number. Use these numbers for your superscript in-text citations.
References	Insert a title called *References* and center it on the page. Use single space for your entries, but leave a blank line between items. For the name-year style, indent entries under the first word.

Glossary of Usage

A, An   Use *a* before words beginning with a consonant and before words beginning with a vowel that sounds like a consonant:

a cat   a house   a one-way street   a union   a history

Use *an* before words that begin with a vowel and before words with a silent *h*.

an egg   an ice cube   an hour   an honor

Accept, Except   *Accept* means *to agree to, to believe*, or *to receive*.

The detective **accepted** his account of the event.

Except, a verb, means *to exclude or leave out*, and *except*, a preposition, means *leaving out*.

Because he did not know the answers, he was **excepted** from the list of contestants and asked to leave.

Except for brussels sprouts, I eat most vegetables.

Advice, Advise   *Advice* is a noun, and *advise* is a verb.

She always offers too much **advice**.

Would you **advise** me about choosing the right course?

Ain't   This is a nonstandard way of saying *am not, is not, has not, have not*, and so on.

All Ready, Already   *All ready* means *prepared; already* means *before* or *by this time*.

The courses for the meal are **all ready** to be served.

When I got home, she was **already** there.

All Right, Alright   *All right* is two words, not one. *Alright* is an incorrect form.

Alot, A Lot   *Alot* is an incorrect form of *a lot*.

Among, Between   Use *among* when referring to three or more things and *between* when referring to two things.

The decision was discussed **among** all the members of the committee.

I had to decide **between** the chocolate pie and the almond ice cream.

Amount, Number   Use *amount* for things or ideas that are general or abstract and cannot be counted. For example, *furniture* is a general term and cannot be counted. That is, we cannot say *one furniture* or *two furnitures*. Use *number* for things that can be counted (for example, *four chairs* or *three tables*).

He had a huge **amount** of work to finish before the deadline.

A **number** of people saw the accident.

An   See the entry for **a, an.**

And   Although some discourage using *and* as the first word in a sentence, it is an acceptable word with which to begin a sentence.

Anybody, Any Body   See the entry for **anyone, any one.**

Anyone, Any One   *Anyone* means *any person at all. Any one* refers to a specific person or thing in a group. There are similar distinctions for other words ending in *-body* and *-one* (for example, *everybody, every body, anybody, any body, someone,* and *some one*).

The teacher asked if **anyone** knew the answer.

Any one of those children could have taken the ball.

As, As If, As Though, Like   Use *as* in a comparison (not *like*) when equality is intended or when the meaning is *in the function of*.

> Celia acted **as** (not *like*) the leader when the group was getting organized. (Celia = leader)

Use *as if* or *as though* for the subjunctive.

> He spent his money **as if** (*or* **as though**) he were rich.

Use *like* in a comparison (not *as*) when the meaning is *in the manner of* or *to the same degree as*.

> The boy swam **like** a fish.

Awhile, A While   *Awhile* is an adverb meaning *a short time* and modifies a verb:

> He talked **awhile** and then left.

A while is an article with the noun *while* and means *a period of time:*

> I'll be there in **a while**.

Bad, Badly   *Bad* is an adjective and is used after linking verbs. *Badly* is an adverb. (See 18b.)

> The wheat crop looked **bad** (not *badly*) because of lack of rain.

> There was a **bad** flood last summer.

> The building was **badly** constructed and unable to withstand strong winds.

Beside, Besides   *Beside* is a preposition meaning *at the side of, compared with*, or *having nothing to do with*. *Besides* is a preposition meaning *in addition to* or *other than*. *Besides* as an adverb means *also* or *moreover*.

> That is **beside** the point.

> **Besides** the radio, they had no contact with the outside world.

> **Besides**, I enjoyed the concert.

Between, Among   See the entry for **among, between**.

Breath, Breathe   *Breath* is a noun, and *breathe* is a verb.

> She held her **breath** when she dived into the water.

> Learn to **breathe** deeply when you swim.

But   Although some people discourage the use of *but* as the first word in a sentence, it can be used to begin a sentence.

Can, May   *Can* expresses ability, knowledge, or capacity:

> He **can** play both the violin and the cello.

May is a verb that expresses possibility or permission. Careful writers avoid using *can* to mean *permission:*

> **May** [not *can*] I sit here?

Choose, Chose   *Choose* is the present tense of the verb, and *chose* is the past tense:

> Jennie should **choose** strawberry ice cream.

> Yesterday, she **chose** strawberry-flavored popcorn.

Cite, Site   *Cite* is a verb that means *to quote an authority or source; site* is a noun referring to *a place*.

> Be sure to **cite** your sources in the paper.

> That is the **site** of the new city swimming pool.

Could of   This is incorrect. Instead use *could have*.

Different from, Different than   *Different from* is always correct, but some writers use *different than* if a clause follows this phrase.

> This program is **different from** the others.

> That is a **different** result **than** they predicted.

Done   The past tense forms of the verb *do* are *did* and *done*. *Did* is the simple form that needs no additional verb as a helper. *Done* is the past form that requires the helper *have*. Some writers make the mistake of interchanging *did* and *done*.

> They ~~done~~ it again. (*or*) They ~~done~~ it again.
> _did_   _have done_

Etc.   This is an abbreviation of the Latin *et cetera*, meaning *and the rest*. It should be used sparingly if at all in formal academic writing. Use instead phrases such as *and so forth* or *and so on*.

Everybody, Every Body   See the entry for **anyone, any one**.

Everyone, Every One   See the entry for **anyone, any one**.

Except, Accept   See the entry for **accept, except**.

Farther, Further   *Farther* is used when actual distance is involved, and *further* is used to mean *to a greater extent, more*.

> The house is **farther** from the road than I realized.

> That was **furthest** from my thoughts at the time.

Fewer, Less   *Fewer* is used for things that can be counted (*fewer trees, fewer people*), and *less* is used for ideas, abstractions, things that are thought of collectively rather than separately (*less trouble, less furniture*), and things that are measured by amount, not number (*less milk, less fuel*).

Gone, Went   Past tense forms of the verb *go*. *Went* is the simple form that needs no additional verb as a helper. *Gone* is the past form that requires the helper *have*. Some writers make the mistake of interchanging *went* and *gone*. (See Section 16b.)

> They ~~gone~~ away yesterday.
> _went (or) have gone_

Good, Well   *Good* is an adjective and therefore describes only nouns. *Well* is an adverb and therefore describes adjectives, other adverbs, and verbs. The word *well* is used as an adjective only in the sense of *in good health*. (See 16b.)

> The stereo works ~~good~~. I feel ~~good~~.
> _well_   _well_

> She is a **good** driver.

Got, Have   *Got* is the past tense of *get* and should not be used in place of *have*. Similarly, *got to* should not be used as a substitute for *must*. *Have got to* is an informal substitute for *must*.

> Do you ~~get~~ any pennies for the meter?
> _have_

> I ~~got to~~ go now.
> _must_

> **Informal:**   You **have got to** see that movie.

Have, Got   See the entry for **got, have**.

Have, Of   *Have*, not *of*, should follow verbs such as *could, might, must,* and *should*.

> They should ~~of~~ called by now.
> _have_

I   Although some people discourage the use of *I* in formal essays, it is acceptable. If you wish to eliminate the use of *I*, see Chapter 9 on passive verbs.

Is When, Is Why, Is Where, Is Because   These are incorrect forms for definitions. See 6f on faulty predication.

Its, It's   *Its* is a personal pronoun in the possessive case. *It's* is a contraction for *it is*.

> The kitten licked **its** paw.   **It's** a good time for a vacation.

Lay, Lie   *Lay* is a verb that needs an object and should not be used in place of *lie*, a verb that takes no direct object. (See 16c.)

He should ~~lay~~ *lie* down and rest awhile.

You can ~~lie~~ *lay* that package on the front table.

Less, Fewer   See the entry for **fewer, less**.

Like, As   See the entry for **as, as if, as though, like**.

Like for   The phrase "I'd like for you to do that" is incorrect. Omit *for*.

May, Can   See the entry for **can, may**.

Number, Amount   See the entry for **amount, number**.

Of, Have   See the entry for **have, of**.

O.K., OK, Okay   These can be used informally but should not be used in formal or academic writing.

Reason. . . Because   This is redundant. Instead of *because*, use *that*.

The reason she dropped the course is ~~because~~ *that* she couldn't keep up with the homework.

> **Less wordy revision:**   She dropped the course **because** she couldn't keep up with the homework.

Reason Why   Using *why* is redundant. Drop the word *why*.

The reason ~~why~~ I called is to remind you of your promise.

Saw, Seen   Past tense forms of the verb *see*. *Saw* is the simple form that needs no additional verb as a helper. *Seen* is the past form that requires the helper *have*. Some writers make the mistake of interchanging *saw* and *seen*. (See 16b.)

They ~~seen~~ *saw* it happen. (*or*) They ~~seen~~ *have seen* it happen.

Set, Sit   *Set* means *to place* and is followed by a direct object. *Sit* means *to be seated*. It is incorrect to substitute *set* for *sit*.

Come in and ~~set~~ *sit* down.

~~Sit~~ *Set* the flowers on the table.

Should of   This is incorrect. Instead use *should have*.

Sit, Set   See the entry for **set, sit**.

Site, Cite   See the entry for **cite, site**.

Somebody, Some Body   See the entry for **anyone, any one**.

Someone, Some One   See the entry for **anyone, any one**.

Suppose to, Use to   These are nonstandard forms for *supposed to* and *used to*.

Than, Then   *Than* introduces the second element in a comparison. *Then* means *at that time, next, after that*, or *in that case*.

She is taller **than** I am.

He picked up the ticket and **then** left the house.

That There, This Here, These Here, Those There   These are incorrect forms for *that, this, these, those*.

That, Which   Use *that* for essential clauses and *which* for nonessential clauses. Some writers, however, also use *which* for essential clauses. (See 23c.)

Their, There, They're   *Their* is a possessive pronoun; *there* means *in, at*, or *to that place*; and *they're* is a contraction for *they are*.

Their house has been sold.

There is the parking lot.

They're both good swimmers.

Theirself, Theirselves, Themself   These are all incorrect forms for *themselves*.

Them   It is incorrect to use *them* in place of either the pronoun *these* or *those*.

Look at ~~them~~ apples.   _those_

Then, Than   See the entry for **than, then**.

To, Too, Two   *To* is a preposition, *too* is an adverb meaning *very* or *also*, and *two* is a number.

He brought his bass guitar **to** the party.

He brought his drums **too**.

He had **two** music stands.

Use to, Suppose to   See the entry for **suppose to, use to**.

Want for   Omit the incorrect *for* in phrases such as "I want *for* you to come here."

Well, Good   See the entry for **good, well**.

Went, Gone   See the entry for **gone, went**.

Where   It is incorrect to use *where* to mean *when* or *that*.

The Fourth of July is a holiday ~~where~~ people watch fireworks.   _when_

I see ~~where~~ there is now a ban on shooting panthers.   _that_

Where. . . at   This is a redundant form. Omit *at*.

This is where the picnic is ~~at~~.

Which, That   See the entry for **that, which**.

While, Awhile   See the entry for **awhile, a while**.

Who, Whom   Use *who* for the subjective case; use *whom* for the objective case.

He is the person **who** signs that form.

He is the person **whom** I asked for help.

Who's, Whose   *Who's* is a contraction for *who is; whose* is a possessive pronoun.

Who's included on that list?

Whose wristwatch is this?

Your, You're   *Your* is a possessive pronoun; *you're* is a contraction for *you are*.

Your hands are cold.

You're a great success.

Glossary of Grammatical Terms

Abstract Nouns   See Chapter 35.

Active Voice   See Chapter 9.

Adjective and Adverb Clauses   See **Dependent Clauses**.

Adjectives   See 18a.

Adverbs   See 18b.

Agreement   See 16a.

Antecedents   Words or groups of words to which pronouns refer

> When the **bell** was rung, **it** sounded very loudly.

> (*Bell* is the antecedent of *it*.)

Articles   See Chapter 36.

Auxiliary Verbs   Verbs used with main verbs in verb phrases.

> **should be** going   **has** taken
> (auxiliary verb)   (auxiliary verb)

Case   See 17a.

Clauses   Groups of related words that contain both subjects and predicates and function either as sentences or as parts of sentences. Clauses are either independent (or main) or dependent (or subordinate). (See Chapter 15 and 23a, b, and c.)

Collective Nouns   Nouns that refer to groups of people or things, such as a *committee, team,* or *jury*. (See 16a.)

Comma Splices   Punctuation errors in which two or more independent clauses in compound sentences are separated only by commas and no coordinating conjunctions. (See 15a.)

> Jessie said he could not help, but (or); that was his usual response.

Common Nouns   See Chapter 35.

Comparative   See 18c.

Complement   When linking verbs link subjects to adjectives or nouns, the adjectives or nouns are complements.

> Phyllis was **tired**.
> (complement)
> She became a **musician**.
> (complement)

Complex Sentences   Sentences with at least one independent clause and at least one dependent clause arranged in any order.

Compound-Complex Sentences   Sentences with at least two independent clauses and at least one dependent clause arranged in any order.

Compound Nouns   Words such as *swimming pool, dropout, roommate,* and *stepmother,* formed of more than one word that could stand on its own.

Compound Sentences   Sentences with two or more independent clauses and no dependent clauses. (See Chapter 15.)

Conjunctions   Words that connect other words, phrases, and clauses in sentences. *Coordinating conjunctions* connect independent clauses; *subordinating conjunctions* connect dependent or subordinating clauses with independent or main clauses.

> **Coordinating**   and, but, for, or, nor, so, yet
> **conjunctions:**
>
> **Some subordinating**   after, although, because, if, since,
> **conjunctions:**   until, while

Conjunctive Adverbs   Words that begin or join independent clauses. (See Chapter 23.)

> consequently, however, therefore, thus, moreover

Connotation   The attitudes and emotional overtones beyond the direct definition of a word. For example, the words *plump* and *fat* both mean *fleshy,* but *plump* has a more positive connotation than *fat*. (See 10d.)

Coordination   Equal importance. Two independent clauses in the same sentence are coordinate because they have equal importance and the same emphasis.

Dangling Modifiers   See 19a.

Demonstrative Pronouns   Pronouns that refer to things.

Denotation   The explicit dictionary definition of a word, as opposed to the connotation of a word. (See 10d.)

Dependent Clauses (Subordinate Clauses)   Clauses that cannot stand alone as complete sentences. (See Chapters 22, 23.)

Direct Discourse   See 26a.

Direct/Indirect Quotations   See 26a.

Direct Objects   Nouns or pronouns that follow a transitive verb and complete the meaning or receive the action of the verb. The direct object answers the question *what?* or *whom?*

Essential and Nonessential Clauses and Phrases   See 23c.

Faulty Parallelism   See 21b.

Faulty Predication   See 6f.

Fragments   Groups of words punctuated as sentences that either do not have both a subject and a complete verb or that are dependent clauses. (See Chapter 14.)

> Whenever we wanted to pick fresh fruit while we were staying on my
> , we would head for the orchard with buckets
> grandmother's farm.

Fused Sentences   Punctuation errors (also called *run-ons*) in which there is no punctuation between independent clauses in the sentence. (See 15b.)

> Jennifer never learned how to ask politely she just took what she wanted.

Gerunds   Verbal forms ending in *-ing* that function as nouns or as parts of verb forms. (See 34e.)

> Arnon enjoys **cooking**.
>   (gerund)
> **Jogging** is another of his pastimes.
>   (gerund)

Homonyms   Words that sound alike but are spelled differently and have different meanings. (hear/here, passed/past, buy/by, etc.) (See 32c.)

Idioms   Expressions meaning something beyond the simple definition or literal translation into another language. See Chapter 39.

Independent Clauses   Clauses that can stand alone as complete sentences because they do not depend on other clauses to complete their meanings. (See 23a.)

Indirect Discourse   See 26a.

Infinitives   Phrases made up of the present form of the verb preceded by *to*. Infinitives can have subjects, objects, complements, or modifiers.

> Everyone wanted **to swim** in the new pool.
>   (infinitive)

Irregular Verbs   See 16b.

Jargon   See 10a.

Linking Verbs   See 16a.

Misplaced Modifiers   See 19b.

Modal Verbs   See 34c.

Modifiers   See Chapter 19.

Nonessential (or Nonrestrictive) Clauses and Phrases   See 23c.

Nouns   Words that name people, places, things, and ideas and have plural or possessive endings. Nouns function as subjects, direct objects, predicate nominatives, objects of prepositions, and indirect objects.

Object of the Preposition   The noun following the preposition. The preposition, its object, and any modifiers make up the prepositional phrase.

For **Daniel**
(object of the preposition for)

She knocked twice **on the big wooden door.**
(prepositional phrase)

Parallel Construction   See Chapter 21.

Participles   Verb forms that may be part of the complete verb or function as adjectives or adverbs. The present participle ends in *-ing*, and the past participle usually ends in *-ed*, *-d*, *-n*, or *-t*. (See **Phrases**.)

Present participles: *running, sleeping, digging*

She is **running** for mayor in this campaign.
(present participle)

Past participles: *walked, deleted, chosen*

The candidate **elected** will take office in January.
(past participle)

Parts of Speech   The eight classes into which words are grouped according to their function, place, meaning, and use in a sentence: nouns, pronouns, verbs, adjectives, adverbs, prepositions, conjunctions, and interjections.

Passive Voice   See Chapter 9.

Person   See 17a.

Personal Pronouns   See 17a.

Phrases   Groups of related words without subjects and predicates.

Verb phrases function as verbs.

She **has been eating** too much sugar.
(verb phrase)

Noun phrases function as nouns.

A major winter storm hit **the eastern coast of Maine.**
(noun phrase)   (noun phrase)

Prepositional phrases usually function as modifiers.

That book **of hers** is overdue at the library.
(prepositional phrase)

Possessive Pronouns   See 17a.

Predication   Words or groups of words that express action or state of beginning in a sentence and consist of one or more verbs, plus any complements or modifiers.

Prepositions   Words that link and relate their objects (usually nouns or pronouns) to some other word or words in a sentence. Prepositions usually precede their objects but may follow the objects and appear at the end of the sentence.

The server gave the check **to my date** by mistake.
(prepositional phrase)

I wonder **what** she is asking **for.**
(object of the preposition)   (preposition)

Pronoun Case   See 17a.

Pronouns   Words that substitute for nouns. (See 17a.) Pronouns should refer to previously stated nouns, called *antecedents*.

When **Josh** came in, **he** brought some firewood.
(antecedent)   (pronoun)

There are seven forms of pronouns: personal, possessive, reflexive, interrogative, demonstrative, indefinite, and relative.

Proper Nouns   See 28a.

Relative Pronouns   Pronouns that show the relationship of a dependent clause to a noun in the sentence. Relative pronouns substitute for nouns already mentioned in sentences; introduce adjective or noun clauses; and include *that, which, who, whom,* and *whose.*

This was the movie **that** won the Academy Award.

Restrictive Clauses and Phrases   See 23c.

Run-On Sentences   See **Fused Sentences** and 15b.

Sentence Fragment   See **Fragments**.

Sentences   Groups of words that have at least one independent clause (a complete unit of thought with a subject and predicate). Sentences can be classified by their structure as simple, compound, complex, and compound-complex.

Simple:	one independent clause
Compound:	two or more independent clauses
Complex:	one or more independent clauses and one or more dependent clauses
Compound-complex:	two or more independent clauses and one or more dependent clauses

Split Infinitives   Phrases in which modifiers are inserted between *to* and the verb. Some people object to split infinitives, but others consider them grammatically acceptable.

to quickly turn   to easily reach   to forcefully enter

Subject   The word or words in a sentence that act or are acted on by the verb or are linked by the verb to another word or words in the sentence. The *simple subject* includes only the noun or other main word or words, and the *complete subject* includes all the modifiers with the subject.

Harvey objected to his roommate's alarm going off at 9:00 a.m.
(Harvey is the subject.)

Every single one of the people in the room heard her giggle.
(The simple subject is one; the complete subject is the whole phrase.)

Subjunctive Mood   See 16e.

Subordinating Conjunctions   Words such as *although, if, until*, and *when* that join two clauses and subordinate one to the other.

She is late. She overslept.

She is late **because** she overslept.

Subordination   The act of placing one clause in a subordinate or dependent relationship to another in a sentence because it is less important and is dependent for its meaning on the other clause.

Suffixes   Word parts added to the ends of words (-ful, -less, etc.).

Superlative Forms of Adjectives and Adverbs   See 18c.

Synonyms   Words with similar meanings (damp/moist, pretty/attractive, etc.).

Tense   See **Verb Tenses**.

Tone   See Chapter 10.

Transitions   Words in sentences that show relationships between sentences and paragraphs. (See Chapter 13.)

Transitive Verbs   See **Verbs**.

Verbals   Words that are derived from verbs but do not act as verbs in sentences. Three types of verbals are infinitives, participles, and gerunds.

Infinitives:	*to* + **verb**
	to say to wind
Participles:	Words used as modifiers or with helping verbs. The present participle ends in -*ing*, and many past participles end in -*ed*.
	The dog is **panting**. (present participle)
	He bought only **used** clothing. (past participle)
Gerunds:	Present participles used as nouns.
	Smiling was not a natural act for her. (gerund)

Verb Conjugations   The forms of verbs in various tenses. (See Chapter 34 and 16b.)

Verbs Words or groups of words (verb phrases) in predicates that express action, show a state of being, or act as a link between the subject and the rest of the predicate. Verbs change form to show time (tense), mood, and voice and are classified as transitive, intransitive, and linking verbs. (See 16b and Chapter 34.)

Transitive verbs:	Require objects to complete the predicate.

He **cut** the cardboard **box** with his knife.
(transitive verb) *(object)*

Intransitive verbs:	Do not require objects.

My ancient cat often **lies** on the porch.
(intransitive verb)

Linking verbs:	Link the subject to the following noun or adjective.

The trees **are** bare.
(linking verb)

Verb Tenses The times indicated by the verb forms in the past, present, or future. (See 16b and 34a.)

Voice Verbs are either in the *active* or *passive* voice. (See Chapter 9.) Voice can also refer to levels of formality used in writing. (See Chapter 10.)

Credits

Index

Correction Symbols

Symbol	Problem	Section
abbr	abbreviation error	31
adj	adjective error	18
adv	adverb error	18
agr	agreement error	16a, 17b
art	article error	36
awk	awkward construction	6, 20
ca	case error	17a
cap(s)	capitalization error	28
cit	citation missing/format error	45–48
coh	coherence needed	1, 6
cs	comma splice	15a
dm	dangling modifier	19a
frag	fragment	14
fs	fused/run-on sentence	15b
hyph	hyphenation error	27a
ital	italics error	29
lc	use lowercase	28
log	logic	1a-e, 2, 6f
mm	misplaced modifier	19b
¶/no¶	new paragraph/do not begin new paragraph	1e-f
num	number	30
//	parallelism error	21
pass	unneeded passive voice	9
pl	plural needed	32b, 35
pred	predication error	6f
prep	preposition error	37
p	punctuation error	27
.	period error	27c
?	question mark error	27c
!	exclamation mark error	27c
,	comma error	22, 23
;	semicolon error	25
:	colon error	27b
'	apostrophe error	24
" "	quotation marks error	26
—	dash error	27d
( )	parentheses error	27f
ref	reference error	17b
shft	shift error	20
sp	spelling error	32
sxt	sexist language	12
trans	transition needed	1g, 13
usage	usage error	Glossary of Usage
var	variety needed	7
v	verb error	16b, 34
vt	verb tense error	34a
w	wordy	8
wc	word choice/wrong word	10, 11, 12
x	obvious error	
^	insert	
∼/tr	transpose	
ℓ	delete	

Contents